Discourse and Social Change

Norman Fairclough

Polity Press

First published in 1992 by Polity Press in association with Blackwell Publishers Ltd.
First published in paperback 1993

Reprinted 1994, 1995, 1996, 1998, 1999, 2000

Editorial office:
Polity Press
65 Bridge Street
Cambridge CB2 1UR, UK

Marketing and production:
Blackwell Publishers Ltd
108 Cowley Road
Oxford OX4 1JF, UK

Published in the USA by
Blackwell Publishers Inc.
350 Main Street
Malden MA 02148, USA

ISBN 0–7456–0674–1
ISBN 0–7456–1218–0 (pbk)

A CIP catalogue record for this book is available from
the British Library and the Library of Congress.

Typeset in 11 on 13 pt Garamond
by Graphicraft Typesetters Ltd., Hong Kong
Printed in Great Britain by TJ International, Padstow, Cornwall
This book is printed on acid-free paper.

For my mother, and in memory of my father

Contents

Preface

The idea of writing this book came from discussions with a number of colleagues at Lancaster University about discourse analysis as a method in social research, in particular sociologists Paul Bagguley, Scott Lash and Celia Lury, Mick Dillon of the Politics Department, and Susan Condor of the Psychology Department. I have also benefited from the encouragement and enthusiasm of colleagues and students in Linguistics, especially Romy Clark, Roz Ivanic, Hilary Janks, Stef Slembrouk, and Mary Talbot. Mary Talbot also provided the conversational narrative sample in chapter 5. I am grateful to Gunther Kress and John Thompson for their very helpful comments on an earlier draft. Last but by no means least, I have had invaluable support and tolerance during the writing process from Vonny, Simon and Matthew.

Acknowledgements

The newspaper article on p. 106 is reproduced by kind permission of *The Sun*. I am grateful to Cambridge University Press and to Dr S. Levinson for permission to use the figure on p. 163, to Lancaster University for permission to reproduce the text on pp. 212–13 and to MGN Limited for permission to reproduce the article on p. 111.

Introduction

Today individuals working in a variety of disciplines are coming to recognize the ways in which changes in language use are linked to wider social and cultural processes, and hence are coming to appreciate the importance of using language analysis as a method for studying social change. But there does not yet exist a method of language analysis which is both theoretically adequate and practically usable. My main objective in this book, therefore, is to develop an approach to language analysis which can contribute to filling this gap – an approach which will be particularly useful for investigating change in language, and will be usable in studies of social and cultural change.

To achieve this, it is necessary to draw together methods for analysing language developed within linguistics and language studies, and social and political thought relevant to developing an adequate social theory of language. Among the former, I include work within various branches of linguistics (vocabulary, semantics, grammar), pragmatics, and above all the 'discourse analysis' that has been developed recently mainly by linguists (the various senses of 'discourse' and 'discourse analysis' are discussed shortly); and I include among the latter the work of Antonio Gramsci, Louis Althusser, Michel Foucault, Jürgen Habermas and Anthony Giddens (see references). Such a synthesis is long overdue, but there are various factors which have militated against it being satisfactorily achieved so far. One is the isolation of language studies from other social sciences, and the domination of linguistics by formalistic and cognitive paradigms. Another is the traditional lack of interest in language on the part of other social sciences, and a tendency to see language as transparent: while linguistic data such as interviews are widely used, there has been a tendency to believe that the social content of such data can be read off without attention to the language itself. These positions and attitudes are now changing. Boundaries between social sciences are weakening, and a greater diversity of theory and practice is developing within disciplines. And these changes have been accompanied by a 'linguistic turn' in social theory, which has resulted in language being accorded a more central role within social phenomena.

Previous attempts at synthesizing language studies and social theory have thus had limited success. For example, a group of linguists in Britain in the 1970s developed a 'critical linguistics' by combining the theories and methods of text analysis of 'systemic linguistics' (Halliday 1978) with theories of ideology. Somewhat earlier in France, Michel Pêcheux and his associates began to develop an approach to discourse analysis which drew especially upon work by the linguist Zellig Harris, and Althusser's reworking of a Marxist theory of ideology. Both of these attempts suffer from an imbalance between the social and linguistic elements of the synthesis, though they have complementary strengths and weaknesses: in the former, the linguistic analysis and the treatment of language texts is well developed, but there is little social theory and the concepts of 'ideology' and 'power' are used with little discussion or explanation, whereas in Pêcheux's work the social theory is more sophisticated but linguistic analysis is treated in very narrow, semantic terms. Moreover, both attempts are based upon a static view of power relations, with an overemphasis upon how the ideological shaping of language texts contributes to reproducing existing power relations. Little attention is paid to struggle and transformation in power relations and the role of language therein. There is similar emphasis upon the description of texts as finished products, and little attention to processes of text production and interpretation, or the tensions that characterize these processes. As a consequence, these attempts at synthesis are not suitable for investigating language dynamically, within processes of social and cultural change. (See chapter 1 for a more detailed discussion of these approaches, and some reference to more recent attempts to improve and develop them.)

The synthesis that I shall attempt in this book will, like Pêcheux's, centre around 'discourse analysis' and the concept of 'discourse'. Discourse is a difficult concept, largely because there are so many conflicting and overlapping definitions formulated from various theoretical and disciplinary standpoints (see van Dijk 1985; McDonell 1986, for some of the range). In linguistics, 'discourse' is sometimes used to refer to extended samples of spoken dialogue, in contrast with written 'texts'. Text analysis' and 'discourse analysis' in this sense do not share the traditional limitation of linguistic analysis to sentences or smaller grammatical units; instead, they focus upon higher-level organizational properties of dialogue (e.g. turn-taking, or the structure of conversational openings and closings) or of written texts (e.g. the structure of a crime report in a newspaper). More commonly, however, 'discourse' is used in linguistics to refer to extended samples of either spoken or written language. In addition to preserving the emphasis upon higher-level organizational features, this sense of 'discourse' emphasizes interaction between speaker and addressee or between writer and reader, and therefore processes of producing and interpreting speech and writing, as well as the situational context of language use. 'Text' is regarded here as one dimension of discourse: the written or spoken 'product' of the process of text production. (On this 'text-and-interaction' view of discourse, see Widdowson 1979.) Finally, 'discourse' is also used for different types of language used in different sorts of social situation (e.g. 'newspaper discourse', 'advertising discourse', 'classroom discourse', 'the discourse of medical consultations').

On the other hand, 'discourse' is widely used in social theory and analysis, for example in the work of Michel Foucault, to refer to different ways of structuring areas of knowledge and social practice. Thus the discourse of 'medical science' is currently the dominant one in the practice of health care, though it contrasts with various wholistic 'alternative' discourses (e.g. those of homeopathy and acupuncture) as well as popular 'folk' discourses. Discourses in this sense are manifested in particular ways of using language and other symbolic forms such as visual images (see Thompson 1990). Discourses do not just reflect or represent social entities and relations, they construct or 'constitute' them; different discourses constitute key entities (be they 'mental illness', 'citizenship' or 'literacy') in different ways, and position people in different ways as social subjects (e.g. as doctors or patients), and it is these social effects of discourse that are focused upon in discourse analysis. Another important focus is upon historical change: how different discourses combine under particular social conditions to produce a new, complex discourse. A contemporary example is the social construction of the AIDS disease, in which various discourses (e.g. discourses of venereology, of cultural 'invasion' by 'aliens', of pollution) are combined to constitute a new discourse of AIDS. This more social-theoretical sense of discourse will be discussed further in chapter 2.

My attempt at drawing together language analysis and social theory centres upon a combination of this more social-theoretical sense of 'discourse' with the 'text-and-interaction' sense in linguistically-oriented discourse analysis. This concept of discourse and discourse analysis is three-dimensional. Any discursive 'event' (i.e. any instance of discourse) is seen as being simultaneously a piece of text, an instance of discursive practice, and an instance of social practice. The 'text' dimension attends to language analysis of texts. The 'discursive practice' dimension, like 'interaction' in the 'text-and-interaction' view of discourse, specifies the nature of the processes of text production and interpretation, for example which types of discourse (including 'discourses' in the more social-theoretical sense) are drawn upon and how they are combined. The 'social practice' dimension attends to issues of concern in social analysis such as the institutional and organizational circumstances of the discursive event and how that shapes the nature of the discursive practice, and the constitutive/constructive effects of discourse referred to above.

I should add that 'text' is used in this book in a sense which is quite familiar in linguistics but not elsewhere, to refer to any product whether written or spoken, so that the transcript of an interview or a conversation, for example, would be called a 'text'. The emphasis in this book is upon language and therefore linguistic texts, but it is quite appropriate to extend the notion of discourse to cover other symbolic forms such as visual images, and texts which are combinations of words and images, for example in advertising (see Hodge and Kress 1988). I shall use the term 'discourse' without an article to refer to language use seen in the above three-dimensional way (e.g. 'the positioning of social subjects is achieved in discourse'), and I shall also refer to 'discourse types' which are drawn upon when people engage in discourse, meaning conventions such as genres and styles. In chapter 4 I shall also begin using the term 'discourse' with an article ('a discourse', 'discourses', 'the discourse of biology') in something like the social-theoretical sense for a particular class of discourse types or conventions. I shall also refer to the 'discourse practices' of particular institutions, organizations or societies (in contrast to 'discursive practice' as one analytically distinguishable dimension of discourse).

The case for the multidimensional concept of discourse and discourse analysis sketched out above is made in chapters 1–3. Chapter 1 is a survey of approaches to discourse analysis which are linguistically-oriented, that is, they focus upon texts and text analysis. I shall argue that these approaches give insufficient attention to important social aspects of discourse, for which one needs to draw upon social theory. Chapter 2 reviews such social perspectives upon discourse in the work of Michel Foucault, a social theorist who has been a major influence in the development of discourse analysis as a form of social analysis. The chapter goes on to argue that greater attention to texts and language analysis would increase the value of discourse analysis as a method in social research. Chapter 3 then presents my multidimensional approach as a synthesis of socially- and linguistically-oriented views of discourse, moving towards what I call a 'social theory of discourse'. This approach is elaborated and applied to various sorts of discourse in later chapters of the book.

I suggested at the beginning of this introduction that changes in language use are an important part of wider social and cultural changes. This is increasingly the case, but the claim needs more explanation and justification. Claims about the social importance of language are not new. Social theory in recent decades has given language a more central place in social life (see Thompson 1984). Firstly, within Marxist theory, Gramsci (1971) and Althusser (1971) have stressed the significance of ideology for modern social reproduction, and others such as Pêcheux (1982) have identified discourse as the pre-eminent linguistic material form of ideology (see pp. 30–5 below; by 'reproduction' I mean the mechanisms through which societies sustain their social structures and social relations over time). Secondly, Foucault (1979) has highlighted the importance of technologies in modern forms of power, and it is clear that these are centrally instantiated in language (see pp. 51–4 below). Thirdly, Habermas (1984) has focused upon the colonization of the 'lifeworld' by the 'systems' of the economy and the state, which he sees in terms of a displacement of 'communicative' uses of language – oriented to producing understanding – by 'strategic' uses of language – oriented to success, to getting people to do things. The elevation of language and discourse within the social sphere is variously reflected in work on, for example, gender relations (Spender 1980) or the media (van Dijk 1985b) which focuses upon language, and sociological research which takes conversation as its data (Atkinson and Heritage 1984).

What is open to question is whether such theory and research recognizes an importance that language has always had in social life but which has previously not been sufficiently acknowledged, or actually reflects an increase in the social importance of language. Although both may be true, I believe that there has been a significant shift in the social functioning of language, a shift reflected in the salience of language in the major social changes which have been taking place over the last few decades. Many of these social changes do not just involve language, but are constituted to a significant extent by changes in language practices; and it is perhaps one indication of the growing importance of language in social and cultural change that attempts to engineer the direction of change increasingly include attempts to change language practices. Let me give some examples.

Firstly, in many countries there has recently been an upsurge in the extension of the market to new areas of social life: sectors such as education, health care and the arts have been required to restructure and reconceptualize their activities as the production and marketing of commodities for consumers (Urry 1987). These changes have profoundly affected the activities, social relations, and social and professional identities of people working in such sectors. A major part of their impact comprises changes in discourse practices, that is, changes in language. In education, for example, people find themselves under pressure to engage in new activities which are largely defined by new discourse practices (such as marketing), and to adopt new discourse practices within existing activities (such as teaching). This includes 'rewordings' of activities and relationships, for example rewording learners as 'consumers' or 'clients', courses as 'packages' or 'products'. It also includes a more subtle restructuring of the discourse practices of education – the types of discourse (genres, styles, etc.) which are used in it – and a 'colonization' of education by types of discourse from outside, including those of advertising, management, and counselling.

Again, industry is moving towards what is being called 'post-Fordist' production (Bagguley and Lash 1988; Bagguley 1990), in which workers no longer function as individuals performing repetitive routines within an invariant production process, but as teams in a flexible relation to a fast-changing process. Moreover, traditional employee–firm relations have been seen by managements as dysfunctional in this context; they have therefore attempted to transform workplace culture, for example by setting up institutions which place employees in a more participatory relation with management, such as 'quality circles'. To describe these changes as 'cultural' is not just rhetoric: the aim is new cultural values, workers who are 'enterprising', self-motivating and, as Rose (MS) has put it, 'self-steering'. These changes in organization and culture are to a significant extent changes in discourse practices. Language use is assuming greater importance as a means of production and social control in the workplace. More specifically, workers are now being expected to engage in face-to-face and group interaction as speakers and listeners. Almost all job descriptions in white-collar work, even at the lowest levels, now stress communication skills. One result is that people's social identities as workers are coming to be defined in terms that have traditionally been seen not as occupational, but as belonging to the sphere of private life. One striking feature of changes of this sort is that they are transnational. New styles of management and devices such as 'quality circles' are imported from more economically successful countries like Japan, so that changes in the discourse practices of workplaces come to have a partly international character. The new global order of discourse is thus characterized by widespread tensions between increasingly international imported practices and local traditions.

There are many other examples of change: changes in relations between doctors and patients, between politicians and the public, between women and men in workplaces and in the family, all of which are partly constituted by new discourse practices. Moreover, the increasing salience of discourse in social transformations is being matched as I suggested above by a concern to control discourse: to bring about changes in discourse practices as part of the engineering of social and cultural change. We are witnessing a 'technologization of discourse' (Fairclough 1990b), in which discursive technologies as a type of 'technologies of government' (Rose and Miller 1989) are being systematically applied in a variety of organizations by professional technologists who research, redesign, and provide training in discourse practices. Social psychologists involved in 'skills training' were an early example of this development (see Argyle 1978). Discursive technologies such as interviewing or counselling are coming to be treated as context-free techniques or skills which can be applied in various different domains. And institutional discourse practices are being widely subjected to simulation: in particular, conversational discourse practices which traditionally belong in the private sphere are being systematically simulated within organizations. (For further discussion of discourse technologization see pp. 215–18 below.)

My objective, then, is to develop an approach to discourse analysis which could be used as one method amongst others for investigating social changes such as those referred to above. For a method of discourse analysis to be useful in such contexts, it would need to fulfil a number of minimum conditions. I shall comment on four of these, and in the process elaborate a little on the sketch of my approach that I gave earlier. Firstly, it would need to be a method for multidimensional analysis. My three-dimensional approach enables relationships between discursive and social change to be assessed, and detailed properties of texts to be related systematically to social properties of discursive events as instances of social practice.

Secondly, it would need to be a method for multifunctional analysis. Changing discourse practices contribute to change in knowledge (including beliefs and common sense), social relations, and social identities; and one needs a conception of discourse and a method of analysis which attends to the interplay of these three. A good starting point is a systemic theory of language (Halliday 1978) which sees language as multifunctional, and sees texts as simultaneously representing reality, enacting social relations, and establishing identities. This theory of language can fruitfully be combined with the emphasis upon socially constructive properties of discourse in social-theoretical approaches to discourse such as Foucault's.

Thirdly, it would need to be a method for historical analysis. Discourse analysis should focus upon structuring or 'articulatory' processes in the construction of texts, and in the longer-term constitution of 'orders of discourse' (that is, total configurations of discursive practices in particular institutions, or indeed in a whole society). On the level of texts, I see these processes in terms of 'intertextuality' (see pp. 84–5 and chapter 4 below): texts are constructed through other texts being articulated in particular ways, ways which depend upon and change with social circumstances. On the level of orders of discourse, relationships among and boundaries between discourse practices in an institution or the wider society are progressively shifted in ways which accord with directions of social change.

Fourthly, it would need to be a critical method. Relationships between discursive, social and cultural change are typically not transparent for the people involved. Nor is technologization of discourse. 'Critical' implies showing connections and causes which are hidden; it also implies intervention, for example providing resources for those who may be disadvantaged through change. In this connection, it is important to avoid an image of discursive change as a unilinear, top-down process: there is struggle over the structuring of texts and orders of discourse, and people may resist or appropriate changes coming from above, as well as merely go along with them (see pp. 68–70 and chapter 7 below).

To conclude this introduction, I shall give a brief preview of the treatment of discursive change in chapters 3–7. Chapter 3 presents my synthesis of socially and linguistically-oriented views of discourse. My account of analysis in the dimension of discursive practice centres upon the concept of intertextuality. My account of analysis in the dimension of social practice, however, centres upon the concepts of ideology and especially hegemony, in the sense of a mode of domination which is based upon alliances, the incorporation of subordinate groups, and the generation of consent. Hegemonies within particular organizations and institutions and at a societal level are produced, reproduced, contested and transformed in discourse. Moreover, the structuring of discourse practices in particular ways within orders of discourse can be seen, where it comes to be naturalized and win widespread acceptance, as itself a form of (specifically cultural) hegemony. It is the combination of the concepts of intertextuality and hegemony that makes the framework of chapter 3 a useful one for investigating discursive change in relation to social and cultural change. Which prior texts and text types are drawn upon in a given instance (a particular 'discursive event'), and how they are articulated, depends upon how the discursive event stands in relation to hegemonies and hegemonic struggles – whether, for example, it is contesting existing hegemonic practices and relations, or on the contrary taking them as given. The approach to discursive change set out in chapter 3 combines a view of text and discursive practice which derives from Bakhtin via Kristeva's concept of intertextuality (Bakhtin 1981 and 1986; Kristeva 1986a), and a view of power which derives from Gramsci's theory of hegemony (Gramsci 1971; Buci-Glucksmann 1980).

The framework of chapter 3 is elaborated in the chapters which follow. Chapter 4 takes up the concept of intertextuality in terms of a distinction between 'manifest' intertextuality (the explicit presence of other texts in a text) and 'interdiscursivity' (the constitution of a text from a configuration of text types or discourse conventions). I suggest a way of differentiating and relating 'genres', 'discourses', 'styles' and 'activity types' as different sorts of discourse conventions. The chapter also discusses intertextuality in relation to the social distribution of texts and the transformations they undergo, and in relation to the construction of social identity in discourse. In chapters 5 and 6 the emphasis is upon text analysis. These chapters address aspects of the vocabulary, grammar, cohesion, text structure, force, and coherence of texts (see p. 75 below for these terms). They also develop the view of discourse analysis as multifunctional: chapter 5 is mainly concerned with the function of discourse in constituting social identities and social relations, whereas the focus in chapter 6 is upon constituting, reproducing and changing systems of knowledge and belief in discourse. In chapter 7 the emphasis is upon the social practice dimension of discourse, and specifically upon certain broad tendencies of change affecting contemporary orders of discourse (the 'democratization', 'commodification', and 'technologization' of discourse), and their relationship to social and cultural changes.

The analyses of change in chapters 4–7 feature a range of fields and institutions, with detailed analysis of samples of discourse. One issue addressed in chapter 4 is the way in which the mass media are shifting the boundary between the public and private spheres of social life. This not only involves questions of subject matter in media discourse, such as the treatment of aspects of private life as (public) news, but is also manifested intertextually in a mixing of discourse practices for the private sphere with those of the public sphere, with the result that some sections of the media use a stereotypical version of popular speech. Another issue is the pressure on service industries to treat their services as commodities and their clients as consumers, which is evident in the mixing of the discourse practices of information-giving and advertising. In chapter 5 I discuss changes in the social identities of professional workers and their clients and in the nature of interaction between them, focusing upon doctors and patients. I suggest that changes in doctor–patient identities and relations are discursively realized in a shift away from formal medical interviews to more conversational consultations, which may incorporate the discourse practices of counselling into those of more traditional medicine. Chapter 6 includes samples from two antenatal care booklets which exemplify contrasting representations of antenatal processes. I go on to discuss the engineering of semantic change as part of an attempt to effect cultural change, referring specifically to speeches by a minister in the Thatcher government on the theme of 'enterprise culture'. Chapter 7 returns to the theme of commodification and the mixing of information-giving and advertising, this time with reference to education, using the example of a university prospectus.

One of the aims of this book is to persuade readers that discourse analysis is an interesting sort of analysis to do, and to provide them with the resources for doing it. The final chapter of the book, chapter 8, draws together the material introduced in chapters 3–7 in the form of a set of guidelines for doing discourse analysis. These guidelines deal with the collection, transcription and coding of texts, and with the use of results, as well as with analysis.

1

Approaches to Discourse Analysis

My objective in this chapter is to describe briefly a number of recent and current approaches to discourse analysis, as a context and basis for the elaboration of my approach in chapters 3–8. Discourse analysis has now become a very diverse area of study, with a variety of approaches in each of a number of disciplines (some of the variety is represented in van Dijk 1985a). The survey of approaches in this chapter is therefore necessarily selective. I have chosen approaches which in some degree combine close analysis of language texts with a social orientation to discourse. This accords with my aim in later chapters to achieve an effective and usable combination of textual analysis and other modes of social analysis. I have also treated approaches selectively, focusing upon aspects of them which are closest to my priorities in this book.

The approaches surveyed can be divided into two groups according to the nature of their social orientation to discourse, distinguishing 'non-critical' and 'critical' approaches. Such a division is not absolute. Critical approaches differ from non-critical approaches in not just describing discursive practices, but also showing how discourse is shaped by relations of power and ideologies, and the constructive effects discourse has upon social identities, social relations and systems of knowledge and belief, neither of which is normally apparent to discourse participants. The approaches I have designated as basically non-critical are: the framework for describing classroom discourse in Sinclair and Coulthard (1975); ethnomethodological work in 'Conversation analysis'; the model for therapeutic discourse in Labov and Fanshel (1977); and a recent approach to discourse analysis developed by social psychologists Potter and Wetherell (1987). The critical approaches I have included are: the 'critical linguistics' of Fowler et al. (1979), and the French approach to discourse analysis developed on the basis of Althusser's theory of ideology by Pêcheux (Pêcheux 1982). The chapter concludes with a summary of key issues in discourse analysis drawn from this survey, which will serve as a point of departure for the presentation of my own approach in chapter 3.

Sinclair and Coulthard

Sinclair and Coulthard (1975; see also Coulthard 1977) worked towards a general descriptive system for analysing discourse, but they decided to focus upon the classroom because it is a formal situation whose discourse practice is likely to be governed by clear rules. Their descriptive system is based upon units which are assumed to be in the same relationship to each other as units in early forms of systemic grammar (Halliday 1961): there is a 'rank scale' of units, with units of higher rank being made up of units of the rank below. So, in grammar a sentence is made up of clauses, which are made up of groups, and so forth. Likewise, in classroom discourse, there are five units of descending rank – lesson, transaction, exchange, move, act – such that a lesson is made up of transactions, which are made up of exchanges, and so on.

Sinclair and Coulthard have little to say about the 'lesson', but they do suggest a clear structure for the 'transaction'. Transactions consist of exchanges. They are opened and closed by 'boundary exchanges' which consist minimally of 'framing moves' with or without other moves. For example, 'Well, today I thought we'd do three quizzes' consists of a framing move ('well') and a 'focusing' move which tells the class what the transaction will be about. Between the boundary exchanges there is usually a sequence of 'informing', 'directing' or 'eliciting' exchanges, in which respectively statements and requests (or commands) are made and questions are asked, usually by the teacher.

Let us look at the structure of one type of exchange, the

eliciting exchange. It typically consists of three moves: 'initiating', 'response' and 'feedback'. For example:

TEACHER: Can you tell me why do you eat all that food?
             Yes.
PUPIL: To keep you strong.
T: To keep you strong. Yes. To keep you strong.
             Why do you want to be strong?

The teacher's first contribution is an initiating move, the pupil's contribution is a response, and the first line of the teacher's second contribution is feedback; the second line is another initiating move. Notice that one contribution ('utterance') can consist of more than one move. The consistent presence of feedback presupposes that teachers have the power to evaluate pupils' contributions (one would rarely risk doing that outside a learning situation), and shows that much of classroom discourse is concerned with testing what pupils know, and training them to say things which are relevant according to criteria laid down by the schools.

A move consists of one or more acts. Sinclair and Coulthard distinguish 22 acts for classroom discourse, some of which (such as 'bid', when a child asks for the right to respond, perhaps by raising a hand) are quite specific to this discourse type. Others are less so: the initiating move of an eliciting exchange includes an 'elicitation', for example, while the initiating move of a directing exchange includes a 'directive'.

Acts are functional rather than formal categories, and a major issue is the relationship between them and the formal categories of grammar (this issue has received much attention within pragmatics, see Levinson 1983; Leech and Thomas 1989). It is well known that there are no simple correspondences. For example, an interrogative sentence (a 'grammatical question') can be a directive as well as an elicitation (e.g. 'Can you close the curtains?'), and a declarative sentence ('grammatical statement') can be either of these or an 'informative' act (e.g. 'The curtains aren't closed' can be asking for confirmation, requesting someone to close them, or just giving information). Sinclair and Coulthard refer to what they call 'situation' and 'tactics' for determining what function a sentence has in a particular piece of discourse. The former brings in situational factors which are relevant: for example, if children know talking is not allowed in class, a declarative sentence from the teacher ('You're talking') will probably be interpreted as a command to stop. Like Labov and Fanshel (see below), Sinclair and Coulthard propose interpretative rules which take account of both the linguistic form of sentences and situational factors. 'Tactics' deals with the influence of the sequential position of a sentence in the discourse upon its interpretation. For example, a declarative sentence such as 'Perhaps it's different from the woman's point of view', coming after a feedback in a series of eliciting exchanges (i.e. where one would expect an initiating move), is likely to be interpreted as an elicitation despite the fact that most declaratives are not elicitations, and most elicitations are interrogative sentences.

The strength of the Sinclair and Coulthard framework is in the pioneering way in which it draws attention to systematic organizational properties of dialogue and provides ways of describing them. Its limitations are the absence of a developed social orientation to discourse, and insufficient attention to interpretation. These limitations can be related to their choice of data: they concentrate upon a traditional teacher-centred mode of classroom discourse, and their data does not reflect the diversity of current classroom practices. This makes classroom discourse seem more homogeneous than it actually is, and naturalizes dominant practices by making them appear to be the only practices. It presents them as simply 'there' and available for description, rather than as having been put there through processes of contestation with alternative practices, and as having been 'invested' (see p. 88 below) with particular ideologies (e.g. views of learning and learners), and as helping to sustain particular relations of power within society. In short, the Sinclair and Coulthard approach lacks a developed social orientation in failing to consider how relations of power have shaped discourse practices, and in failing to situate classroom discourse historically in processes of social struggle and change. A striking characteristic of contemporary classroom practice is its diversity; one wants to know why the traditional classroom discourse they describe is under pressure, and what is at stake.

The homogeneity of the data also draws attention away from the ambivalence of classroom discourse, and the diversity of possible interpretations. Consider this example from Coulthard (1977: 108):

TEACHER:	What kind of person do you think he is?
	Do you – what are you laughing at?
PUPIL:	Nothing.
T:	Pardon?
P:	Nothing.
T:	You're laughing at nothing, nothing at all?
P:	No.
	It's funny really 'cos they don't think as though they were there they might not like it and it sounds rather a pompous attitude.

Sinclair and Coulthard see this in terms of the pupil misinterpreting the situation, and so taking the teacher's question about laughter as disciplinary rather than dialogical in intent. But such examples also point to the potential heterogeneity of classroom discourse, the co-existence in schools of a repertoire of classroom discourses, which producers and interpreters of text need to take account of. This implies attention to discourse processes, both interpretation and production, whereas the emphasis in Sinclair and Coulthard is on texts as discourse products (though the category of 'tactics' implies some attention to interpretation). This also makes their position as analysts problematical, since analysts interpret texts rather than just describe them. In claiming to describe their data are not Sinclair and Coulthard actually interpreting it in a teacher-oriented way, for example, by seeing the pupil as 'misinterpreting' the teacher rather than, perhaps, being non-commital in response to an ambivalent question from the teacher? After all, 'nothing' is also ambivalent: it could mean 'I can't tell you what's making me laugh here.' This raises another problem with the framework: it forces decisions about the functions of utterances, whereas utterances are often really ambivalent for interpreters, rather than just ambiguous, as recent work in pragmatics has shown (see Levinson 1983), that is, their meanings are not clearly decidable.

Conversation Analysis

Conversation analysis (CA) is an approach to discourse analysis which has been developed by a group of sociologists who call themselves 'ethnomethodologists'. Ethnomethodology is an interpretative approach to sociology which focuses upon everyday life as a skilled accomplishment, and upon methods which people use for 'producing' it (Garfinkel 1967; Benson and Hughes 1983). Ethnomethodologists tend to avoid general theory, and discussion or use of concepts such as class, power or ideology, which are of central concern to mainstream sociology. Some ethnomethodologists take a particular interest in conversation and in the methods conversationalists use for producing and interpreting it (Schenkein 1978; Atkinson and Heritage 1984). Conversation analysts have concentrated mainly upon informal conversation between equals (e.g. telephone conversations), though some recent work has shifted to institutional types of discourse, where power asymmetries are more obvious (Button and Lee 1987). CA contrasts with the Sinclair and Coulthard approach by highlighting discourse processes, and correspondingly giving more attention to interpretation as well as production. Its conception of interpretation and process is a narrow one, however, as I shall argue below, and CA is comparable to Sinclair and Coulthard in its orientation to discovering structures in texts.

Conversation analysts have produced accounts of various aspects of conversation: conversational openings and closings; how topics are established, developed and changed; how people tell stories in the course of conversations; how and why people 'formulate' conversations (e.g. give their gist, suggest what they imply). Work on turn-taking, how conversationalists alternate in taking turns at speaking, has been particularly impressive and influential. Sacks, Schegloff and Jefferson (1974) propose a simple but powerful set of turn-taking rules. These rules apply at the completion of a 'turn-constructional unit': conversationalists build their turns with units such as a complex sentence, a simple sentence, a phrase, even a word, and participants are able to determine what this unit is and predict its point of completion with great accuracy. The rules are ordered: (i) the current speaker may select the next speaker; (ii) if not, the next speaker may 'self-select' by starting to produce a turn; (iii) if not, the current speaker may continue. Sacks, Schegloff and Jefferson argue that these rules account for many observed features of conversation: that overlaps between speakers occur but are generally short, that a great many transitions between turns occur with no gap and no overlap, and so forth. Despite the generality of the rules, they allow for considerable variation in such features as the order and length of turns.

CA has laid considerable emphasis upon the 'sequential implicativeness' of conversation – the claim that any utterance will constrain what can follow it. 'Adjacency pairs' such as question-and-answer or complaint-and-apology are particularly clear examples: a question produced by one speaker sequentially implicates an answer from another. Evidence for x sequentially implicating y includes (i) the fact that whatever occurs after x will be taken as y if at all possible (for instance, if 'Is that your wife?' is followed by 'Well, it's not my mother', the latter is likely to be taken as an implied positive answer; and (ii) the fact that if y does not occur, its absence is noticed, and is commonly grounds for an inference (for example, if teachers fail to give feedback to learners' responses, this may be taken as implicitly rejecting them). According to Atkinson and Heritage (1984: 6), 'virtually every utterance occurs at some structurally defined place in talk.' One implication of this is that turns display an analysis of prior turns, giving constant evidence in the text of how utterances are interpreted.

Another implication is that the sequential position alone of an utterance is enough to determine its meaning. Yet this is highly questionable, on the twin grounds that (i) the effects of sequence upon meaning vary according to discourse type, and (ii), as I suggested in discussing Sinclair and Coulthard, a variety of discourse types may be drawn upon during an interaction, with participants as producers and interpreters constantly having to negotiate their positions in relation to this repertoire. Consider this extract from a medical interview which I analyse in chapter 5 (pp. 144–9 below):

PATIENT:	and I think . that's one of the reasons why I drank s⌈o much you ⌈know – ⌈and em
DOCTOR:	⌊hm ⌊hm hm⌊hm are you
	you back are you back on it have you started drinking ⌈again
P:	⌊no
D:	oh you haven't (un⌈clear)
P:	⌊no . but em one thing that the lady on the Tuesday said to me

I shall suggest in my analysis of this fragment of an interview that it is a mixture of medical interview and counselling. Within such a mixture, what does sequence tell the interpreter about the doctor's question in his first turn? In a more conventional medical interview, a doctor's question immediately after a patient has alluded to a possibly dangerous medical condition (here, drinking) would probably be taken as a medical probe, requiring full attention from both participants. In a counselling session, such a question might be taken in a more conversational way as an aside showing that the counsellor is in tune with the patient's problems. Here the patient seems to take it as an aside: she gives perfunctory one-word answers to the main question and the doctor's acknowledgement of (and perhaps check upon?) the answer, and changes the subject back to her narrative of recent events. To make such an interpretative decision, the patient needs more than information about sequence: she needs to make judgements about the nature of the social event, the social relationship between herself and the doctor, and the discourse type. This implies a view of discourse processes and interpretation which is more complex than that generally assumed in CA – a view that can accommodate, for example, producers and interpreters negotiating their way within repertoires of discourse types. The example also suggests that analysis itself is a process of interpretation, and therefore a contentious and problematic practice. One gets little sense of this in CA. Yet, like Sinclair and Coulthard, analysts tend to interpret data on the basis of a shared orientation among participants to a single discourse type (though see Jefferson and Lee 1981). One effect is to give an overly harmonious and co-operative picture of conversation.

There is also a neglect of power as a factor in conversation. In the processes of negotiation I have referred to, some participants typically have more muscle than others, and in many types of discourse (e.g. classroom discourse) we do not find shared rules for turn-taking where participants have equal rights and obligations, but an asymmetrical distribution of rights (e.g. to self-select, to interrupt, to 'hold the floor' across several turns) and obligations (e.g. to take a turn if nominated to do so). In such cases it is evident that producing discourse is part of wider processes of producing social life, social relationships, and social identities; yet much CA in its harmonious reading of interaction between equals gives the impression that producing discourse is an end in itself.

Despite different disciplinary starting points and theoretical orientations, the Sinclair and Coulthard and CA approaches have rather similar strengths and limitations: both have made important contributions to a new appreciation of the nature of structures in dialogue, but both have an undeveloped social orientation to discourse (in this respect CA suffers from the same inadequacies as Sinclair and Coulthard), and neither provides a satisfactory account of discourse processes and interpretation, though CA gives considerable insight into certain aspects of interpretation.

Labov and Fanshel

Labov and Fanshel (1977) is a study by a linguist and a psychologist of the discourse of the psychotherapeutic interview. Unlike Sinclair and Coulthard and CA, Labov and Fanshel assume the heterogeneity of discourse, which they see as reflecting the 'contradictions and pressures' (p. 35) of the interview situation. They agree with Goffman (1974) that shifts between 'frames' are a normal feature of conversation, and identify in their data a configuration of different 'styles' associated with different frames: 'interview style', 'everyday style' used in patients' narratives about 'life since the last visit' (N, for 'narrative', below) and 'family style' (F below), the style usually used in family situations, for expressing strong emotions.

Interviews are divided into 'cross-sections', corresponding approximately in extent to Sinclair and Coulthard's 'exchanges', though cross-sections can also be parts of monologues. The analysis of cross-sections emphasizes the existence of parallel verbal and paralinguistic 'streams of communication', the latter covering such features as pitch, volume, and voice qualifiers such as 'breathiness', and carrying implicit meanings which are 'deniable'. One variable between discourse types is the relative importance of the paralinguistic channel: in therapeutic discourse, contradictions between the explicit meanings of the verbal channel and the implicit meanings of the paralinguistic channel are a key feature.

The analysis produces an 'expansion' of each cross-section, a formulation of the text which makes explicit what was implicit, by providing referents for pronouns, verbalizing the implicit meanings of the paralinguistic cues, introducing relevant factual material from other parts of the data, and making explicit some of the shared knowledge of the participants. Expansions are open-ended, and can be elaborated indefinitely. Here is a sample text, analysed in terms of styles, and its expansion:

> <ɴAn-nd so—when—I called her t'day, I said, <ꜰ'Well, when do you plan t'come home?'>ꜰ>ɴ

> <ɴWhen I called my mother today (Thursday), I actually said,
> <ꜰ'Well, in regard to the subject which we both know is
> important and is worrying me, when are you leaving my sister's
> house where {2} your obligations have already been fulfilled and
> {4} returning as I am asking you to a home where {3} your primary
> obligations are being neglected, since you should do this as
> {HEAD-MO} head of our household?'>ꜰ>ɴ

The symbols in curly brackets precede propositions which are recurrently taken as given. Some of these are specific to the particular interaction; others such as {HEAD-MO}, 'mother is the head of the household', have general implications in the culture for role obligations; and others are part of the standing assumptions of therapy (e.g. 'the therapist does not tell the patient what to do') or the culture (e.g. 'one should take care of oneself'). Propositions are rarely explicitly formulated, yet the main issue in an interaction may be whether an event is or is not an instance of some proposition. Moreover, propositions consti-tute implicit connections between parts of an interaction that are important for its coherence.

The cross-section is then analysed as an 'interaction' (glossed as an 'action which affects the relations of self and others'). Any utterance is assumed to be simultaneously performing a number of actions which are hierarchically ordered so that higher-level actions are performed by means of lower-level ones (a rela-tionship marked by 'thereby' below). Thus for the sample above (I have simplified the Labov and Fanshel representation):

> Rhoda (the patient) continues the narrative, and gives information
> to support her assertion that she carried out the suggestion {S}.

> Rhoda requests information on the time her mother intends to come home, and thereby requests indirectly that her mother come home, thereby carrying out the suggestion {S}, thereby challenging her mother indirectly for not performing properly her role as head of the household, simultaneously admitting her own limitations, simultaneously asserting again that she carried out the suggestion.

The proposition {S} is the (therapist's) suggestion that one should express one's needs to other people. Such representations are based upon discourse rules proposed by Labov and Fanshel for interpreting the surface forms of utterances as particular sorts of action. For example, there is a 'rule of indirect requests' which specifies the conditions under which questions ('requests for information') are taken as requests for action. The analysis is completed with 'sequencing rules' for combining cross-sections together.

Labov and Fanshel refer to their approach as 'comprehensive' discourse analysis, and its exhaustiveness is certainly impressive, though also, as they point out, very time-consuming. They themselves identify a number of problems with it: paralinguistic cues are notoriously difficult to interpret, expansions can be endlessly expanded and there is no obviously motivated cut-off point, and expansions have the effect of flattening out important differences between foregrounded and backgrounded elements in discourse. I want, however, to focus my discussion upon two important insights in their approach which need to be taken further.

The first is the view that discourse may be stylistically heterogeneous due to contradictions and pressures in the speech situation. In the case of therapeutic discourse, for example, the suggestion is that use of 'everyday' and 'family' style is part of a patient strategy to establish some parts of the talk as immune to the intrusive expertise of the therapist. I have mentioned above the similarity of this to Goffman's concept of frames. The principle of the heterogeneity of discourse is a central element in my discussion of 'intertextuality' (pp. 84–5 below). I shall mention here just two differences between my position and Labov and Fanshel's. First, the embedding of one style within another, as in the sample above, is only one form of heterogeneity, and it often takes more complex forms where styles are difficult to separate. Secondly, their view of heterogeneity is too static: they see therapeutic discourse as a stable configuration of styles, but they do not analyse heterogeneity dynamically as historical shifts in configurations of styles. The main value of the heterogeneity principle seems to lie in investigating discursive change within wider social and cultural change (see pp. 96–7 below for an elaboration of this perspective).

The second insight is that discourse is constructed upon implicit propositions which are taken for granted by participants, and which underpin its coherence. Again, this is an important principle whose potential and implications are not developed by Labov and Fanshel. In particular, they do not attend to the ideological character of some of these propositions – such as the role obligations associated with being a mother, or the individualistic ideology of the self in the proposition 'one should take care of oneself' – or to the ideological work of therapy in reproducing them without challenge, which is reminiscent of critiques of therapy as a mechanism for fitting people back into conventional social roles. In other words, Labov and Fanshel stop short of a *critical* analysis of therapeutic discourse, while providing valuable analytical resources for such an analysis.

Potter and Wetherell

As a final example of a non-critical approach to discourse analysis, I shall discuss Potter and Wetherell's (1987) use of discourse analysis as a method in social psychology. This is interesting in the present context, first because it shows how discourse analysis can be used to study issues which have traditionally been approached with other methods, and second because it raises the question of whether discourse analysis is concerned primarily with the 'form' or the 'content' of discourse. (See the criticism by Thompson (1984: 106–8) of Sinclair and Coulthard for being 'formalistic' and neglecting the content of classroom discourse.)

Potter and Wetherell's advocacy of discourse analysis as a method for social psychologists is based upon a single argument which is successively applied to several major areas of social-psychological research. The argument is that traditional social

psychology has misconceived and indeed 'suppressed' key properties of the language materials it uses as data; that discourse is
'constructive' and hence 'constitutes' objects and categories; and
that what a person says does not remain consistent from one
occasion to another, but varies according to the functions of talk.
The argument is first applied to research on attitudes: traditional
research assumed people have consistent attitudes to 'objects'
such as 'coloured immigrants', whereas discourse analysis shows
not only that people produce different and even contradictory
evaluations of an object according to the context, but also that the
object itself is constructed differently depending upon its evaluation (so 'coloured immigrants' is a construction which many
people would reject). The argument is then applied to the study
of how people use rules, how people produce explanatory
accounts (excuses, justifications, etc.) of their behaviour, and
so forth, arguing in each case for the superiority of discourse
analysis over other methods, such as experimental methods.

Potter and Wetherell contrast the prioritization of content
in their approach with a prioritization of form in social-
psychological 'speech accommodation theory'. The latter is concerned with how people modify their speech according to who
they are talking to, and thus with the variability of linguistic form
according to context and function; whereas in the former they are
concerned with the variability of linguistic content. In some cases,
the focus is the propositional content of utterances – for example,
in researching attitudes, what New Zealand respondents say
about whether Polynesian immigrants ought to be repatriated –
and upon the sorts of argument within which such propositions
function. In other cases, the focus is upon vocabulary and
metaphor – for example, the predicates (verbs, adjectives) and
metaphors used in association with 'community' in media reports
of the inner-city disturbances in Britain in 1980.

In fact the form-content distinction is not as clear as it may
appear to be. There are aspects of content which clearly edge over
into matters of form; for example, metaphor may be a question of
fusing different domains of meaning, but it is also a question of
what words are used in a text, which is an aspect of its form.
And, conversely, aspects of form edge over into content: the
mixture of styles in therapeutic discourse identified by Labov and
Fanshell is on one level a mixture of forms (they refer for example

to intonational contours which are typical of 'family' style) but is also significant in terms of content, for instance in terms of the construction of the patient as a particular sort of 'self' or subject.

Potter and Wetherell's analytical framework is impoverished in comparison with other approaches: their 'content' amounts to limited aspects of the 'ideational' or conceptual meaning of discourse, which leaves untouched other (broadly, 'interpersonal') dimensions of meaning and associated aspects of form. ('Ideational' and 'interpersonal' meaning are more fully explained on pp. 64–5 below.) It is in Potter and Wetherell's treatment of 'the self' that these analytical limitations become most apparent. In contrast with traditional treatments of the self in social psychology, they adopt a constructivist position which emphasizes the variable constitution of the self in discourse. Yet they are unable properly to operationalize this theory in their discourse analysis, because (as I argue below, pp. 140–4) different selves are implicitly signalled through configurations of many diverse features of verbal (as well as bodily) behaviour, and one needs a richer analytical apparatus than Potter and Wetherell's to describe them.

Like other approaches referred to, Potter and Wetherell's is insufficiently developed in its social orientation to discourse. There is a one-sided individualistic emphasis upon the rhetorical strategies of speakers in their discourse analysis. The discussion of the self is an apparent exception, because a constructivist view of the self emphasizes ideology and the social shaping of the self in discourse, but this theory fits uneasily with the predominant orientation of the book and is not operationalized in discourse analysis. Finally, there is a tendency for the strategic or rhetorical activity of the self in using categories, rules, etc. to be posed as an alternative to the subjection of the self, rather than for the two to be seen in a dialectical synthesis (see p. 65 below for an elaboration of this view).

Critical Linguistics

'Critical linguistics' was the approach developed by a group based at the University of East Anglia in the 1970s (Fowler et al. 1979; Kress and Hodge 1979). They tried to marry a method of linguistic text analysis with a social theory of the functioning of language in political and ideological processes, drawing upon the functionalist linguistic theory associated with Michael Halliday (1978, 1985) and known as 'systemic linguistics'.

In view of its disciplinary origins, it is not surprising that critical linguistics was eager to distinguish itself from mainstream linguistics (then more heavily dominated by the Chomskyan paradigm than it is now) and sociolinguistics (see Fowler et al. 1979: 185–95). Two 'prevalent and related dualisms' in linguistic theory are rejected: the treatment of language systems as autonomous and independent of the 'use' of language, and the separation of 'meaning' from 'style' or 'expression' (or 'content' from 'form'). Against the first dualism, critical linguistics asserts with Halliday that 'language is as it is because of its function in social structure' (Halliday 1973: 65), and argues that the language that people have access to depends upon their position in the social system. Against the second dualism, critical linguistics supports Halliday's view of the grammar of a language as systems of 'options' amongst which speakers make 'selections' according to social circumstances, assuming that formal options have contrasting meanings, and that choices of forms are always meaningful. Sociolinguistics is criticized for merely establishing correlations between language and society rather than looking for deeper causal relations, including the effects of language upon society: 'language serves to confirm and consolidate the organizations which shape it' (Fowler et al. 1979: 190).

The quotation from Halliday in the last paragraph reads more fully: 'language is as it is because of its function in the social structure, and the organization of behavioural meanings should give some insight into its social foundations' (Halliday 1973: 65). Kress suggests (1989: 445) that critical linguistics developed the claim in the second part of the quotation but not really that in the first: it 'attempted to "read off" structurings of "social foundations" from "the organization of behavioural meanings"' in texts. Critical linguistics again takes a Hallidayan position, in contrast with the practice of mainstream linguistics and sociolinguistics, in taking complete texts (spoken or written) as the object of analysis. The 'Sapir-Whorf hypothesis' that languages embody particular world-views is extended to varieties within a language; particular texts embody particular ideologies or theories, and the aim is the 'critical interpretation' of texts: 'recovering the social meanings expressed in discourse by analysing the linguistic structures in the light of their interactional and wider social contexts' (Fowler et al. 1979: 195–6). The objective is to produce an analytic method which is usable by people who may, for example, be historians rather than specialists in linguistics.

For textual analysis, critical linguists draw heavily upon Halliday's work in 'systemic grammar' (see Halliday 1985), as well as using concepts from other theories such as 'speech act' and 'transformation'. Critical linguistics differs from other approaches in the attention it gives to the grammar and vocabulary of texts. There is much reference to 'transitivity', the aspect of the grammar of a clause or sentence that relates to its ideational meaning, that is, the way it represents reality (for a detailed discussion of transitivity, see pp. 177–85 below). The grammar provides different 'process types' and associated 'participants' as options, and systematic selection of a particular process type may be ideologically significant. For example, the Communist newspaper *The Morning Star* (21 April 1980) formulates part of a report on a health service union day of action as an actional process with workers ('northerners') as the actor: 'Parliament was hit by hundreds of northerners.' This might have been formulated as a 'relational' process in which the meaning of 'workers taking action' is less prominent (e.g. 'There was a lobby of Parliament by hundreds of northerners').

Another related focus is upon grammatical processes of 'transformation' looked at either in real time (for example, the transformations associated with the development of a story in a newspaper over a period of days, discussed in Trew 1979), or more abstractly, for example where what might have been formulated as a clause ('x criticized y a lot') is actually formulated in a transformed way as a 'nominalization' ('there was much criticism'). Nominalization is the conversion of a clause into a nominal or noun, here 'criticism' from 'x criticized y'. Another transformation is 'passivization', the conversion of an active clause into a passive clause (e.g. the headline 'Demonstrators are Shot (by Police)', rather than 'Police Shoot Demonstrators'). Such transformations may be associated with ideologically significant features of texts such as the systematic mystification of agency: both allow the agent of a clause to be deleted.

A further focus is upon aspects of clause grammar which have to do with its interpersonal meanings, that is, a focus on the way social relations and social identities are marked in clauses. This is the grammar of 'modality' (see pp. 158–62 below for examples and discussion). The approach to vocabulary is based upon the assumption that different ways of 'lexicalizing' domains of meaning may involve ideologically different systems of classification, so there is an interest in how areas of experience may come to be 'relexicalized' on different classificatory principles, for example in the course of political struggle. (See p. 194 below for more detail.)

In critical linguistics, there tends to be too much emphasis upon the text as product, and too little emphasis upon the processes of producing and interpreting texts. For example, although the aim of critical linguistics is said to be critical *interpretation* of texts, little attention is given to the processes and problems of interpretation, either those of the analyst-interpreter or those of the participant-interpreter. Thus in analysis, the relationship between textual features and social meanings tends to be portrayed as straightforward and transparent: despite an insistence that 'there is no predictable one-to-one association between any one linguistic form and any specific social meaning' (Fowler et al. 1979: 198), in practice values are attributed to particular structures (such as passive clauses without agents) in a rather mechanical way. But texts may be open to different interpretations depending on context and interpreter, which means that the social meanings (including ideologies) of discourse cannot simply be read off from the text without considering patterns and variations in the social distribution, consumption and interpretation of the text. It may be that 'ideology is linguistically mediated and habitual for an acquiescent, uncritical reader' (Fowler et al. 1979: 190), but readers are often critical. Once critical linguistics has established ideological meanings for a text, it tends to take their ideological effects for granted.

Another limitation of critical linguistics is that it places a one-sided emphasis upon the effects of discourse in the social reproduction of existing social relations and structures, and correspondingly neglects both discourse as a domain in which social struggles take place, and change in discourse as a dimension of wider social and cultural change. This is not unconnected with my comments in the last paragraph: interpretation is an active process in which the meanings arrived at depend upon the resources deployed and the social position of the interpreter, and one can construe texts as merely producing ideological effects upon a passive recipient only if one ignores this dynamic process. What is at issue more generally is the exclusively top-down view of power and ideology in critical linguistics, which accords with an emphasis one finds also in the Althusserian approach of the Pêcheux group (discussed below) on social stasis rather than change, social structures rather than social action, and social reproduction rather than social transformation. There is a need for a social theory of discourse based upon a revaluation of these dualisms as poles in relationships of tension, rather than opting for one member of each pair and rejecting the other as if they were mutually exclusive.

A final comment is that the language–ideology interface is too narrowly conceived in critical linguistics. Firstly, aspects of texts other than grammar and vocabulary may be of ideological significance, for example the overall argumentative or narrative structure of a text. Secondly, critical linguistics has dealt mainly with written monologue, and has had relatively little to say about ideologically important aspects of the organization of spoken dialogue (such as turn-taking), though there is some discussion of pragmatic dimensions of utterances such as their politeness features (see pp. 162–6 below). Thirdly, because of the relative neglect of processes of interpretation, the emphasis is heavily upon the realization of ideologies in texts. What is backgrounded is the sense in which processes of interpretation involve interpreters in making assumptions which are not in the text and which may have an ideological nature (see p. 84 below for an example). (Fairclough 1989b has a fuller discussion.)

Critical linguists have recently been voicing their own criticisms of earlier work (Kress 1989; Fowler 1988a) including some of those I have voiced above, and certain members of the group have been closely involved in the development of a somewhat different approach (Hodge and Kress 1988; Kress and Threadgold 1988) which they call 'social semiotics'. In contrast with critical linguistics, there is a concern with a variety of semiotic systems including language, and with the interplay between language and visual semiosis. Discourse processes of text production and interpretation have become a central concern, and there is more overt attention to developing a social theory of discourse, with an orientation to struggle and historical change in discourse which is centred in an attempt to develop a theory of genre.

Pêcheux

Michel Pêcheux and his collaborators (Pêcheux et al. 1979; Pêcheux 1982) have developed a critical approach to discourse analysis which, like critical linguistics, attempts to combine a social theory of discourse with a method of text analysis, working mainly on written political discourse. Their research has been consciously linked to political developments in France, especially the relationship between the Communist and Socialist parties in the 1970s, and a comparison of their political discourse.

The major source for Pêcheux's approach in social theory was Althusser's Marxist theory of ideology (1971). Althusser emphasized the relative autonomy of ideology from the economic base, and the significant contribution of ideology to reproducing or transforming economic relations. He also argued that ideology, far from being just disembodied 'ideas', occurs in material forms. Furthermore, ideology works through constituting ('interpellating') persons as social subjects, fixing them in subject 'positions' while at the same time giving them the illusion of being free agents. These processes take place within various institutions and organizations such as education, the family, or the law, which in Althusser's view function as ideological dimensions of the state – what he called 'ideological state apparatuses' (ISAs).

Pêcheux's contribution to this theory has been to develop the idea of language as one crucially important material form of ideology. He uses the term 'discourse' to stress the ideological nature of language use. Discourse 'shows the effects of ideological struggle within the functioning of language, and, conversely, the existence of linguistic materiality within ideology' (Pêcheux, quoted in Courtine 1981). An ISA can be conceived of as a complex of interrelated 'ideological formations', each corresponding roughly to a class position within the ISA. Pêcheux suggests that each such position incorporates a 'discursive formation' (DF), a term he borrowed from Foucault. A DF is 'that which in a given ideological formation...determines *"what can and should be said"* ' (Pêcheux 1982: 111, original italics). This is understood in specifically semantic terms: words 'change their meaning according to the positions of those who "use" them' (Pêcheux et al. 1979: 33). Further, although two different discursive formations may have certain words or expressions in common, the relationships between these and other words and expressions will differ in the two cases, and so too will the meanings of these shared words or expressions, because it is their relationship to others that determines their meaning. For example, 'militant' means different things in trade-union discourse (where it might be a synonym of 'activist' and an antonym of 'apathetic') and right-wing conservative discourse (where it might be a synonym of 'subversive' and an antonym of 'moderate'). Moreover, social subjects are constituted in relation to particular DFs and their meanings; these DFs are, according to Pêcheux, linguistic facets of '"domains of thought"...socio-historically constituted in the form of points of stabilization which produce the subject and simultaneously *along with him* what he is given to see, understand, do, fear and hope' (Pêcheux 1982: 112–13, original italics).

DFs are positioned within complexes of related DFs referred to as 'interdiscourse', and the specific meanings of one DF are determined 'from outside' by its relationship to others within interdiscourse. The particular 'state' of interdiscourse at a particular time (what DFs are contained within it and in what relationships) depends upon the state of ideological struggle within an ISA. However, this external determination of DFs is something that subjects are typically not aware of; subjects tend to perceive themselves mistakenly as the source of the meanings of a DF, when in fact they are their effects. Pêcheux refers to 'preconstructeds', ready-formed elements which circulate between DFs, which are perceived as what is 'given' or known to or already said by participants, whereas they actually originate outside subjects, in interdiscourse. An example would be expressions like 'the postwar increase in living standards', or 'the Soviet threat', which cross from one DF to another as ready-made expressions, along with their presuppositions (that there has been an increase, and that there is a threat).

An important qualification is that subjects do not always totally identify with a DF. Subjects may distance themselves from a DF by using metadiscursive markers (see p. 122 below) such as 'the so-called x', 'what you call an x', and the 'x'. Pêcheux calls this 'counter-identification' – distancing oneself from existing practices without replacing them with new ones. Where such a replacement does occur, we have the more radical situation of 'disidentification', which involves 'the "overthrow-rearrangement" of the complex of ideological formations (and of the discursive formations which are imbricated with them)' (Pêcheux 1982: 159). However, Pêcheux sees the possibility of disidentification as specifically tied to the revolutionary theory and practice of Marxism-Leninism, in the organizational form of the Communist Party.

The method of analysis is called 'automatic analysis of discourse' because part of the procedure is computerized in order to identify DFs in a corpus of texts. Pêcheux et al. (1979: 33) note that the composition of a corpus itself embodies 'a hypothesis about the existence of one or more DFs' which 'dominate' its constituent texts, and suggest that such a hypothesis ought to come from specialist disciplines such as history or sociology rather than discourse analysts themselves, to avoid circularity. Putting a corpus together on the basis of a hypothesis is tantamount to imposing homogeneity upon the domain of texts, and the corpus is further homogenized through the exclusion of parts of texts whose 'conditions of production' (hence whose dominating DFs) are different from the main ones.

The first part of the procedure is a linguistic analysis of the text into clauses (i.e. simple sentences) using the 'transformational' procedures of the linguist Zellig Harris (1963). For example, 'I regret her departure' would be analysed as two clauses, 'I regret', '(that) she has departed'. Graphs are produced which show what sort of relationships there are between the clauses (co-ordination, subordination, complementation, etc.). These graphs are then subjected to a second, computerized, procedure to determine which words and expressions are in a relationship of 'substitution', that is, which can occur in the same positions in clauses which are similar in their grammatical structure and which are similarly related to other clauses. For example, 'militants' and 'subversives' are in a relationship of substitution in 'We should watch out for militants who disrupt industry', 'The nation must guard against subversives who undermine our institutions'. When words or expressions are placed in a relationship of substitution in a text, semantic relationships are set up between them – such as relationships of synonymy (A implies B, and B implies A) or implication (A implies B, but B does not imply A) – which are likely to be distinctive for the DF with which the text is associated. The procedure focuses upon certain 'key words', words of exceptional social or political significance (e.g. 'struggle' in political discourse). (For a more detailed description of the method of analysis, see Maingueneau 1976; Thompson 1984: 238–47.) Finally, the results of the analytical procedures need to be interpreted, though little attention is given to problems associated with interpretation, and the method seems rather *ad hoc*.

The strength of Pêcheux's approach, and the reason for regarding it as critical, is that it marries a Marxist theory of discourse with linguistic methods of text analysis. However, the treatment of texts is unsatisfactory. As I indicated above, they are homogenized before analysis through the way the corpus is constituted (Courtine and Marandin 1981: 22–3), and the effect of applying transformational procedures to analyse texts into separate clauses is to obliterate distinctive features of textual organization. Moreover, these procedures allow for a selective focus upon parts of texts, which means that sentences rather than whole texts are effectively the objects of analysis. Texts are also treated as products, just as they are by critical linguistics, and the discourse processes of text production and interpretation are given little attention. They are analysed in narrowly semantic terms (a criticism I also directed at Potter and Wetherell) with a predetermined focus upon 'key words': only ideational dimensions of meaning are attended to, while interpersonal dimensions which have to do with social relations and social identities are not, and properties of the meaning of utterances in context are neglected in favour of more abstract meaning relations. Many aspects of the form and organization of texts which other approaches attend to are ignored. In sum, rather than the analyst attempting to come to grips with what is distinctive about the text and the discursive event, texts are treated as evidence for a priori hypotheses about DFs. There is a similar tendency in Althusserian theory to overemphasize reproduction – how subjects are positioned within formations and how ideological domination is secured – at the expense of transformation – how subjects may contest and progressively restructure domination and formations through their practice. I suggested a similar emphasis occurs in critical linguistics. Correspondingly, there is a one-sided view of the subject as positioned, as an effect; the capacity of subjects to act as agents, and even to transform the bases of subjection themselves, is neglected. The theory of 'disidentification' as change externally generated by a particular political practice is an implausible alternative to building the possibility of transformation into one's view of discourse and the subject.

'Second generation' discourse analysis in the Pêcheux tradition has altered the approach in fundamental ways, partly in response to criticisms and partly under the influence of political changes in France (Maldidier 1984: xi–xiv). Some studies of political discourse (e.g. Courtine 1981) have highlighted discursive strategies of alliance, and combinations of different DFs which make discourse highly heterogeneous and ambiguous. These properties are not easily accommodated in the earlier vision in which monolithic DFs have static relationships of opposition. Discourse has come to be characterized as possessing 'constitutive heterogeneity' (Authier-Revuz 1982), having inherent properties of 'dialogism' and 'intertextuality' in the terms of a different theoretical tradition (see Bakhtin 1981; Kristeva 1986a; and pp. 84–5 below), and earlier work was seen along the lines of my criticism above as procedures for imposing homogeneity. Interdiscourse has come to be seen as 'a process of constant restructuring' in which the delimitation of a DF is 'fundamentally unstable, being not a permanent boundary separating an interior and an exterior, but a frontier between different DFs which shifts according to what is at stake in ideological struggle' (Courtine 1981: 24). Given the constitutive heterogeneity of discourse, particular parts of a text will often be ambivalent, raising questions for the interpreter about which DFs are most relevant to their interpretation, and, as Pêcheux observes in one of his last papers (1988), giving discourse analysis the character of an interpretative rather than a straightforwardly descriptive discipline. At the same time, there is an abandonment of the 'theoreticist illusion' that radical transformations of interdiscourse are 'authorized by the existence of Marxism-Leninism' (Pêcheux 1983: 32). With a new focus upon the particular discursive 'event', a dialectical view of discourse emerges, and the possibility of transformations becomes inherent in the heterogeneous and contradictory nature of discourse: 'any given discourse is the potential sign of a movement within the sociohistorical filiations of identification, inasmuch as it constitutes, at the same time, a result of these filiations and the work ...of displacement within their space' (Pêcheux 1988: 648).

Conclusion

I want to conclude this survey by drawing together the main issues so far in the form of a set of statements which can be regarded as desiderata for an adequate critical approach to discourse analysis. This will give a preliminary picture of the approach I begin developing in chapter 3, and indicate its relationship to those already discussed. At the same time, it will help identify areas in which the linguistically-oriented tradition of discourse analysis reviewed in this chapter is weak and underdeveloped, and in which it needs to be strengthened by drawing upon accounts of language and discourse in social theory.

1 The object of analysis is linguistic texts, which are analysed in terms of their own specificity (compare Pêcheux). Selections of texts to represent a particular domain of practice should ensure the diversity of practices is represented (compare Sinclair and Coulthard) and avoid homogenization (compare Pêcheux).

2 In addition to texts as 'products' of processes of text production and interpretation, these processes themselves are analysed (compare Sinclair and Coulthard and Critical linguistics, and see the approach to critical discourse analysis in van Dijk (1988) for detailed attention to discourse processes). Analysis itself is seen as interpretation, and analysts seek to be sensitive to their own interpretative tendencies and social reasons for them (compare Sinclair and Coulthard, Conversation analysis, Critical linguistics).

3 Texts may be heterogeneous and ambiguous, and configurations of different discourse types may be drawn upon in producing and interpreting them (Labov and Fanshel; compare Conversation analysis, 'first generation' Pêcheux group).

4 Discourse is studied historically and dynamically, in terms of shifting configurations of discourse types in discourse processes, and in terms of how such shifts reflect and constitute

wider processes of social change ('second generation' Pêcheux group, social semiotics; compare Labov and Fanshel, 'first generation' Pêcheux group, Critical linguistics).

5 Discourse is socially constructive (Critical linguistics, Pêcheux, Potter and Wetherell), constituting social subjects, social relations, and systems of knowledge and belief, and the study of discourse focuses upon its constructive ideological effects (Pêcheux, Critical linguistics; compare Labov and Fanshel).

6 Discourse analysis is concerned not only with power relations in discourse (compare Conversation analysis), but also with how power relations and power struggle shape and transform the discourse practices of a society or institution ('second generation' Pêcheux group; compare non-critical approaches, Critical linguistics).

7 Analysis of discourse attends to its functioning in the creative transformation of ideologies and practices as well as its functioning in securing their reproduction (compare Pêcheux, Critical linguistics).

8 Texts are analysed in terms of a diverse range of features of form and meaning (e.g. properties of dialogue and text structure as well as vocabulary and grammar) appertaining to both the ideational and interpersonal functions of language (compare Potter and Wetherell, Pêcheux).

What is envisaged is a discourse analysis focused upon variability, change, and struggle: variability between practices and heterogeneity within them as a synchronic reflex of processes of historical change which are shaped by struggle between social forces. Although points 4, 5 and 6 receive some support especially within the critical approaches to discourse analysis I have discussed above, we need to go to social theory to find full and explicit developments of them. Foucault provides valuable insights on all of them, as I shall argue in chapter 2. However, neither the critical tradition in linguistically-oriented discourse analysis nor Foucault deal satisfactorily with point 7 – the way in which discourse contributes both to the reproduction and to the transformation of societies. This duality of discourse is of central importance in the framework I present in chapter 3, and the neglect of it in Foucault's writings is associated with major theoretical and methodological weaknesses in his work.

2

Michel Foucault and the Analysis of Discourse

> Has not the practice of revolutionary discourse and scientific discourse over the past two hundred years freed you from this idea that words are wind, an external whisper, a beating of wings that one has difficulty in hearing in the serious matter of history?
>
> Michel Foucault, *The Archaeology of Knowledge*

Foucault has had a huge influence upon the social sciences and humanities, and the popularization of the concept of 'discourse' and of discourse analysis as a method can partly be attributed to that influence. It is important to examine his work in some detail for two reasons. Firstly, Foucault's approach to discourse analysis is widely referred to as a model by social scientists, and since I am advocating a different approach to discourse analysis in studies of social and cultural change, the relationship between the two needs to be made clear. There is a major contrast here between textually- (and therefore linguistically-) oriented discourse analysis (henceforth abbreviated as TODA) such as mine, and Foucault's more abstract approach. I also need to give reasons why social scientists should consider using TODA; I shall argue at the end of the chapter that it can lead to more satisfactory social analyses.

The second reason for a chapter on Foucault has already been alluded to: the development of an approach to discourse analysis which is theoretically adequate as well as practically usable requires a synthesis of linguistically-oriented discourse analysis and the insights of recent social theory on language and discourse. Foucault's work makes an important contribution to a social theory of discourse in such areas as the relationship of discourse and power, the discursive construction of social subjects and knowledge, and the functioning of discourse in social change. As I pointed out at the end of chapter 1, these are areas where linguistically-oriented approaches are weak and undeveloped.

However, given that Foucault's approach to discourse and the intellectual context within which it developed are so different from my own, one cannot simply 'apply' Foucault's work in discourse analysis; it is, as Courtine says, a matter of 'putting Foucault's perspective to work' (1981: 40) within TODA, and trying to operationalize his insights in actual methods of analysis. The prominence given to discourse in Foucault's earlier work is a consequence of positions which he took up in relation to the conduct of research in the human sciences. He opted for a focus upon discursive practices in an effort to move beyond the two major alternative modes of investigation available to social research – structuralism and hermeneutics (Dreyfus and Rabinow 1982: xiii–xxiii). Foucault is concerned with discursive practices as constitutive of knowledge, and with the conditions of transformation of the knowledge associated with a discursive formation into a science.

This intellectual context helps to explain major differences between Foucault's discourse analysis and that of TODA. In the first place, Foucault was concerned in some phases of his work with a quite specific sort of discourse – the discourse of the human sciences, such as medicine, psychiatry, economics, and grammar. TODA, on the other hand, is in principle concerned with any sort of discourse – conversation, classroom discourse, media discourse, and so forth. Secondly, as I have already indicated, whereas the analysis of spoken and written language texts is a central part of TODA, it is not a part of Foucault's discourse analysis. His focus is upon the 'conditions of possibility' of discourse (Robin 1973: 83), upon 'rules of formation' which define the possible 'objects', 'enunciative modalities', 'subjects', 'concepts' and 'strategies' of a particular type of discourse (these terms are explained below). Foucault's emphasis is upon the domains of knowledge which are constituted by such rules.

I quoted above Courtine's view that we should 'put Foucault's perspective to work' within TODA. The notion of 'Foucault's perspective', however, can be misleading, given the shifts of emphasis within Foucault's work (clearly described in Davidson 1986). In his earlier 'archaeological' work, the focus was on types of discourse ('discursive formations' – see below) as rules for constituting areas of knowledge. In his later 'genealogical' studies, the emphasis shifted to relationships between knowledge and power. And in the work of Foucault's last years, the concern was 'ethics', 'how the individual is supposed to constitute himself as a moral subject of his own actions' (Rabinow 1984: 352). Although discourse remains a concern throughout, the status of discourse changes, and so do the implications for TODA.

In this chapter I shall first give an account and evaluation of conceptions of discourse in Foucault's archaeological studies (especially Foucault 1972), and then go on to discuss how the status of discourse changes in Foucault's genealogical work (focusing upon Foucault 1979 and 1981). The main objective in these sections will be to identify a number of valuable perspectives upon and insights into discourse and language in Foucault's work, which ought to be integrated into the theory of TODA, and where appropriate operationalized in its methodology. I conclude, however, by discussing certain weaknesses in Foucault's work which limit its value for TODA, and how TODA might help strengthen social analysis, including social analysis within the Foucaultian tradition. What I am offering is thus a reading of Foucault from a particular point of view; fuller and more balanced accounts and critiques are available elsewhere (e.g. Dreyfus and Rabinow 1982; Hoy 1986; Dews 1987; Fraser 1989).

Foucault's 'Archaeological' Works

Foucault's earlier 'archaeological' studies (I shall be referring particularly to Foucault 1972) include two major theoretical insights about discourse which need to be incorporated within TODA. The first is a constitutive view of discourse, which involves seeing discourse as actively constituting or constructing society on various dimensions: discourse constitutes the objects of knowledge, social subjects and forms of 'self', social relationships, and conceptual frameworks. The second is an emphasis on the interdependency of the discourse practices of a society or institution: texts always draw upon and transform other contemporary and historically prior texts (a property commonly referred to as the 'intertextuality' of texts – see p. 84 below), and any given type of discourse practice is generated out of combinations of others, and is defined by its relationship to others (a perspective recognized by Pêcheux in the primacy he ascribed to 'interdiscourse' – see p. 31 above). Although the focus of Foucault (1972) is upon the discursive formations of the human sciences, his insights are transferable to all types of discourse.

What does Foucault mean by 'discourse' and 'discourse analysis' in his 'archaeological' works? He sees discourse analysis as concerned with analysing 'statements' (the usual translation of French 'énoncés'; it is somewhat misleading in implying that 'énoncés' are only assertions, as opposed to questions, orders, threats, and so forth). According to one formulation (Foucault 1972: 107–8), the analysis of statements is one of a number of ways of analysing 'verbal performances'. The others are 'a logical analysis of propositions, a grammatical analysis of sentences, a psychological or contextual analysis of formulations'. The discursive analysis of statements does not replace these other types of analysis, but nor can it be reduced to them. One consequence is that for Foucault, discourse analysis is not to be equated with linguistic analysis, nor discourse with language. Discourse analysis is concerned not with specifying what sentences are possible or 'grammatical', but with specifying sociohistorically variable 'discursive formations' (sometimes referred to as 'discourses'), systems of rules which make it possible for certain statements but not others to occur at particular times, places and institutional locations. The conception of linguistic analysis that Foucault is appealing to is dated (Foucault 1972 was written in 1969), and the sort of rules he is concerned with would seem to be what sociolinguists working in the 1970s came to call 'sociolinguistic rules', social rules of language use. However, Foucault's perspective is very different from any found in sociolinguistics; part of this difference is the lack of concern with language texts referred to above.

A discursive formation consists of 'rules of formation' for the particular set of statements which belong to it, and more specifically rules for the formation of 'objects', rules for the formation of 'enunciative modalities' and 'subject positions', rules for the formation of 'concepts', and rules for the formation of 'strategies' (Foucault 1972: 31–9). These rules of formation are constituted by combinations of prior discursive and non-discursive elements (examples are given below), and the process of articulating these elements makes discourse a social practice (Foucault uses the expression 'discursive practice'). I shall discuss each type of rule in turn, giving a summary of Foucault's position, and indicating briefly its potential interest and implications for discourse analysis.

The Formation of Objects

The essential insight in respect of the formation of objects is that the 'objects' of discourse are constituted and transformed in discourse according to the rules of some particular discursive formation, rather than existing independently and simply being referred to or talked about in a particular discourse. By 'objects' Foucault means objects of knowledge, the entities which particular disciplines or sciences recognize within their fields of interest, and which they take as targets for investigation. (This sense of 'objects' can be extended beyond formally organized disciplines or sciences to the entities recognized in ordinary life.) Foucault gives the example of the constitution of 'madness' as an object in the discourse of psychopathology from the nineteenth century onwards; other examples might be the constitution of 'nation' and 'race', or 'freedom' and 'enterprise' (see Keat and Abercrombie 1990) in contemporary media and political discourse, or of 'literacy' in educational discourse. According to Foucault, 'mental illness was constituted by all that was said in all the statements that named it, divided it up, described it, explained it...' (1972: 32). Moreover, madness is not a stable object, but is subject to continuous transformations both between discursive formations and within a given discursive formation. This means that a discursive formation needs to be defined in such a way as to allow for the transformation of its objects, and Foucault suggests that 'the unity of a discourse is based not so much on the permanence and uniqueness of an object as on the space in which various objects emerge and are continuously transformed' (1972: 32).

What is of major significance here for discourse analysis is the view of discourse as constitutive – as contributing to the production, transformation, and reproduction of the objects (and, as we shall see shortly, the subjects) of social life. This entails that discourse is in an active relation to reality, that language signifies reality in the sense of constructing meanings for it, rather than that discourse is in a passive relation to reality, with language merely referring to objects which are taken to be given in reality. The referential view of the relationship between language and reality has been generally presupposed within linguistics and approaches to discourse analysis based within linguistics.

The 'space' Foucault refers to here is defined for a given discourse formation in terms of a relationship; a relationship between specific 'institutions, economic and social processes, behavioural patterns, systems of norms, techniques, types of classification, modes of characterization' (1972: 45); a relationship which constitutes the rules of formation for objects. In terms of the example of psychopathology, Foucault writes:

> If, in a particular period in the history of our society, the delinquent was psychologized and pathologized, if criminal behaviour could give rise to a whole series of objects of knowledge (homicide (and suicide), crimes passionels, sexual offences, certain forms of theft, vagrancy), this was because a group of particular relations was adopted for use in psychiatric discourse. The relation between planes of specification like penal categories and degrees of diminished responsibility, and planes of psychological characterization (facilities, aptitudes, degrees of development or involution, different ways of reacting to the environment, character types, whether acquired or hereditary). The relation between the authority of medical decision and the authority of judicial decision...The relation between the filter formed by judicial interrogation, police information, investigation, and the whole machinery of judicial information, and the filter formed by the medical questionnaire, clinical examinations, the search for antecedents, and biographical accounts. The relation between the family, sexual and penal norms of the behaviour of individuals, and the table of pathological symptoms and diseases of which they are the signs. The relationship between therapeutic confinement in hospital...and punitive confinement in prison...(1972: 43–4)

Foucault is suggesting here that a discursive formation constitutes objects in ways which are highly constrained, where the constraints on what happens 'inside' a discursive formation are a function of the interdiscursive relations between discursive formations, and the relations between discursive and non-discursive practices that make up that discursive formation. The stress on interdiscursive relations has important implications for discourse analysis, since it places at the centre of the agenda the investigation of the structuring or articulation of discursive formations in relation to each other within what I shall call, using a Foucaultian term, institutional and societal 'orders of discourse' – the totality of discursive practices within an institution or society, and the relationships between them (see Fairclough 1989a: 29, and p. 68 below). The view that the articulation of orders of discourse is decisive for the constitution of any one discursive formation, and ought therefore to be a central focus of discourse analysis, is variously expressed in the work of Pêcheux (in his concept of 'interdiscourse': see chapter 2 above), Bernstein (1982), and Laclau and Mouffe (1985).

The Formation of Enunciative Modalities

Foucault's main thesis with respect to the formation of 'enunciative modalities' is that the social subject that produces a statement is not an entity which exists outside of and independently of discourse, as the source of the statement (its 'author'), but is on the contrary a function of the statement itself. That is, statements position subjects – those who produce them, but also those they are addressed to – in particular ways, so that 'to describe a formulation *qua* statement does not consist in analysing the relations between the author and what he says (or wanted to say, or said without wanting to); but in determining what position can and must be occupied by any individual if he is to be the subject of it' (1972: 95–6).

This view of the relationship between subject and statement is elaborated through a characterization of discursive formations as being made up of particular configurations of 'enunciative modalities'. Enunciative modalities are types of discursive activity such as describing, forming hypotheses, formulating regulations, teaching, and so forth, each of which has its own associated subject positions. So, for example, teaching as a discursive activity positions those who take part as 'teacher' or 'learner'. As in the case of 'objects', the rules of formation for enunciative modalities are constituted for a particular discursive formation by a complex group of relations. Foucault sums these up for clinical discourse:

> If, in clinical discourse, the doctor is in turn the sovereign direct questioner, the observing eye, the touching finger, the organ that deciphers signs, the point at which previously formulated descriptions are integrated, the laboratory technician, it is because a whole group of relations is involved...between a number of distinct elements, some of which concerned the status of doctors, others the institutional and technical site [hospital, laboratory, private practice, etc.] from which they spoke, others their position as subjects perceiving, observing, describing, teaching, etc. (1972: 53)

This articulation of enunciative modalities is historically specific and open to historical change; attention to the social conditions under which such articulations are transformed and the mechanisms of their transformation is a significant part of researching discursive change in relation to social change (see pp. 96–9 and chapter 7 below). Rather than postulating a unitary 'subject of medicine' which would give coherence to these various enunciative modalities and subject positions, Foucault suggests that these various modalities and positions manifest the dispersion or fragmentation of the subject. In other words, a doctor is constituted through a configuration of enunciative modalities and subject positions which is held in place by the current rules of medical discourse. Foucault's work is a major contribution to the decentering of the social subject in recent social theories (see Henriques et al. 1984), the view of the subject as constituted, reproduced and transformed in and through social practice, and the view of the subject as fragmented.

What is of particular significance in the present context is that Foucault attributes a major role to discourse in the constitution of social subjects. By implication, questions of subjectivity, social identity, and 'selfhood' ought to be of major concern in theories of discourse and language, and in discursive and linguistic analysis. In fact, they have received very little attention indeed in mainstream linguistics, linguistically- and textually-oriented discourse analysis, sociolinguistics, or linguistic pragmatics. These academic disciplines have almost always held the sort of pre-social view of the social subject that has been widely rejected in recent debates on subjectivity. According to this view, people enter social practice and interaction with social identities which are preformed, which affect their practice, but are not affected by it. In terms of language, it is widely taken for granted in these disciplines that a person's social identity will affect how they use language, but there is little sense of language use – discursive practices – affecting or shaping social identity. Subjectivity and social identity are marginal issues in language studies, generally not going beyond theories of 'expression' and 'expressive meaning': the identity (social provenance, gender, class, attitudes, beliefs, and so forth) of a speaker is 'expressed' in the linguistic forms and meanings she chooses.

As against this, I shall take up Foucault's position by placing the question of the effects of discursive practice upon social identity at the centre of TODA, theoretically and methodologically. This view has significant consequences for the claims of discourse analysis to be a major method of social research: an expressive theory of subjectivity in discourse allows discourse to be seen as a secondary and marginal dimension of social practice, whereas a constitutive theory does not. However, there are important reservations. Foucault's insistence upon the subject as an effect of discursive formations has a heavily structuralist flavour which excludes active social agency in any meaningful sense. This is unsatisfactory, for reasons I go into in the final section. The position on discourse and subjectivity I shall advocate in chapter 3 (pp. 90–1 below) is a dialectical one, which sees social subjects as shaped by discursive practices, yet also capable of reshaping and restructuring those practices.

The Formation of Concepts

By 'concepts', Foucault means the battery of categories, elements and types which a discipline uses as an apparatus for treating its field of interest: he gives the example of subject, predicate, noun, verb, and word as concepts of grammar. But as in the case of objects and enunciative modalities, a discursive formation does not define a unitary set of stable concepts in well-defined relations to each other. The picture is rather one of shifting configurations of changing concepts. Foucault proposes to approach the formation of concepts within a discursive formation through a description of how the 'field of statements' associated with it, in which its concepts 'appeared and circulated', is organized. This strategy gives rise to a rich account (1972) of the many different sorts of relationship that may exist within and between texts. This is helpful in developing intertextual and interdiscursive perspectives in TODA, particularly since these perspectives have received scant attention in linguistics or in linguistically-oriented discourse analysis.

Within the 'field of statements' of a discursive formation, there are relationships along various dimensions. One class of relationships is between the statements of a single text, for example the relationships of sequence and dependence. Foucault refers to 'various rhetorical schemata according to which groups of statements may be combined (how descriptions, deductions, definitions, whose succession characterizes the architecture of a text, are linked together)' in ways that depend on the discursive formation (1972: 57). Such intratextual relations have been investigated more recently within text linguistics. Other relationships are 'interdiscursive', concerning the relationship between different discursive formations or different texts. Interdiscursive relations can be differentiated according to whether they belong to fields of 'presence', 'concomitance' or 'memory'. Foucault defines a field of presence as 'all statements formulated elsewhere and taken up in discourse, acknowledged to be truthful, involving exact description, well-founded reasoning, or necessary presupposition', as well as 'those that are criticized, discussed, judged...rejected or excluded' (pp. 57–8), either explicitly or implicitly. A field of concomitance consists more specifically of statements from different discursive formations, and is linked to the issue of relationships between discursive formations. Finally, a field of memory consists of statements 'that are no longer accepted or discussed' through which 'relations of filiation, genesis, transformation, continuity, and historical discontinuity can be established' (pp. 98–9). Foucault adds relations of a statement to 'all the formulations whose subsequent possibility is determined by' it, and those whose status (e.g. as literature) the statement shares.

Foucault sums up this perspective in the claim that 'there can be no statement that in one way or another does not reactualize others' (1972: 98). His treatment of relations between statements is reminiscent of writings on genre and dialogism by Bakhtin (1981, 1986), which Kristeva introduced to western audiences with the concept of intertextuality (1986a: 37). And as I noted above, Pêcheux adopts a similar perspective in giving primacy to 'interdiscourse' in his theory of discourse. Although distinctions between Foucault's various types of relation are not always clear, what he is providing here is the basis for systematic investigation of relations within and between texts and types of discourse. I shall draw a distinction between 'intertextuality', relations between texts, and 'interdiscursivity', relations between discursive formations or more loosely between different types of discourse (see pp. 117–18 below). Interdiscursivity involves the relations between other discursive formations which according to Foucault constitute the rules of formation of a given discursive formation (see the sections above on the formation of objects and enunciative modalities).

In discussing relationships within fields of statements, Foucault (1972: 97–8) makes some valuable comments upon the notion of 'context', and specifically upon how the 'situational context' of a statement (the social situation in which it occurs) and its verbal context (its position in relation to other statements which precede and follow it) determine the form it takes, and the way it is interpreted. It is a commonplace in sociolinguisitics that statements (or 'utterances') are so determined. The important additional observation that Foucault makes is that the relationship between an utterance and its verbal and situational context is not a transparent one: how context affects what is said or written, and how it is interpreted, varies from one discursive formation to another. For instance, aspects of the social identity of a speaker such as gender, ethnicity or age which are likely to substantially affect forms and meanings in a conversation may have little effect in a conference of biologists. Again, the fact that an utterance from one participant appears immediately after a question from another may constitute a stronger cue to take that utterance as answering the question in a cross-examination than in a casual conversation. One cannot therefore simply appeal to 'context' to explain what is said or written or how it is interpreted, as many linguists in sociolinguistics and pragmatics do: one must take a step back to the discursive formation and the articulation of discursive formations in orders of discourse to explicate the context-text-meaning relationship.

The Formation of Strategies

The rules of formation discussed so far constitute a field of possibilities for the creation of theories, themes, or what Foucault calls 'strategies', not all of which are actually realized. The rules for the formation of strategies determine which possibilities are realized. They are constituted by a combination of interdiscursive and nondiscursive constraints on possible strategies (1972: 66–70). Foucault suggests, for instance, that 'economic discourse, in the Classical period, is defined by a certain constant way of relating possibilities of systematization interior to a discourse, other discourses that are exterior to it, and a whole non-discursive field of practices, appropriation, interests and desires' (1972: 69). Notice the reiteration here of interdiscursive relations as constraints upon a discursive formation. Foucault notes that possible relationships between discourses include analogy, opposition, complementarity, and 'relations of mutual delimitation' (p. 67).

The discussion of non-discursive constraints here is the nearest Foucault comes in this earlier work to acknowledging that discourse is determined 'from outside': the predominant position taken on the relationship between discursive and non-discursive practice suggests rather that the former has primacy over the latter. Foucault refers first to the function of the discourse in a field of non-discursive practices, such as 'the function carried out by economic discourse in the practice of emergent capitalism' (1972: 69); second to the 'rules and processes of appropriation' of discourse, in the sense that the 'right to speak' and 'ability to understand' as well as the right to draw upon 'the corpus of already formulated statements' are unequally distributed between social groups (p. 68); third to 'the *possible positions of desire in relation to discourse*: discourse may in fact be the place for a phantasmatic representation, an element of symbolization, a form of the forbidden, an instrument of derived satisfaction' (p. 68, Foucault's italics).

Foucault associates the rules for the formation of strategies with the 'materiality' of statements. The non-discursive constraints just referred to establish relationships between statements and institutions. By the 'materiality' of a statement, Foucault means not its property of being uttered at a particular time or place, but the fact of it having a particular status within particular institutional practices.

From Archaeology to Genealogy

I have already referred to the shifts of focus in the course of Foucault's work. My concern now is with the shift from archaeology to genealogy, and its implications for Foucault's conception of discourse.

Foucault makes the following succinct explanation of the relationship between archaeology and genealogy:

> 'Truth' is to be understood as a system of ordered procedures for the production, regulation, distribution, circulation and operation of statements.
>
> 'Truth' is linked in a circular relation with systems of power which produce and sustain it, and to effects of power which it induces and which extend it. A 'regime' of truth. (Rabinow 1984: 74)

The first proposition is, I hope, a recognizable summary of archaeology as I have outlined it above. The second shows in brief the effect of genealogy upon archaeology: it adds power, or, in Davidson's words, its focus is in 'the mutual relations between systems of truth and modalities of power' (1986: 224). The shift to genealogy represents a decentering of discourse. Whereas in Foucault (1972) the intelligibility of systems of knowledge and truth was attributed to rules of discourse which were conceived as autonomous – and indeed the relationship of non-discursive to discursive practice was apparently regulated by these rules – in Foucault's major genealogical study *Discipline and Punish* (1979) discourse is secondary to systems of power.

At the same time, however, the view of the nature of power in modern societies which Foucault develops in his genealogical studies (see Fraser 1989) places discourse and language at the heart of social practices and processes. The character of power in modern societies is tied to problems of managing populations. Power is implicit within everyday social practices which are pervasively distributed at every level in all domains of social life, and are constantly engaged in; moreover, it 'is tolerable only on condition that it masks a substantial part of itself. Its success is proportional to its ability to hide its own mechanisms' (1981: 86). Power does not work negatively by forcefully dominating those who are subject to it; it incorporates them, and is 'productive' in the sense that it shapes and 'retools' them to fit in with its needs. Modern power was not imposed from above by particular collective agents (e.g. classes) upon groups or individuals; it developed 'from below' in certain 'microtechniques' (such as 'examination' in its medical or educational senses: see below), which emerged in institutions such as hospitals, prisons and schools at the beginning of the modern period. Such techniques imply a dual relation between power and knowledge in modern society: on the one hand, the techniques of power are developed on the basis of knowledge which is generated, for example, in the social sciences; on the other hand, the techniques are very much concerned with exercising power in the process of gathering knowledge. Foucault coins the term 'bio-power' to refer to this modern form of power, which has emerged since the seventeenth century: bio-power 'brought life and its mechanisms into the realm of explicit calculations and made knowledge/power an agent of transformation of human life' (1981: 143).

This conception of power suggests that discourse and language are of central importance in the social processes of modern society: the practices and techniques that Foucault places so much weight upon – interview, counselling, and so forth – are to a substantial degree discursive practices. Thus analysing institutions and organizations in terms of power entails understanding and analysing their discursive practices. But Foucault's view of power implies not only greater attention to discourse in social analysis, but also more attention to power in discourse analysis; these questions about discourse and power arise neither in Foucault's archaeological studies, nor in linguistically-oriented approaches to discourse analysis. As Shapiro points out: 'Foucault takes the language–politics connection to a higher level of abstraction, one that permits us to go beyond the linguistically reflected power exchanges between persons and groups to an analysis of the structures within which they are deployed' (1981: 162).

Some of these issues are raised by Foucault himself in a study (1984) which explores various procedures through which discursive practices are socially controlled and constrained: 'in every society, the production of discourse is at once controlled, selected, organized and redistributed by a certain number of procedures whose role is to ward off its powers and dangers, to gain mastery over its chance events, to evade its ponderous, formidable, materiality' (p. 109). Among the 'procedures' that Foucault examines are constraints upon what can be said, by whom, and on what occasions; oppositions between the discourses of reason and madness, and between true and false discourse; the effects of attributions of authorship, boundaries between disciplines, and attribution of canonical status to certain texts; and social constraints on access to certain discursive practices – Foucault notes in this connection that 'any system of education is a political way of maintaining or modifying the appropriation of discourses, along with the knowledges and powers which they carry' (p. 123). A significant emphasis in Foucault (1984) is upon power struggle over the determination of discursive practices: 'Discourse.is not simply that which translates struggles or systems of domination, but is the thing for which and by which there is struggle, discourse is the power which is to be seized' (p. 110).

The move from archaeology to genealogy involves a shift of emphasis in terms of which dimensions of discourse are given prominence. Whereas the discursive formations of Foucault (1972) are characterized in terms of particular disciplines (e.g. the discourses of psychopathology, political economy, and natural history, though Foucault resists the idea of a simple correspondence between discourses and disciplines), the salient discourse categories of Foucault (1979, 1981) are of a more 'generic' character (e.g. interview and counselling, as discursive practices associated respectively with what Foucault calls 'examination' and 'confession: see below). That is, they point to various forms of interaction which are structured in particular ways and involve particular sets of participants (e.g. interviewer and interviewee), which can be used in various disciplines or institutions and are thus compatible with various discursive formations (so there are medical, sociological, job and media interviews). The contrast for some writers is between 'discourses' and 'genres' (see Kress 1988, and pp. 125–8 below).

Two major 'technologies' of power analysed by Foucault are 'discipline' (with 'examination' as its core technique, Foucault 1979) and 'confession' (Foucault 1981). A primary and initially surprising concern of genealogical analysis is how techniques work upon 'bodies', that is, how they affect the detailed normalized forms of control over bodily dispositions, habits and movements which are discernible in modern societies, most obviously in the drilling of the body in military training and analogous processes in industry, education, medicine, and so forth. The modern technology of discipline is geared to producing what Foucault calls 'docile bodies', and bodies which are adapted to the demands of modern forms of economic production. Discipline is manifest in such diverse forms as the architecture of prisons, schools or factories which are designed to allocate to each inmate a space (cell, desk, bench, etc.) which can be subjected to constant observation; the division of the educational or working day into strictly demarcated parts; the disciplining of bodily activity in connection with, for instance, traditional teaching of handwriting, which 'presupposes a gymnastics – a whole routine whose rigorous code invests the body in its entirety' (1979: 152); or 'normalizing judgement', the ways in which systems of punishment constantly measure individuals against norms. Although discipline is a technology for handling masses of people, it does so in a highly individualizing way, in a way which isolates and focuses in on each and every individual in turn and subjects them to the same normalizing procedures. In accordance with Foucault's emphasis on the productivity of power, disciplinary power produces the modern individual (1979: 194).

The 'examination' implements 'power relations that make it possible to extract and constitute knowledge' (1979: 185). Foucault isolates three distinctive properties of the examination (1979: 187–92). First, 'the examination transformed the economy of visibility into the exercise of power.' Foucault contrasts feudal power, where the powerful sovereign was highly visible whereas those who were subject to power 'could remain in the shade', and modern disciplinary power wherein power is invisible but its subjects spotlighted. Constant visibility on the one hand keeps the individual subjected, and on the other allows individuals to be treated and 'arranged' like objects. The examination 'is, as it were, the ceremony of this objectification'. Second, 'the examination also introduces individuality into the field of documentation': examination is associated with the production of records about people. This has two consequences: 'the constitution of the individual as a describable, analysable object', and the manipulation of records to arrive at generalizations about populations, averages, norms, etc. The latter is, Foucault suggests, the humble point of origin of the human sciences. Third, 'the examination, surrounded by all its documentary techniques, makes each individual a "case": a case which at one and the same time constitutes an object for a branch of knowledge and a hold for a branch of power.' Foucault contrasts the traditional practice of writing chronicles of the great to stand as monuments, with the modern disciplinary writing of case histories to subject and objectify.

If the examination is the technique of objectifying people, the confession is the technique of subjectifying them. 'Western man', Foucault writes, 'has become a confessing animal' (1981: 174). The compulsion to delve into and talk about oneself, and especially one's sexuality, in an ever widening set of social locations (originally religion, but then love relationships, family relationships, medicine, education, and so forth) appears on the face of it to be a liberating resistance to objectifying bio-power. Foucault, however, believes that this is an illusion: confession draws more of the person into the domain of power.

Foucault defines confession in overtly discursive terms as a 'ritual of discourse', what one might call a genre in terms more familiar within TODA. Confession is defined first by topic – 'the speaking subject is also the subject of the statement' – and then by the power relationship between those involved: 'one does not confess without the presence (or virtual presence) of a partner who is not simply the interlocutor but the authority who requires the confession, prescribes and appreciates it, and intervenes in order to judge, forgive, console, and reconcile' (1981: 61). Confession has the peculiar feature that the very act of doing it changes the person who does it; it 'exonerates, redeems, and purifies him; it unburdens him of his wrongs, liberates him and promises him salvation' (p. 62). Furthermore, the value of a confession is increased by the obstacles and resistance one has to overcome to make it.

Although Foucault's account of confession is more explicitly discursive than his account of examination (he refers to the former as a 'discursive form' as well as a 'ritual of discourse'), I would suggest that both are clearly associated with particular discourse genres. In the case of examination, these would include medical examination, educational examining, and many varieties of interview. In the case of confession, they would include not only religious confession but also therapeutic discourses and varieties of counselling. One of Foucault's themes is how confession gained scientific status in the nineteenth century, and he notes in this connection that examination and confession were combined in the interrogation, the 'exacting questionnaire', and hypnosis.

The techniques of power which Foucault draws attention to are relevant to types of discourse which have become salient in modern society, and which seem to be closely associated with its modes of social organization and its cultural values. These culturally salient genres, especially interviewing and counselling, and those associated with management and advertising, appear to be 'colonizing' the orders of discourse of various contemporary institutions and organizations. In this process, they have undergone a dramatic expansion of functions as they have moved across boundaries between institutions, generating many sub-types and variants (therapeutic, educational, employment and consumer counselling, for example). Interview and counselling represent respectively objectifying and subjectifying genres corresponding to the objectifying technique of examination and the subjectifying technique of confession, and the modes of discourse which bureaucratically 'handle' people like objects on the one hand, and modes of discourse which explore and give voice to the self, appear to be two foci of the modern order of discourse.

In this respect, Foucault's genealogical perspective points to directions of research into discourse which are important to the concerns of this book: the investigation of historical transformations in the discursive practices of orders of discourse, and their relationship to wider processes of social and cultural change (see pp. 96–9 and chapter 7 below). There are important issues of causality here: to what extent do discursive changes constitute these wider social or cultural changes, as opposed to merely 'reflecting' them? And how far, therefore, can wider processes of change be researched through analysis of changing discursive practices? There is also the question of how widespread and how effective are conscious efforts by institutional agents to engineer changes in discursive practices, drawing upon social scientific research (e.g. into interview techniques), often simulating the informal conversation discursive practices of the private sphere in public domains on the basis of calculations of their effectiveness (e.g. in putting interviewees at ease), and training institutional personnel in new discursive techniques. I refer to this process of intervention as the 'technologization of discourse': discourse itself is now widely subject to the technologies and techniques Foucault identified with the modern workings of power (see further pp. 215–18 below).

Foucault and Textually-Oriented Discourse Analysis

The major insights into discourse that I have identified in Foucault's work can be summarized as follows. In his earlier archaeological work, there are two claims of particular importance:

1 the constitutive nature of discourse – discourse constitutes the social, including 'objects' and social subjects;
2 the primacy of interdiscursivity and intertextuality – any discursive practice is defined by its relations with others, and draws upon others in complex ways.

Three further substantive points emerge from Foucault's genealogical work:

3 the discursive nature of power – the practices and techniques of modern 'biopower' (e.g. examination and confession) are to a significant degree discursive;

4   the political nature of discourse – power struggle occurs both in and over discourse;
5   the discursive nature of social change – changing discursive practices are an important element in social change.

These constitute a rich set of theoretical claims and hypotheses to try to incorporate and operationalize within TODA.

There are, however, certain difficulties for TODA in Foucault's work, such as his neglect of textual analysis, and his view of discourse as constitutive. The purpose of this final section is to discuss these difficulties, and to indicate respects in which TODA should not follow Foucault.

As I have indicated above, a major contrast between Foucault and TODA is that Foucault's analysis of discourse does not include discursive and linguistic analysis of real texts. Yet the inclusion of such analysis may be a means of overcoming certain weaknesses which commentators have found in Foucault's work. I am not suggesting a reduction of discourse analysis to textual or linguistic analysis. The issue is rather whether analysis should include actual instances of discourse. When they are included, in TODA, they should be subjected not just to linguistic forms of textual analysis, but to analysis on three dimensions: analysis of the text, analysis of discourse processes of text production and interpretation (including the question of which discourse types and genres are drawn upon, and how they are articulated), and social analysis of the discursive 'event' in terms of its social conditions and effects at various levels (situationally, institutionally, societally). (See also pp. 71–3 below.) So what I am advocating is textual analysis in conjunction with other types of analysis, and the main issue is whether specific instances (and texts) should be analysed.

The relevant weaknesses in Foucault's work have to do with conceptions of power and resistance, and questions of struggle and change. Foucault is charged with exaggerating the extent to which the majority of people are manipulated by power; he is accused of not giving enough weight to the contestation of practices, struggles between social forces over them, possibilities of dominated groups opposing dominant discursive and non-discursive systems, possibilities of change being brought about in power relations through struggle, and so forth (Lecourt 1972;

Macdonell 1986). It is not that Foucault ignores such matters: he is interested in change, for instance, since he devotes a whole chapter of Foucault (1972) to 'change and transformations', in which he stresses throughout that the rules of formation of discursive formations define not static objects and concepts but the fields of their possible transformation. And in Foucault (1982), there is a full discussion of forms of struggle. It is rather that in the totality of his work and in the major analyses, the dominant impression is one of people being helplessly subjected to immovable systems of power. Foucault certainly insists that power necessarily entails resistance, but he gives the impression that resistance is generally contained by power and poses no threat. This would seem to be so, for instance, in what Foucault calls the 'reverse discourse' of homosexuality. Preoccupation with homosexuality in the discourses of nineteenth-century psychiatry and jurisprudence resulted in homosexuality beginning to 'speak in its own name...often in the same vocabulary, using the same categories by which it was medically disqualified' (1981: 101). It is thus a resistant discourse which does not go outside the parameters of its discourse formation.

These problems seem to be connected with the absence of a concept of practice in Foucault's analyses, including the absence of text and textual analysis. By 'practice' I mean real instances of people doing or saying or writing things. Foucault (1972) does refer to practice, when he introduces the concept of 'discursive practice', but he defines it in a confusing way as 'rules' which underlie actual practice: a discursive practice is 'a system of anonymous, historical rules' (p. 117). In other words, practice is being reduced to its converse, structures, using that term in the broad sense of the resources which underlie and are necessary for (as well as being a product of) practice. It appears to be always structures that are in focus, be it the rules of formation of Foucault (1972), or techniques such as the examination in Foucault (1979). Yet Foucault is of course claiming to talk about practice: his focus upon structures is intended to account for what can and does actually happen.

The questionable assumption is that one can extrapolate from structure to practice, that one can arrive at conclusions about practice without directly analysing real instances of it, including texts. This would seem to imply, for instance, that practice is considerably more uniform than we have reason to believe; that the extent to which and ways in which practice is determined by structures are less variable than they would appear to be; and that the determination of which rules or sets of rules are drawn upon in practice is more straightforward than it actually is. In brief, what is missing is any sense that practice has properties of its own which (i) cannot be reduced to the implementation of structures; (ii) imply that how structures figure in practice cannot be assumed, but has to be determined; and (iii) ultimately help to shape structures.

There is a further absence associated with this focus on structures: that of the detailed mechanisms of change. How did the structures come to be as they are? How do the structures get to be different? As Taylor (1986: 90) says with reference to Foucault, 'for purposes of such diachronic explanation, we can question whether we ought to speak of a priority of language over act. There is a circular relation. Structures of action or languages are only maintained by being renewed constantly in action/speech. And it is in action/speech that they also fail to be maintained, that they are altered.' In other words, structures are reproduced but also transformed in practice.

But if structures may be reproduced or transformed in practice, what is it that determines actual outcomes in different instances? More generally, what is it that determines the cumulative outcomes of practice in particular social domains or institutions, and differences between them in the reproductive as opposed to transformative tendencies of discourse? I would want to suggest that structures are reproduced or transformed depending the state of relations, the 'balance of power', between those in struggle in a particular sustained domain of practice, such as the school or the workplace. Too great a focus upon structures is tantamount to taking a one-sided perspective in respect of these struggles – the perspective of the powerful, of those whose problem is preserving social order and sustaining domination. The Gramscian conceptualization of power in terms of hegemony is superior to Foucault's conception of power in that it avoids such imbalances (Gramsci 1971; Hall 1988). In this approach, hegemony is conceived as an unstable equilibrium built upon alliances and the generation of consent from subordinate classes and groups, whose instabilities are the constant focus of struggles (see pp. 91–6 below for further discussion). Foucault's neglect of practice and of detailed mechanisms of change goes along with a neglect of struggle, other than modes of 'resistance' which are assumed not to have the capacity fundamentally to transform structures.

The absence of a focus upon practice and struggle can help to explain why Foucault's analyses come across as 'terribly one-sided' in another respect (Taylor 1986: 81). The techniques of power which feature in the genealogical studies are interpreted as unambivalent tools of domination and manipulation. But consider the case of counselling as a form of confession in contemporary society. Counselling is indeed used to bring the insides of people's heads into the domain of power/knowledge, but it is also a technique for asserting the value and individuality of people in a society which increasingly treats them (as Foucault has shown us) as ciphers. Counselling is highly ambivalent and the manifest complexity of its relationship to power must rule out any claim that its liberating dimensions are just illusory. A more fruitful way forward is the investigation of how counselling works as a discourse technique in practice, including a study of struggles in discourse over its contradictory orientations to domination and emancipation (see pp. 221–2 below).

There are, however, some comments in Foucault on the 'tactical polyvalence of discourses' which do point in this direction:

> There is not, on the one side, a discourse of power, and opposite it, another discourse that runs counter to it. Discourses are tactical elements or blocks operating in the field of force relations; there can exist different and even contradictory discourses within the same strategy; they can, on the contrary, circulate without changing their form from one strategy to another, opposing strategy. We must not expect the discourses on sex to tell us, above all, what strategy they derive from, or what moral divisions they accompany, or what ideology – dominant or dominated – they represent; rather we must question them on the two levels of their tactical productivity (what reciprocal effects of power and knowledge they ensure) and their strategical integration (what conjunction and what force relationship make their utilization necessary in a given episode of the various confrontations that occur). (1981: 101–2)

I shall discuss such a perspective below (p. 67) in terms of discourses and orders of discourse being amenable to political and ideological 'investment', without being necessarily so invested, or invested in a particular direction.

The notion of the tactical polyvalence of discourses is a valuable insight into processes of ideological struggle in discourse as they might be envisaged in a hegemonic model. Yet Foucault himself is resistant to the concept of ideology, and resistant also to the idea of analysis as a form of ideological critique. These positions arise from Foucault's relativism: truth is relative to particular discursive formations, particular systems of power/knowledge, which are therefore not open to critique from positions outside or above them. It has been pointed out, however, that Foucault's position is a contradictory one, in that he appears to be committed to certain forms of critique which are at odds with his relativism, so that he ends up being ambivalent about critique (Dews 1987; Fraser 1989). In the account of TODA in chapter 3 below, I shall differ from Foucault in using the concept of ideology, and assuming that TODA is a form of ideological critique. However, the criticisms of Foucault and others mean that one must be careful to avoid some of the cruder conceptions of ideology (see Thompson 1990).

My final reservation about Foucault relates to his valuable insights into the constitutive properties of discourse. While I accept that both 'objects' and social subjects are shaped by discursive practices, I would wish to insist that these practices are constrained by the fact that they inevitably take place within a constituted, material reality, with preconstituted 'objects' and preconstituted social subjects. The constitutive processes of discourse ought therefore to be seen in terms of a dialectic, in which the impact of discursive practice depends upon how it interacts with the preconstituted reality. With respect to 'objects', it is perhaps helpful to use both the terms 'referring' and 'signifying': discourse includes reference to preconstituted objects, as well as the creative and constitutive signification of objects. Here again, analyses of real practice and real text are an important corrective to Foucault's overstatement of the constitutive effects of discourse. For example, studies of media discourse which have focused upon how particular texts are interpreted as well as upon how they are organized have suggested a highly complex picture, in which texts may be interpreted from various more or less compliant or oppositional positions, making highly problematic any schematic view of the effect of discourse upon the constitution of, for example, social subjects. This sort of example also indicates that the process of constituting subjects always takes place within particular forms of interaction between preconstituted subjects, where the forms of interaction influence the constitutive process (see Dews 1987: 198). It also suggests that constituted social subjects are not merely passively positioned but are capable of acting as agents, and amongst other things of negotiating their relationship with the multifarious types of discourse they are drawn into.

To sum up, I am suggesting that TODA is likely to strengthen social analysis, essentially by ensuring attention to concrete instances of practice and the textual forms and processes of interpretation associated with them. Such attention to the detail of particular cases can help social analysts avoid the schematism and one-sidedness which limit Foucault's work, be it in relation to the effects of power and possibilities of resistance, the constitution of social subjects, or the social and cultural values associated with particular genres such as counselling. It can also help to relate general statements about social and cultural change to the precise mechanisms and modalities of the effects of change in practice.

3

A Social Theory of Discourse

In this chapter I present a view of discourse and a framework for discourse analysis which will be elaborated and illustrated in the rest of the book. My approach is dictated by the objectives set out in the Introduction: to bring together linguistically-oriented discourse analysis and social and political thought relevant to discourse and language, in the form of a framework which will be suitable for use in social scientific research, and specifically in the study of social change. The first two chapters have identified a number of achievements and limitations of previous work, and chapter 3 is written in the light of that discussion without being directly based upon it. I begin with a discussion of the term 'discourse', and go on to analyse discourse in a three-dimensional framework as text, discursive practice, and social practice. These three dimensions of analysis are discussed in turn, and I conclude by setting out my approach to investigating discursive change in its relationship with social and cultural change.

Discourse

My focus is upon language, and accordingly I use 'discourse' more narrowly than social scientists generally do to refer to spoken or written language use. I shall be using the term 'discourse' where linguists have traditionally written about 'language use', 'parole' or 'performance'. In the tradition initiated by Ferdinand de Saussure (1959), parole is regarded as not amenable to systematic study because it is essentially individual activity: individuals draw in unpredictable ways according to their wishes and intentions upon a language, a 'langue', which is itself systematic and social. Linguists in this tradition identify parole in order to dismiss it, for the implication of the Saussurean position is that any systematic study of language must be a study of the system itself, the langue, and not of its 'use'.

De Saussure's position has come under sustained attack from sociolinguists who have asserted that language use is shaped socially and not individually. They have argued that variation in language use is systematic and amenable to scientific study, and that what makes it systematic is its correlation with social variables: language varies according to the nature of the relationship between participants in interactions, the type of social event, the social goals people are pursuing in an interaction, and so forth (Downes 1984). While this clearly represents an advance on the dominant Saussurean tradition in mainstream linguistics, it has two main limitations. Firstly, the emphasis tends to be one-sidedly upon how language varies according to social factors, which suggests that types of social subject, social relations, and situation exist quite independently of language use, and precludes the possibility of language use actually contributing to their constitution, reproduction and change. Secondly, the 'social variables' which are seen as correlating with linguistic variables are relatively surface features of social situations of language use, and there is no sense that properties of language use may be determined in a more global sense by the social structure at a deeper level – social relations between classes and other groups, ways in which social institutions are articulated in the social formation, and so forth – and may contribute to reproducing and transforming it.

In using the term 'discourse', I am proposing to regard language use as a form of social practice, rather than a purely individual activity or a reflex of situational variables. This has various implications. Firstly, it implies that discourse is a mode of action, one form in which people may act upon the world and especially upon each other, as well as a mode of representation. This is a view of language use which has been made familiar, though often in individualistic terms, by linguistic philosophy and linguistic pragmatics (Levinson 1983). Secondly, it implies that there is a dialectical relationship between discourse and social structure, there being more generally such a relationship between social practice and social structure: the latter is both a condition for, and an effect of, the former. On the one hand, discourse is shaped and constrained by social structure in the widest sense and at all levels: by class and other social relations at a societal level, by the relations specific to particular institutions such as law or education, by systems of classification, by various norms and conventions of both a discursive and a non-discursive nature, and so forth. Specific discursive events vary in their structural determination according to the particular social domain or institutional framework in which they are generated. On the other hand, discourse is socially constitutive. This is the import of Foucault's discussion of the discursive formation of objects, subjects and concepts. Discourse contributes to the constitution of all those dimensions of social structure which directly or indirectly shape and constrain it: its own norms and conventions, as well as the relations, identities and institutions which lie behind them. Discourse is a practice not just of representing the world, but of signifying the world, constituting and constructing the world in meaning.

We can distinguish three aspects of the constructive effects of discourse. Discourse contributes first of all to the construction of what are variously referred to as 'social identities' and 'subject positions' for social 'subjects' and types of 'self' (see Henriques et al. 1984; Weedon 1987). We should, however, recall the discussion of Foucault on this issue in chapter 2 and my observations there about overstating the constructivist position. Secondly, discourse helps construct social relationships between people. And thirdly, discourse contributes to the construction of systems of knowledge and belief. These three effects correspond respectively to three functions of language and dimensions of meaning which coexist and interact in all discourse – what I shall call the 'identity', 'relational', and 'ideational' functions of language. The identity function relates to the ways in which social identities are set up in discourse, the relational function to how social relationships between discourse participants are enacted and negotiated, the ideational function to ways in which texts signify the world and its processes, entities and relations. The identity and relational functions are grouped together by Halliday (1978) as the 'interpersonal' function. Halliday also distinguishes a 'textual' function which can be usefully added to my list: this concerns how bits of information are foregrounded or backgrounded, taken as given or presented as new, picked out as 'topic' or 'theme', and how a part of a text is linked to preceeding and following parts of the text, and to the social situation 'outside' the text.

Discursive practice is constitutive in both conventional and creative ways: it contributes to reproducing society (social identities, social relationships, systems of knowledge and belief) as it is, yet also contributes to transforming society. For example, the identities of teachers and pupils and the relationships between them which are at the heart of a system of education depend upon a consistency and durability of patterns of speech within and around those relationships for their reproduction. Yet they are open to transformations which may partly originate in discourse: in the speech of the classroom, the playground, the staffroom, educational debate, and so forth.

It is important that the relationship between discourse and social structure should be seen dialectically if we are to avoid the pitfalls of overemphasizing on the one hand the social determination of discourse, and on the other hand the construction of the social in discourse. The former turns discourse into a mere reflection of a deeper social reality, the latter idealistically represents discourse as the source of the social. The latter is perhaps the more immediately dangerous pitfall, given the emphasis in contemporary debates on the constitutive properties of discourse. Let us look at an example to see how this pitfall can be avoided without compromising the constitutiveness principle. Parent-child relationships in the family, the determination of what positions of 'mother', 'father' and 'child' are socially available as well as the placing of real individuals in these positions, the nature of the family, and of the home, are all constituted partly in discourse, as cumulative (and in fact contradictory) outcomes of complex and diverse processes of talk and writing. This could easily lead to the idealist conclusion that realities of the social world such as the family merely emanate from people's heads. However, there are three provisos which together help to block this. First, people are always confronted with the family as a real institution (in a limited number of variant forms) with concrete practices, existing relations and identities which have themselves been constituted in discourse, but reified into institutions and practices. Second, the constitutive effects of discourse work in conjunction with those of other practices, such as the distribution of household tasks, dress, and affective aspects of behaviour (e.g. who gets emotional). Third, the constitutive work of discourse necessarily takes place within the constraints of the dialectical determination of discourse by social structures (which in this case include but go beyond the reality of family structures), and, as I shall argue below, within particular power relations and struggles. Thus the discursive constitution of society does not emanate from a free play of ideas in people's heads but from a social practice which is firmly rooted in and oriented to real, material social structures.

A dialectical perspective is also a necessary corrective to an overemphasis on the determination of discourse by structures, discursive structures (codes, conventions and norms) as well as non-discursive structures. From this point of view, the capacity of the word 'discourse' to refer to the structures of convention which underlie actual discursive events as well as the events themselves is a felicitous ambiguity, even if from other points of view it can be confusing. Structuralism (represented, for example, by Pêcheux's approach described in chapter 1 above) comes to treat discursive practice and the discursive event as mere instantiations of discursive structures, which are themselves represented as unitary and fixed. It sees discursive practice in terms of a model of mechanistic (and therefore pessimistic) causality. The dialectical perspective sees practice and the event as contradictory and in struggle, with a complex and variable relationship to structures which themselves manifest only a temporary, partial and contradictory fixity.

Social practice has various orientations – economic, political, cultural, ideological – and discourse may be implicated in all of these without any of them being reducible to discourse. For example, there are a number of ways in which discourse may be said to be a mode of economic practice: discourse figures in variable proportions as a constituent of economic practice of a basically non-discursive nature, such as building bridges or producing washing machines; there are forms of economic practice which are of a basically discursive nature, such as the stock market, journalism, or writing soap operas for television. Moreover, a society's sociolinguistic order may be at least in part structured as a market where texts are produced, distributed and consumed like commodities (in 'culture industries': Bourdieu 1982).

But it is discourse as a mode of political and ideological practice that is most germane to the concerns of this book. Discourse as a political practice establishes, sustains and changes power relations, and the collective entities (classes, blocs, communities, groups) between which power relations obtain. Discourse as an ideological practice constitutes, naturalizes, sustains and changes significations of the world from diverse positions in power relations. As this wording implies, political and ideological practice are not independent of each other, for ideology is significations generated within power relations as a dimension of the exercise of power and struggle over power. Thus political practice is the superordinate category. Furthermore, discourse as a political practice is not only a site of power struggle, but also a stake in power struggle: discursive practice draws upon conventions which naturalize particular power relations and ideologies, and these conventions themselves, and the ways in which they are articulated, are a focus of struggle. I shall argue below that Gramsci's concept of hegemony provides a fruitful framework for conceptualizing and investigating political and ideological dimensions of discursive practice.

Rather than particular types of discourse having inherent political or ideological values, I shall say that different types of discourse in different social domains or institutional settings may come to be politically or ideologically 'invested' (Frow 1985) in particular ways. This implies that types of discourse may also come to be invested in different ways – they may come to be 'reinvested'. (I shall give an example at the end of the discussion of discursive change below.)

How we conceive of the discursive conventions and norms which underlie discursive events is an issue of some importance. I have already alluded to the structuralist view that there are well-defined sets of conventions or codes which are merely instantiated in discursive events. This extends into a view of sociolinguistic domains as constituted by a set of such codes in complementary distribution, such that each has its own functions and situations and conditions of appropriacy which are sharply demarcated from those of others. (I have criticized views of sociolinguistic variation based upon the concept of 'appropriacy' in Fairclough forthcoming b.) Approaches of this sort trace systematic variation within speech communities according to sets of social variables, including setting (e.g. classroom, playground, staffroom, and assembly are different school settings), types of activity and social purpose (e.g. teaching, project work or testing in a classroom), and speaker (e.g. teacher as opposed to pupil). In this view, the code is primary, and a set of codes is merely a sum of its parts.

A position which is more fruitful for the historical orientation to discursive change in this book is that of French discourse analysts who suggest that 'interdiscourse', the complex interdependent configuration of discursive formations, has primacy over its parts and has properties which are not predictable from its parts (see the discussion of Pêcheux in chapter 1 above). Interdiscourse is furthermore the structural entity which underlies discursive events, rather than the individual formation or code: too many discursive events manifest an orientation to configurations of code elements and to their boundaries for the existent (but special case) of the discursive event built out of normative instantiation of a single code to be regarded as the rule. An example would be 'mixed genres' which combine elements of two or more genres, such as 'chat' in television chat shows, which is part conversation and part entertainment and performance (see Tolson 1990 for an analysis of 'chat'). I shall however use the Foucaultian term 'order of discourse' rather than interdiscourse, because it suggests more clearly the sorts of configuration envisaged.

Let us use the looser term 'element', rather than code or formation, for the parts of an order of discourse (I shall come to the nature of these elements below). In contrast with accounts based upon theories of 'appropriacy', where a single and constant relationship of complementarity between elements is assumed, I assume that the relationship may be or become a contradictory one. The boundaries between elements may be lines of tension. Consider, for instance, the diverse subject positions for a single individual across different settings and activities of an institution, along the lines of the dispersion of the subject in the formation of enunciative modalities, in Foucault's terms (see pp. 43–5 above). It is feasible that boundaries between settings and practices should be so naturalized that these subject positions are lived as complementary. Under different social circumstances, the same boundaries might become a focus of contestation and struggle, and the subject positions and the discursive practices associated with them might be experienced as contradictory. For instance, pupils may accept that narratives of their own experience in their own social dialects are 'appropriate' in designated discussion sections of lessons, but not in designated teaching sections or in written work; or again, the contradictions between what is allowed in one place but not in another may become a basis for struggle to shift boundaries between discussion, teaching and writing. The acceptability of personal experience narratives, even in a strictly delimited part of classroom activity, may be a compromise outcome of earlier boundary struggles to get them into the classroom in the first place.

What applies for boundaries between subject positions and associated discursive conventions applies generally for elements of orders of discourse. It applies also for boundaries between distinct orders of discourse. The school and its order of discourse may be experienced as being in a complementary and non-overlapping relationship with adjacent domains such as the home or neighbourhood, or on the other hand perceived contradictions between such domains may become the basis for struggles to redefine their boundaries and relationships, struggles to extend the properties of the parent – child relationship and its discursive conventions to the teacher – pupil relationship or vice-versa, for example, or to extend peer relationships and practices in the neighbourhood and the street into the school.

The outcomes of such struggles are rearticulations of orders of discourse, both of relations between elements in 'local' orders of discourse such as that of the school, and of relations between local orders of discourse in a societal order of discourse. Consequently, boundaries between elements (as well as local orders of discourse) may shift between relatively strong or relatively weak (see Bernstein 1981) depending upon their current articulation: elements may be discrete and well-defined, or they may be fuzzy and ill-defined.

Nor should it be assumed that these 'elements' are themselves internally homogeneous. A consequence of the articulatory struggle I am envisaging is that new elements are constituted through the redrawing of boundaries between old elements. An element may therefore be heterogeneous in its origins, and while that historical heterogeneity may not be experienced as such when conventions are highly naturalized, it may be experienced in different conditions as a contradiction within the element. An example would be a familiar teaching style which consists of the teacher engaging in a structured question – answer routine with pupils to elicit from them predetermined information. This style is not necessarily experienced in terms of a contradiction arising from teachers purporting to ask their pupils when they are actually in the business of telling them, but it is open to being experienced in this way. If we apply the concept of investment here, we can say that elements, local orders of discourse, and societal orders of discourse are potentially experienced as contradictorily structured, and thereby open to having their existing political and ideological investments become the focus of contention in struggles to deinvest/reinvest them.

The elements I have referred to may be very variable in 'scale'. There are cases where they appear to correspond to a conventional understanding of a fully-fledged code or 'register' (Halliday 1978), as a bloc of variants at different levels with distinctive phonological patterns, vocabulary, grammatical patterns, turn-taking rules, and so on. Examples of such cases are the discourse of bingo sessions, or cattle auctions. In other cases, however, the variables are smaller scale: particular turn-taking systems, vocabularies which incorporate particular classification schemes, scripts for genres such as crime reports or oral narratives, sets of politeness conventions, and so forth. One point of contrast between orders of discourse is the extent to which such elements do solidify into relatively durable blocs. I shall suggest (pp. 125–8 below) a small number of different types of element: genres, styles, activity types, and discourses.

It may be enlightening at this point to recall a quotation from Foucault (p. 42 above) referring to the rules of formation of objects in psychopathology. The 'relations' which Foucault identifies as having been adopted in psychiatric discourse to enable the formation of the 'objects' he refers to, can be interpreted as relations between discursive elements of different scales:

'planes of specification' and 'planes of psychological characterization' are at least partially constituted in vocabularies, whereas the 'judicial interrogation' and the 'medical questionnaire' are discursive elements of a generic type (on genre, see p. 126). Note, however, that they are not just discursive elements. Police investigation, clinical examination, and therapeutic and punitive confinement may have discursive components but they are not *per se* discursive entities. Foucault's descriptions highlight the mutual imbrication of the discursive and the non-discursive in the structural conditions for social practice. In this light, orders of discourse may be regarded as discursive facets of social orders, whose internal articulation and rearticulation have the same nature.

The focus so far has been mainly upon what makes discourse like other forms of social practice. I now need to correct the balance by addressing the question of what makes discursive practice specifically discursive. Part of the answer is evidently language: discursive practice is manifested in linguistic form, in the form of what I shall refer to as 'texts', using 'text' in Halliday's broad sense of spoken as well as written language (Halliday 1978). If being an instance of social (political, ideological, etc.) practice is one dimension of a discursive event, being a text is another.

However, this is not enough. These two dimensions are mediated by a third which focuses on discourse as a specifically discursive practice. 'Discursive practice' does not here contrast with 'social practice': the former is a particular form of the latter. In some cases, the social practice may be wholly constituted by the discursive practice, while in others it may involve a mixture of discursive and non-discursive practice. Analysis of a particular discourse as a piece of discursive practice focuses upon processes of text production, distribution and consumption. All of these processes are social and require reference to the particular economic, political and institutional settings within which discourse is generated. Production and consumption have a partially sociocognitive nature, in that they involve cognitive processes of text production and interpretation which are based upon internalized social structures and conventions (hence the 'socio-' prefix). In the account of these sociocognitive processes, one concern is to specify which (elements of) orders of discourse (as well as other social resources, called 'members' resources') are drawn upon, and how, in the production and interpretation of meanings. The central concern is to trace explanatory connections between ways (normative, innovative, etc.) in which texts are put together and interpreted, how texts are produced, distributed and consumed in a wider sense, and the nature of the social practice in terms of its relation to social structures and struggles. One can neither reconstruct the production process nor account for the interpretation process purely by reference to texts: they are respectively traces of and cues to these processes, and can be neither produced nor interpreted without members' resources. A way of linking this emphasis on discursive practice and processes of text production, distribution and consumption to the text itself is to focus upon the intertextuality of the latter: see the section 'Discursive Practice' below.

This three-dimensional conception of discourse is represented diagrammatically in figure 3.1. It is an attempt to bring together three analytical traditions, each of which is indispensable for discourse analysis. These are the tradition of close textual and linguistic analysis within linguistics, the macrosociological tradition of analysing social practice in relation to social structures, and the interpretivist or microsociological tradition of seeing social practice as something which people actively produce and make sense of on the basis of shared commonsense procedures. I accept the interpretivist claim that we must try to understand how members of social communities produce their 'orderly' or 'accountable' worlds. I take analysis of the sociocognitive processes within discursive practice to be partly dedicated to this objective (though I suggest below that it has 'macro' as well as 'micro' dimensions). I would argue, however, that in so producing their world, members' practices are shaped in ways of which they are usually unaware by social structures, relations of power, and the nature of the social practice they are engaged in whose stakes always go beyond producing meanings. Thus their procedures and practices may be politically and ideologically invested, and they may be positioned as subjects (and 'members') by them. I would also argue that members' practice has outcomes and effects upon social structures, social relations, and social struggles around them, of which again they are usually unaware. And finally, I would argue that the procedures which members use are

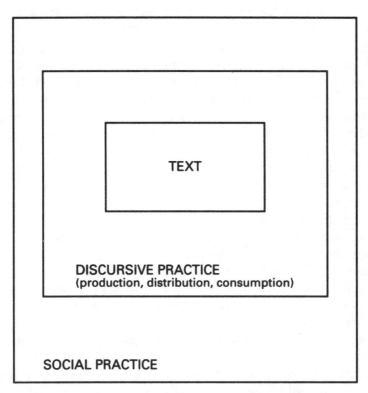

Figure 3.1 Three-dimensional conception of discourse

themselves heterogeneous and contradictory, and contested in struggles which partly have a discursive nature. The part of the procedure which deals with the analysis of texts can be called 'description', and the parts which deal with analysis of discourse practice and with analysis of the social practice of which the discourse is a part can be called 'interpretation'. (See further pp. 198–9 below on this distinction.)

Discourse as Text

For reasons which will become clear later, one never really talks about features of a text without some reference to text production and/or interpretation. Because of this overlap, the division of analytical topics between text analysis and analysis of discursive practice (and so between the analytical activities of description and interpretation) is not a sharp one. Where formal features of texts are most salient, topics are included here; where productive and interpretative processes are most salient, topics are dealt with under analysis of discursive practice, even though they involve formal features of texts. What I give under these two headings is a broad analytical framework or model; selective more detailed accounts of analytical topics will be found in chapters 4 and 5.

It is a sensible working hypothesis to assume that any sort of textual feature is potentially significant in discourse analysis. This raises a major difficulty. Language analysis is a complex and sometimes quite technical sphere in its own right, which incorporates many types and techniques of analysis. Although a background in linguistics may in principle be a prerequisite to doing discourse analysis, discourse analysis is in fact a multidisciplinary activity, and one can no more assume a detailed linguistic background from its practitioners than one can assume detailed backgrounds in sociology, psychology or politics. In these circumstances, what I have set out to do is (i) offer in this chapter a very general analytical framework which is intended to give readers a large-scale map of the terrain; (ii) identify for more detailed treatment and illustration in chapters 4–6 selective analytical focuses which seem especially fruitful in discourse analysis; (iii) dispense as far as possible with forbidding technicality and jargon; and (iv) provide references for those who wish to pursue particular lines of analysis.

Some of the categories in the framework for text analysis below appear to be oriented to language forms, while others appear to be oriented to meanings. This distinction is a misleading one, however, because in analysing texts one is always simultaneously addressing questions of form and questions of meaning. In the terminology of much of twentieth-century linguistics and semiotics, one is analysing 'signs', that is words or longer stretches of text which consist of a meaning combined with a form, or a 'signified' combined with a 'signifier' (see de Saussure 1959). Saussure and others within the linguistics tradition have emphasized the 'arbitrary' nature of the sign, the view that there is no motivated or rational basis for combining a particular signifier with a particular signified. As against this, critical approaches to discourse analysis make the assumption that signs are socially motivated, i.e. that there are social reasons for combining particular signifiers with particular signifieds. (I am grateful to Gunther Kress for discussions on this issue.) This may be a matter of vocabulary – 'terrorist' and 'freedom fighter' are contrasting combinations of signifier and signified, and the contrast between them is a socially motivated one – or a matter of grammar (see examples below), or other dimensions of language organization.

Another important distinction in relation to meaning is between the meaning potential of a text, and its interpretation. Texts are made up of forms which past discursive practice, condensed into conventions, has endowed with meaning potential. The meaning potential of a form is generally heterogeneous, a complex of diverse, overlapping and sometimes contradictory meanings (see Fairclough 1990a), so that texts are usually highly ambivalent and open to multiple interpretations. Interpreters usually reduce this potential ambivalence by opting for a particular meaning, or a small set of alternative meanings. Providing we bear in mind this dependence of meaning upon interpretation, we can use 'meaning' both for the potentials of forms, and for the meanings ascribed in interpretation.

Text analysis can be organized under four main headings: 'vocabulary', 'grammar', 'cohesion', and 'text structure'. These can be thought as ascending in scale: vocabulary deals mainly with individual words, grammar deals with words combined into clauses and sentences, cohesion deals with how clauses and sentences are linked together, and text structure deals with large-scale organizational properties of texts. In addition, I distinguish a further three main headings which will be used in analysis of discursive practice rather than text analysis, though they certainly involve formal features of texts: the 'force' of utterances, i.e. what sorts of speech acts (promises, requests, threats etc.) they constitute; the 'coherence' of texts; and the 'intertextuality' of texts. Together, these seven headings constitute a framework for analysing texts which covers aspects of their production and interpretation as well as formal properties of text.

The main unit of grammar is the clause, or 'simple sentence', for example the newspaper headline 'Gorbachev Rolls Back the Red Army. The main elements of clauses are usually called 'groups' or 'phrases', for example 'the Red Army', 'Rolls Back'. Clauses combine to make up complex sentences. My comments here will be restricted to certain aspects of the clause.

Every clause is multifunctional, and so every clause is a combination of ideational, interpersonal (identity and relational), and textual meanings (see pp. 64–5 above). People make choices about the design and structure of their clauses which amount to choices about how to signify (and construct) social identities, social relationships, and knowledge and belief. Let me illustrate with the newspaper headline above. In terms of ideational meaning, the clause is transitive: it signifies a process of a particular individual acting physically (note the metaphor) upon an entity. We might well see here a different ideological investment from other ways of signifying the same events, for example 'The Soviet Union Reduces its Armed Forces', or 'The Soviet Army Gives up 5 Divisions'. In terms of interpersonal meaning, the clause is declarative (as opposed to interrogative, or imperative), and contains a present tense form of the verb which is categorically authoritative. The writer-reader relationship here is that between someone telling what is the case in no uncertain terms, and someone being told; these are the two subject positions set up in the clause. Thirdly, there is a textual aspect: 'Gorbachev' is topic or theme of the clause, as the first part of a clause usually is: the article is about him and his doings. On the other hand, if the clause were made into a passive, that would make 'the Red Army' the theme: 'The Red Army is Rolled Back (by Gorbachev)'. Another possibility offered by the passive is the deletion of the (bracketed) agent, because the agent is unknown, already known, judged irrelevant, or perhaps in order to leave agency and hence responsibility vague. The Critical linguistics approach is particularly interesting on grammar (Fowler et al. 1979; Kress and Hodge 1979). Leech, Deuchar and Hoogenraad (1982) is an accessible introduction to grammar, and Halliday (1985) is a more advanced account of a form of grammar particularly useful in discourse analysis.

'Vocabulary' can be investigated in a great many ways, and the comments here and in chapter 6 are very selective. One point that needs to be made is that it is of limited value to think of a language as having a vocabulary which is documented in 'the' dictionary, because there are a great many overlapping and competing vocabularies corresponding to different domains, institutions, practices, values, and perspectives. The terms 'wording', 'lexicalization' and 'signification' (on these and other aspects of vocabulary, see Kress and Hodge 1979; Mey 1985) capture this better than 'vocabulary', because they imply processes of wording (lexicalizing, signifying) the world which happen differently in different times and places and for different groups of people.

One focus for analysis is upon alternative wordings and their political and ideological significance, upon such issues as how domains of experience may be 'reworded' as part of social and political struggles (the example of rewording 'terrorists' as 'freedom fighters' or vice-versa is well known), or how certain domains come to be more intensively worded than others. Another focus is word meaning, and particularly how the meanings of words come into contention within wider struggles: I shall suggest that particular structurings of the relationships between words and the relationships between the meanings of a word are forms of hegemony. A third focus is upon metaphor, upon the ideological and political import of particular metaphors, and conflict between alternative metaphors.

In looking at 'cohesion' (see Halliday and Hasan 1976; Halliday 1985), one is looking at how clauses are linked together into sentences, and how sentences are in turn linked together to form larger units in texts. Linkage is achieved in various ways: through using vocabulary from a common semantic field, repeating words, using near-synonyms, and so forth; through a variety of referring and substituting devices (pronouns, definite article, demonstratives, ellipsis of repeated words, and so forth); through using conjunctive words, such as 'therefore', 'however', 'and' and 'but'. Focusing upon cohesion is a way into what Foucault refers to as 'various rhetorical schemata according to which groups of statements may be combined (how descriptions, deductions, definitions, whose succession characterizes the architecture of a text, are linked together' (see p. 46 above). These schemata, and particular aspects of them such as the argumentative structure of texts, vary across discourse types, and it is interesting to explore such variations as evidence of different modes of rationality, and changes in modes of rationality as discourse practices change.

'Text structure' (see de Beaugrande and Dressler 1981; Coulthard 1977; Brown and Yule 1983; Stubbs 1983) also concerns the 'architecture' of texts, and specifically higher-level design features of different types of text: what elements or episodes are combined in what ways and what order to constitute, for example, a crime report in a newspaper, or a job interview. Such structuring conventions can give a lot of insight into the systems of knowledge and belief and the assumptions about social relationships and social identities that are built into the conventions of text types. As these examples suggest, we are concerned with the structure of monologue and dialogue. The latter involves turn-taking systems and conventions for organizing the exchange of speaker turns, as well as conventions for opening and closing interviews or conversations.

Discursive Practice

Discursive practice, as I indicated above, involves processes of text production, distribution, and consumption, and the nature of these processes varies between different types of discourse according to social factors. For example, texts are produced in specific ways in specific social contexts: a newspaper article is produced through complex routines of a collective nature, by a team whose members are variously involved in its different stages of production – accessing sources such as press agency reports, transforming these sources (often themselves already texts) into a draft report, deciding where to place the report in the newspaper, and editing the report (for a detailed account, and more generally on discourse processes, see van Dijk 1988).

There are other ways in which the concept of 'text producer' is more complicated than it may seem. It is useful to deconstruct the producer into a set of positions, which may be occupied by the same person or by different people. Goffman (1981: 144) suggests a distinction between 'animator', the person who actually makes the sounds, or the marks on paper, 'author', the one who puts the words together and is responsible for the wording, and 'principal', the one whose position is represented by the words. In newspaper articles, there is some ambiguity about the relationship between these positions: the principal is often a 'source' outside the newspaper, but some reports do not make that clear, and give the impression that the principal is the newspaper (its editor, or a journalist); and texts which are collectively authored are often written as if they were authored by an individual journalist (who might at best be animator). (See Fairclough 1988b for an example.)

Texts are also consumed differently in different social contexts. This is partly a matter of the sort of interpretative work which is applied to them (such as close scrutiny, or semi-focused attention in the course of doing other things), and partly of the modes of interpretation which are available; recipes, for instance, are not usually read as aesthetic texts, or academic articles as rhetorical texts, though both kinds of reading are possible. Consumption like production may be individual or collective: compare love letters with administrative records. Some texts (official interviews, great poems) are recorded, transcribed, preserved, re-read; others (unsolicited publicity, casual conversations) are transitory, unrecorded, thrown away. Some texts (political speeches, textbooks) are transformed into other texts. Institutions have specific routines for 'processing' texts: a medical consultation is transformed into a medical record which may be used to compile medical statistics (see pp. 130–3 below for a discussion of such 'intertextual chains'). Furthermore, texts have variable outcomes of an extra-discursive as well as a discursive sort. Some texts lead to wars or to the destruction of nuclear weapons; others to people losing or gaining jobs; others again change people's attitudes, beliefs or practices.

Some texts have a simple distribution – a casual conversation belongs only to the immediate context of situation in which it occurs – whereas others have a complex distribution. Texts produced by political leaders, or texts within international arms negotiation, are distributed across a range of different institutional domains, each of which has its own patterns of consumption, and its own routines for reproducing and transforming texts. Television viewers, for instance, receive a transformed version of a speech given by Thatcher or Gorbachev, which is consumed in accordance with particular viewing habits and routines. Producers within sophisticated organizations such as government departments produce texts in ways which anticipate their distribution, transformation, and consumption, and have multiple audiences built into them. They may anticipate not only 'addressees' (those directly addressed), but also 'hearers' (those not addressed directly, but assumed to be part of audience), and 'overhearers' (those who do not constitute part of the 'official' audience but are known to be *de facto* consumers (for example, Soviet officials are overhearers in communications between NATO governments). And each of these positions may be multiply occupied.

As I indicated above, there are specifically 'sociocognitive' dimensions of text production and interpretation, which centre upon the interplay between the members' resources which discourse participants have internalized and bring with them to text processing, and the text itself, as a set of 'traces' of the production process, or a set of 'cues' for the interpretation process. These processes generally proceed in a nonconscious and automatic way, which is an important factor in determining their ideological effectiveness (see further below), though certain aspects of them are more easily brought to consciousness than others.

Processes of production and interpretation are socially constrained in a double sense. Firstly, they are constrained by the available members' resources, which are effectively internalized social structures, norms and conventions, including orders of discourse, and conventions for the production, distribution and consumption of texts of the sort just referred to, and which have been constituted through past social practice and struggle. Secondly, they are constrained by the specific nature of the social practice of which they are parts, which determines what elements of members' resources are drawn upon, and how (in normative or creative, acquiescent or oppositional ways) they are drawn upon. A major feature of the three-dimensional framework for discourse analysis is that it attempts to explore these constraints, especially the second – to make explanatory connections between the nature of the discourse processes in particular instances, and the nature of the social practices they are a part of. Given the focus in this book on discursive and social change, it is this aspect of discursive processes – determining what aspects of members' resources are drawn upon and how – that is of most interest. I return to it below in the discussion of intertextuality.

But first I want to say a little in more general terms about the sociocognitive aspects of production and interpretation, and to introduce two more of the seven dimensions of analysis: 'force' and 'coherence'. The production or interpretation of a text (I shall refer just to interpretation in some of the discussion below) is usually represented as a multilevel process, and a 'bottom-up–

top-down' process. Lower levels analyse a sequence of sounds or marks on paper into sentences. Higher levels are concerned with meaning, the ascription of meanings to sentences, to whole texts, and to parts or 'episodes' of a text which consist of sentences which can be interpreted as coherently connected. Meanings for 'higher' units are in part built up from meanings for 'lower' units. This is 'bottom-up' interpretation. However, interpretation is also characterized by predictions about the meanings of higher-level units early in the process of interpreting them on the basis of limited evidence, and these predicted meanings shape the way lower-level units are interpreted. This is 'top-down' processing. Production and interpretation are partly 'top-down' and partly 'bottom up'. In addition, interpretation is taking place in real time: the interpretation which has already been arrived at for word, or sentence, or episode x will exclude certain otherwise possible interpretations for word, sentence, or episode x + 1 (see Fairclough 1989a).

These aspects of text processing help to explain how interpreters reduce the potential ambivalence of texts, and show part of the effect of context in reducing ambivalence, in a narrow sense of 'context' as that which preceeds (or follows) in a text. However, 'context' also includes what is sometimes called the 'context of situation': interpreters arrive at interpretations of the totality of the social practice of which the discourse is a part, and these interpretations lead to predictions about the meanings of texts which again reduce ambivalence by excluding certain otherwise possible meanings. This is in a sense an elaboration of the 'top-down' properties of interpretation.

A major limitation of the sort of account of sociocognitive processes given above is that it is generally put in universal terms, as if, for example, the effect of context on meaning and the reduction of ambivalence were always the same. But this is not the case. How context affects the interpretation of text varies from one discourse type to another, as Foucault pointed out (see pp. 47–8 above). And differences between discourse types in this respect are socially interesting because they point to implicit assumptions and ground rules which often have an ideological character. Let me illustrate these points through a discussion of 'force' (see Leech 1983; Levinson 1983: Leech and Thomas 1989).

The force of part of a text (often, but not always, a sentence-sized part) is its actional component, a part of its interpersonal meaning, what it is being used to do socially, what 'speech act(s)' it is being used to 'perform' (give an order, ask a question, threaten, promise, etc.). Force is in contrast with 'proposition': the propositional component, which is part of ideational meaning, is the process or relationship that is predicated of the entities. So in the case of 'I promise to pay the bearer on demand the sum of £5', the force is that of a promise, whereas the proposition might be schematically represented as 'x pay y to z'. Parts of texts are typically ambivalent in terms of force, and they may have extensive 'force potential'. For instance, 'Can you carry the suitcase?' could be a question, a request or order, a suggestion, a complaint, and so on. Some analyses of speech acts distinguish between direct and indirect force; we might say in this case that we have something with the direct force of a question which might also have any of the other forces listed as its indirect force. Moreover, it is by no means uncommon for interpretations to remain ambivalent: on occasion, it may not be clear whether we have a simple question, or also a veiled (and so, if challenged, deniable) request.

'Context' in both senses above is an important factor in reducing the ambivalence of force. Sequential position in the text is a powerful predictor of force. In a cross-examination, anything that counsel says to a witness immediately following an answer from the witness is likely to be interpreted as a question (which does not preclude it being simultaneously interpreted as other things, such as an accusation). This helps to explain how it is that forms of words can have forces which seem highly unlikely if one considers them out of context. And, of course, the context of situation, the overall nature of the social context, also reduces ambivalence.

However, before an interpreter can draw upon either context of situation, or indeed sequential context, to interpret the force of an utterance, she must have arrived at an interpretation of what the context of situation is. This is analogous to interpreting text: it involves an interplay between cues and members' resources, but the members' resources in this case is in effect a mental map of the social order. Such a mental map is necessarily just one interpretation of social realities which are amenable to many interpretations, politically and ideologically invested in particular ways. Pin-pointing the context of situation in terms of this mental map provides two bodies of information relevant to determining how context affects the interpretation of text in any particular case: a reading of the situation which foregrounds certain elements, backgrounds others, and relates elements to each other in certain ways; and a specification of which discursive types are likely to be relevant.

Thus one effect upon interpretation of the reading of the situation is to foreground or background aspects of the social identity of participants, so that for example the gender, ethnicity, or age of the text producer are much less likely to affect interpretation in the case of a botany textbook than in the case of a casual conversation or a job interview. Thus the effect of context of situation upon text interpretation (and text production) depends upon the reading of the situation. The effect of sequential context, on the other hand, depends upon discourse type. For example, we cannot assume that a question will always predispose to the same degree the interpretation of the utterance which follows it as an answer; it depends on the discourse type. In classroom discourse, questions strongly predict answers; in conversational discourse within a family, questions may routinely go unanswered without any real sense of infringement or need for repair. A one-sided emphasis on sequential context as determining interpretation without recognition of such variables is an unsatisfactory feature of Conversation analysis, as I argued in chapter 2 above. Moreover, differences between discourse types of this order are socially important: where questions must be answered, the likelihood is that asymmetries of status between sharply demarcated subject roles are taken as given. So investigating the interpretative principles that are used to determine meaning gives insight into the political and ideological investment of a discourse type.

Let us now turn from force to 'coherence' (see de Beaugrande and Dressler 1981: chapter 5; Brown and Yule 1983: chapter 7). Coherence is often treated as a property of texts, but it is better regarded as a property of interpretations. A coherent text is a text whose constituent parts (episodes, sentences) are meaningfully related so that the text as a whole 'makes sense', even though there may be relatively few formal markers of those meaningful relationships – that is, relatively little explicit 'cohesion' (see the last section). The point is, however, that a text only makes sense to someone who makes sense of it, someone who is able to infer those meaningful relations in the absence of explicit markers. But the particualr way in which a coherent reading is generated for a text depends again upon the nature of the interpretative principles that are being drawn upon. Particular interpretative principles come to be associated in a naturalized way with particular discourse types, and such linkages are worth investigating for the light they shed on the important ideological functions of coherence in interpellating subjects. That is, texts set up positions for interpreting subjects that are 'capable' of making sense of them, and 'capable' of making the connections and inferences, in accordance with relevant interpretative principles, necessary to generate coherent readings. These connections and inferences may rest upon assumptions of an ideological sort. For instance, what establishes the coherent link between the two sentences 'She's giving up her job next Wednesday. She's pregnant' is the assumption that women cease to work when they have children. In so far as interpreters take up these positions and automatically make these connections, they are being subjected by and to the text, and this is an important part of the ideological 'work' of texts and discourse in 'interpellating' subjects (see the next section). There is, however, the possibility not only of struggle over different readings of texts, but also of resistance to the positions set up in texts.

Let me now turn to the last of the seven dimensions of analysis, and the one which is most salient in the concerns of this book: 'intertextuality' (see Bakhtin 1981, 1986; Kristeva 1986a). I shall devote the whole of chapter 4 to intertextuality, so discussion here can be quite brief. Intertextuality is basically the property texts have of being full of snatches of other texts, which may be explicitly demarcated or merged in, and which the text may assimilate, contradict, ironically echo, and so forth. In terms of production, an intertextual perspective stresses the historicity of texts: how they always constitute additions to existing 'chains of speech communication' (Bakhtin 1986: 94) consisting of prior texts to which they respond. In terms of distribution, an intertextual perspective is helpful in exploring relatively stable networks which texts move along, undergoing predictable transformations as they shift from one text type to another (for instance, political speeches are often transformed into news reports). And in terms of consumption, an intertextual perspective is helpful in stressing that it is not just 'the text', not indeed just the texts that inter-textually constitute it, that shape interpretation, but also those other texts which interpreters variably bring to the interpretation process.

I shall draw a distinction between 'manifest intertextuality', where specific other texts are overtly drawn upon within a text, and 'interdiscursivity' or 'constitutive intertextuality'. Interdis-cursivity extends intertextuality in the direction of the principle of the primacy of the order of discourse which I discussed above, p. 68. On the one hand, we have the heterogeneous constitu-tion of texts out of specific other texts (manifest intertextual-ity); on the other hand, the heterogeneous constitution of texts out of elements (types of convention) of orders of discourse (interdiscursivity).

The concept of intertextuality sees texts historically as trans-forming the past – existing conventions and prior texts – into the present. This may happen in relatively conventional and norma-tive ways: discourse types tend to turn particular ways of draw-ing upon conventions and texts into routines, and to naturalize them. However, this may happen creatively, with new configura-tions of elements of orders of discourse, and new modes of manifest intertextuality. It is the inherent historicity of an inter-textual view of texts, and the way it so readily accommodates creative practice, that make it so suitable for my present concerns with discursive change, though as I shall argue below (pp. 93–4) it needs to be linked to a theory of social and political change for the investigation of discursive change within wider processes of cultural and social change.

Analysis of discursive practice should, I believe, involve a com-bination of what one might call 'micro-analysis' and 'macro-analysis'. The former is the sort of analysis which conversation analysts excel at: the explication of precisely how participants pro-duce and interpret texts on the basis of their members' resources. But this must be complemented with macro-analysis in order to know the nature of the members' resources (including orders of discourse) that is being drawn upon in order to produce and interpret texts, and whether it is being drawn upon in normative or creative ways. Indeed, one cannot carry out micro-analysis without knowing this. And, of course, micro-analysis is the best place to uncover that information: as such, it provides evidence for macro-analysis. Micro- and macro-analysis are therefore mutual requisites. It is because of their interrelationship that the dimension of discursive practice in my three-dimensional framework can mediate the relationship between the dimensions of social practice and text: it is the nature of the social practice that determines the macro-processes of discursive practice, and it is the micro-processes that shape the text.

One implication of the position I have adopted in this section is that how people interpret texts in various social circumstances is a question requiring separate investigation. While the framework I have presented points to the importance of considering inter-pretation in its own right, it should be noted that empirical studies are not included in this book. (For discussion of research on the interpretation of mass media texts, see Morley 1980 and Thompson 1990: chapter 6.)

Discourse as Social Practice: Ideology and Hegemony

My objective in this section is to spell out more clearly aspects of the third dimension in my three-dimensional framework, dis-course as social practice. More specifically, I shall discuss dis-course in relation to ideology and to power, and place discourse within a view of power as hegemony, and a view of the evolution of power relations as hegemonic struggle. In doing so, I draw upon the classic contributions to twentieth-century Marxism of Althusser and Gramsci, which (despite the increasing contempor-ary unfashionability of Marxism) provide a rich framework for investigating discourse as a form of social practice, though with important reservations, especially in the case of Althusser.

Ideology

The theorization of ideology which has been most influential in recent debate about discourse and ideology is surely that of Althusser (Althusser 1971; Larrain 1979), which I briefly referred to in discussing Pêcheux in chapter 1. In fact, Althusser can be regarded as having provided the theoretical bases for the debate, although Volosinov (1973) was a much earlier substantive contribution.

The theoretical bases I have in mind are three important claims about ideology. First, the claim that it has a material existence in the practices of institutions, which opens up the way to investigating discursive practices as material forms of ideology. Second, the claim that ideology 'interpellates subjects', which leads to the view that one of the more significant 'ideological effects' which linguists ignore in discourse (according to Althusser 1971: 161 n. 16) is the constitution of subjects. Third, the claim that 'ideological state apparatuses' (institutions such as education or the media) are both sites of and stakes in class struggle, which points to struggle in and over discourse as a focus for an ideologically-oriented discourse analysis.

If the debate about ideology and discourse has been heavily influenced by these positions, it has also been plagued by the widely acknowledged limitations of Althusser's theory. In particular, Althusser's work contains an unresolved contradiction between a vision of domination as the one-sided imposition and reproduction of a dominant ideology, in which ideology figures like a universal social cement, and his insistence upon apparatuses as the site and stake of a constant class struggle whose outcome is always in the balance. In effect, it is the former vision which is predominant, and there is a marginalization of struggle, contradiction and transformation.

I shall understand ideologies to be significations/constructions of reality (the physical world, social relations, social identities), which are built into various dimensions of the forms/meanings of discursive practices, and which contribute to the production, reproduction or transformation of relations of domination. (This is similar to the position of Thompson (1984, 1990) that certain uses of language and other 'symbolic forms' are ideological, namely those which serve, in specific circumstances, to establish or sustain relations of domination.) The ideologies embedded in discursive practices are most effective when they become naturalized, and achieve the status of 'common sense'; but this stable and established property of ideologies should not be overstated, because my reference to 'transformation' points to ideological struggle as a dimension of discursive practice, a struggle to reshape discursive practices and the ideologies built into them in the context of the restructuring or transformation of relations of domination. Where contrasting discursive practices are in use in a particular domain or institution, the likelihood is that part of that contrast is ideological.

I maintain that ideology invests language in various ways at various levels, and that we do not have to chose between different possible 'locations' of ideology, all of which seem partly justified and none of which seems entirely satisfactory (see Fairclough 1989b for a more detailed account of the position I adopt here). The key issue is whether ideology is a property of structures or a property of events, and the answer is 'both'. And the key problem is to find, as I have already been suggesting in the discussion of discourse, a satisfactory account of the dialectic of structures and events.

A number of accounts make ideology a property of structures by locating it in some form of convention underlying language practice, be it a 'code', 'structure', or 'formation'. This has the virtue of showing events to be constrained by social conventions, but it has the disadvantage already referred to of tending to defocus the event on the assumption that events are mere instantiations of structures, privileging the perspective of ideological reproduction rather than that of transformation, and tending to represent conventions as more clearly bounded than they really are. Pêcheux in his earlier work is a case in point. Another weakness of the structure option is that it does not recognize the primacy of orders of discourse over particular discourse conventions: we need to take account of ideological investments of (parts of) orders of discourse, not just individual conventions, and of the possibility of diverse and contradictory sorts of investment. An alternative to the structure option is to locate ideology in the discursive event, highlighting ideology as a process, transformation, and fluidity. But this can lead to an illusion of discourse as free processes of formation, unless there is a simultaneous emphasis on orders of discourse.

There is also a textual view of the location of ideology, which one finds in Critical linguistics: ideologies reside in texts. While it is true that the forms and content of texts do bear the imprint of (are traces of) ideological processes and structures, it is not possible to 'read off' ideologies from texts. As I argued in chapter 2, this is because meanings are produced through interpretations of texts, and texts are open to diverse interpretations which may differ in their ideological import, and because ideological processes appertain to discourses as whole social events – they are processes between people – not just to the texts which are moments of such events. Claims to discover ideological processes solely through text analysis run into the problem now familiar in media sociology, that text 'consumers' (readers, viewers) appear sometimes to be quite immune to effects of ideologies which are supposedly 'in' the texts (Morley 1980).

I prefer the view that ideology is located both in the structures (i.e. orders of discourse) which constitute the outcome of past events and the conditions for current events, and in events themselves as they reproduce and transform their conditioning structures. It is an accumulated and naturalized orientation which is built into norms and conventions, as well as an ongoing work to naturalize and denaturalize such orientations in discursive events.

A further substantive question about ideology is what features or levels of text and discourse may be ideologically invested. A common claim is that it is 'meanings', and especially word meanings (sometimes specified as 'content', as opposed to 'form'), that are ideological (e.g. Thompson 1984). Word meanings are important, of course, but so too are other aspects of meaning, such as presuppositions (see pp. 120–1 below), metaphors (see pp. 194–8 below), and coherence. I have already pointed out in the previous section how important coherence is in the ideological constitution of subjects.

A rigid opposition between 'content' or 'meaning' and 'form', is misleading because the meanings of texts are closely intertwined with the forms of texts, and formal features of texts at various levels may be ideologically invested. For example, the representation of slumps and unemployment as akin to natural disasters may involve a preference for intransitive and attributive, rather than transitive, sentence structures ('The currency has lost its value, millions are out of work', as opposed to 'Investors are buying gold, firms have sacked millions'; see pp. 177–85 below for these terms). At a different level, the turn-taking system in a classroom, or the politeness conventions operating between secretary and manager, imply particular ideological assumptions about the social identities of, and social relationships between, teachers and pupils, and managers and secretaries. Further and more detailed examples will be given in the sample texts of chapters 4–6. Even aspects of the 'style' of a text may be ideologically invested: see my analysis (pp. 131–3 below) of how the style of a Department of Trade and Industry brochure contributes to constituting 'the enterprising self' as a type of social identity.

It should not be assumed that people are aware of the ideological dimensions of their own practice. Ideologies built into conventions may be more or less naturalized and automatized, and people may find it difficult to comprehend that their normal practices could have specific ideological investments. Even when one's practice can be interpreted as resistant and contributing to ideological change, one is not necessarily aware in detail of its ideological import. There is a strong case to be made for a mode of language education which emphasizes critical awareness of ideological processes in discourse, so that people can become more aware of their own practice, and be more critical of the ideologically invested discourses to which they are subjected (see Clark et al. 1988; Fairclough forthcoming a).

These comments on awareness can be linked to questions about the interpellation of subjects. The ideal case in the Althusserian account is that of the subject positioned in ideology in a way which disguises the action and effects of the latter, and gives the subject an imaginary autonomy. This suggests discursive conventions of a highly naturalized sort. But people are actually subjected in different and contradictory ways; this consideration begins to cast doubt upon the ideal case. When subjection is contradictory – when a person operating in a single institutional framework and a single set of practices is interpellated from various positions and pulled in different directions, as it were – naturalization may be difficult to sustain. Contradictory interpellation is likely to be manifested experientially in a sense of confusion or uncertainty, and a problematization of conventions (see 'Discursive change' below). These are the conditions under which awareness, as well as a transformatory practice is most likely to develop.

The Althusserian account of the subject overstates the ideological constitution of subjects, and correspondingly understates the capacity of subjects to act individually or collectively as agents, including engagement in critique of, and opposition to, ideological practices (see my reservations about Foucault in this regard, pp. 60–1 above). Here also it is important to adopt the dialectical position I advocated earlier: subjects are ideologically positioned, but they are also capable of acting creatively to make their own connections between the diverse practices and ideologies to which they are exposed, and to restructure positioning practices and structures. The balance between the subject as ideological 'effect', and the subject as active agent, is a variable which depends upon social conditions such as the relative stability of relations of domination.

Is all discourse ideological? I have suggested that discursive practices are ideologically invested in so far as they incorporate significations which contribute to sustaining or restructuring power relations. Relations of power may in principle be affected by discursive practices of any type, even scientific and theoretical. This precludes a categorical opposition between ideology and science or theory, which some writers on language/ideology have suggested (Zima 1981; Pêcheux 1982). But all discourse is not thereby irredeemably ideological. Ideologies arise in societies characterized by relations of domination on the basis of class, gender, cultural group, and so forth, and in so far as human beings are capable of transcending such societies, they are capable of transcending ideology. I do not therefore accept Althusser's view (1971) of 'ideology in general' as a form of social cement which is inseparable from society itself. In addition the fact that all types of discourse are open in principle, and no doubt to some extent in fact, in our society to ideological investment, does not mean that all types of discourse are ideologically invested to the same degree. It should not be too difficult to show that advertising is in broad terms more heavily invested than the physical sciences.

Hegemony

The concept of hegemony, which is the centrepiece of Gramsci's analysis of western capitalism and revolutionary strategy in western Europe (Gramsci 1971; Buci-Glucksmann 1980), harmonizes with the view of discourse I have been advocating, and provides a way of theorizing change in relation to the evolution of power relations which allows a particular focus upon discursive change, but at the same time a way of seeing it as contributing to and being shaped by wider processes of change.

Hegemony is leadership as much as domination across the economic, political, cultural and ideological domains of a society. Hegemony is the power over society as a whole of one of the fundamental economically-defined classes in alliance with other social forces, but it is never achieved more than partially and temporarily, as an 'unstable equilibrium'. Hegemony is about constructing alliances, and integrating rather than simply domi-nating subordinate classes, through concessions or through ideological means, to win their consent. Hegemony is a focus of constant struggle around points of greatest instability between classes and blocs, to construct or sustain or fracture alliances and relations of domination/subordination, which takes economic, political and ideological forms. Hegemonic struggle takes place on a broad front, which includes the institutions of civil society (education, trade unions, family), with possible unevenness be-tween different levels and domains.

Ideology is understood within this framework in terms which anticipate all Althusser's advances (Buci-Glucksmann 1980: 66), in, for instance, its focusing of the implicit and unconscious materialization of ideologies in practices (which contain them as implicit theoretical 'premisses'), ideology being 'a conception of the world that is implicitly manifest in art, in law, in economic activity and in the manifestations of individual and collective life' (Gramsci 1971: 328). While the interpellation of subjects is an Althusserian elaboration, there is in Gramsci a conception of subjects as structured by diverse ideologies implicit in their prac-tice which gives them a 'strangely composite' character (1971: 324), and a view of 'common sense' as both a repository of the diverse effects of past ideological struggles, and a constant target for restructuring in ongoing struggles. In common sense, ideolo-gies become naturalized, or automatized. Moreover, Gramsci conceived of 'the field of ideologies in terms of conflicting, over-lapping, or intersecting currents or formations' (Hall 1988: 55-6), what he referred to as 'an ideological complex' (Gramsci 1971: 195). This suggests a focus upon the processes whereby ideological complexes come to be structured and restructured, articulated and rearticulated. (There is important discussion of hegemony and articulation in Laclau and Mouffe (1985) which constitutes a precedent for my application of these concepts to discourse, though without the analysis of actual texts which I would see as essential to discourse analysis.)

Such a conception of hegemonic struggle in terms of the articulation, disarticulation and rearticulation of elements is in harmony with what I said earlier about discourse: the dialectical view of the relationship between discursive structures and events; seeing discursive structures as orders of discourse conceived as more or less unstable configurations of elements; and adopting a view of texts which centres upon their intertextuality and how they articulate prior texts and conventions. An order of discourse can be seen as the discursive facet of the contradictory and unstable equilibrium which constitutes a hegemony, and the articulation and rearticulation of orders of discourse is correspondingly one stake in hegemonic struggle. Further, discursive practice, the production, distribution, and consumption (including interpretation) of texts, is a facet of hegemonic struggle which contributes in varying degrees to the reproduction or transformation not only of the existing order of discourse (for example, through the ways prior texts and conventions are articulated in text production), but also through that of existing social and power relations.

Let us take Thatcher's political discourse as an example. This can be interpreted as a rearticulation of the existing order of political discourse, which has brought traditional conservative, neo-liberal and populist discourses into a new mix, and has also constituted an unprecedented discourse of political power for a woman leader. This discursive rearticulation materializes an hegemonic project for the constitution of a new political base and agenda, itself a facet of the wider political project of restructuring the hegemony of the bloc centred upon the bourgeoisie in new economic and political conditions. Thatcher's discourse has been described in these terms by Hall (1988), and Fairclough (1989a) shows how such an analysis can be carried out in terms of a conception of discourse similar to that introduced above, in a way which accounts (as Hall does not) for the specific features of the language of Thatcher's political texts. I should add that the rearticulated order of discourse is a contradictory one: authoritarian elements coexist with democratic and egalitarian ones (for instance, the inclusive pronoun 'we', which implies a claim to speak for ordinary people, coexists with use of 'you' as an indefinite pronoun in such examples as 'You get sick of the rain, don't you'), and patriarchal elements with feminist ones. The rearticulation of orders of discourse is, moreover, achieved not only in productive discursive practice but also in interpretation: making sense of Thatcher's texts requires interpreters who are capable of making coherent connections between their heterogeneous elements, and part of the hegemonic project is the constitution of interpreting subjects for whom such connections are natural and automatic.

However, most discourse bears upon hegemonic struggle in particular institutions (the family, schools, courts of law, etc.) rather than at the level of national politics, the protagonists (as it were) being not classes or political forces linked in such relatively direct ways to classes or blocs, but teachers and pupils, police and public, or women and men. Hegemony also provides both a model and a matrix in such cases. It provides a model: in education, for example the dominant groups also appear to exercise power through constituting alliances, integrating rather than merely dominating subordinate groups, winning their consent, achieving a precarious equilibrium which may be undermined by other groups, and doing so in part through discourse and through the constitution of local orders of discourse. It provides a matrix: the achievement of hegemony at a societal level requires a degree of integration of local and semi-autonomous institutions and power relations, so that the latter are partially shaped by hegemonic relations, and local struggles can be interpreted as hegemonic struggles. This directs attention to links across institutions, and links and movement between institutional orders of discourse (see chapter 7 below for an analysis of changes which transcend particular orders of discourse).

Although hegemony would seem to be the predominant organizational form of power in contemporary society, it is not the only one. There are also the remains of a previously more salient form in which domination is achieved by an uncompromising imposition of rules, norms and conventions. This seems to correspond to a code model of discourse, which sees discourse in terms of the instantiation of codes with strong framing and classification (Bernstein 1981) and a highly regimented, normative practice. It contrasts with what we might call the 'articulation' model of discourse described above, which corresponds to a hegemonic organizational form. Code models are highly institution-oriented, whereas articulation models are more client/public-oriented: compare traditional and more recent forms of classroom discourse or doctor-patient discourse (I discuss specific examples of the latter in chapter 5 below). On the other hand, writers on post-modernism suggest an emergent organizational form of power which is rather difficult to pin-point, but which represents a further shift from institution-orientation associated with a postulated decentering of power, and seems to go with a 'mosaic' model of discourse which characterizes discursive practice as a constant minimally constrained rearticulation of elements. Discursive practice which seems to fit in with this model has been identified as 'post-modern' (Jameson 1984), and the clearest example is in advertising (see Fairclough 1989a: 197–211). I shall return to these models of discourse in chapter 7 below, in connection with a discussion of certain broad tendencies affecting contemporary orders of discourse.

To summarize, in the three-dimensional framework for discourse analysis introduced above, I identified as a major concern the tracing of explanatory connection for particular instances of discourse between the nature of the social practices of which they are a part, and the nature of their discursive practice, including sociocognitive aspects of their production and interpretation. The concept of hegemony helps us to do this, providing for discourse both a matrix – a way of analysing the social practice within which the discourse belongs in terms of power relations, in terms of whether they reproduce, restructure or challenge existing hegemonies – and a model – a way of analysing discourse practice itself as a mode of hegemonic struggle, reproducing, restructuring or challenging existing orders of discourse. This gives substance to the concept of the political investment of discourse practices, and, since hegemonies have ideological dimensions, a way of assessing the ideological investment of discourse practices. Hegemony also has the considerable virtue in the present context of facilitating a focus upon change, which is my final concern in this chapter.

Discursive Change

The focus of this book is discursive change in relation to social and cultural change; its rationale has been given in the Introduction in terms of the functioning of discourse in contemporary social life. This should be a double focus, in accordance with the dialectic between orders of discourse and discursive practice or the discursive event. On the one hand, one needs to understand processes of change as they occur in discursive events. On the other hand, one needs an orientation to how processes of rearticulation affect orders of discourse. I now discuss these in turn.

The immediate origins and motivations of change in the discursive event lie in the problematization of conventions for producers or interpreters, which can happen in a variety of ways. For example, the problematization of conventions for interaction between women and men is a widespread experience in various institutions and domains. Such problematizations have their bases in contradictions – contradictions in this case between traditional gendered subject positions into which many of us were socialized, and new gender relations. On a rather different plane, Thatcher's political discourse can be seen to arise out of the problematization of traditional right-wing discursive practices in circumstances where contradictions become apparent between the social relations, subject positions and political practices they are based in, and a changing world. When problematizations arise, people are faced with what Billig et al. (1988) call 'dilemmas'. They often try to resolve these dilemmas by being innovative and creative, by adapting existing conventions in new ways, and so contributing to discursive change. The inherent intertextuality and therefore historicity of text production and interpretation (see p. 84 above) builds creativity in as an option. Change involves forms of transgression, crossing boundaries, such as putting together existing conventions in new combinations, or drawing upon conventions in situations which usually preclude them.

Such contradictions, dilemmas, and subjective apprehensions of problems in concrete situations have their social conditions in structural contradictions and struggle at the institutional and societal levels. To pursue the example of gender relations, the contradictory positioning of individuals in discursive events, and the dilemmas that result from this, originate in structural contradictions in the gender relations within institutions and society as a whole. What crucially determines how these contradictions are reflected in specific events, however, is the relationship of those events to the struggles which are going on around these contradictions. To polarize possibilities which are a great deal more complex, a discursive event may be either a contribution to preserving and reproducing traditional gender relations and hegemonies and may therefore draw upon problematized conventions, or it may be a contribution to transforming those relations through hegemonic struggle and may therefore try to resolve the dilemmas through innovation. Discursive events themselves have cumulative effects upon social contradictions and the struggles around them. To sum up, then, sociocognitive processes will or will not be innovatory and contribute to discursive change depending upon the nature of the social practice.

Let us turn to the textual dimension of discourse. Change leaves traces in texts in the form of the co-occurrence of contradictory or inconsistent elements – mixtures of formal and informal styles, technical and non-technical vocabularies, markers of authority and familiarity, more typically written and more typically spoken syntactic forms, and so forth. In so far as a particular tendency of discursive change 'catches on' and becomes solidified into an emergent new convention, what at first are perceived by interpreters as stylistically contradictory texts come to lose their patchwork effect and be 'seamless'. Such a process of naturalization is essential to establishing new hegemonies in the sphere of discourse.

This leads to our second focus, change in orders of discourse. As producers and interpreters combine discursive conventions, codes and elements in new ways in innovatory discursive events, they are of course cumulatively producing structural changes in orders of discourse: they are disarticulating existing orders of discourse, and rearticulating new orders of discourse, new discursive hegemonies. Such structural changes may affect only the 'local' order of discourse of an institution, or they may transcend institutions and affect the societal order of discourse. The focus of attention in investigating discursive change should keep alternating between the discursive event and such structural changes, because it is not possible to appreciate the import of the former for wider processes of social change without attending to the latter, just as it is not possible to appreciate how discourse contributes to social change without attending to the former.

Let me illustrate the sorts of issue one might investigate within studies of change in orders of discourse by referring to two related types of change which are currently affecting the societal order of discourse. (There is a more detailed discussion of these in chapter 7 below.) One is an apparent democratization of discourse which involves the reduction of overt markers of power asymmetry between people of unequal institutional power – teachers and pupils, managers and workers, parents and children, doctors and patients – which is evident in a great many different institutional domains. The other is what I have called 'synthetic personalization' (Fairclough 1989a), the simulation of private, face-to-face, discourse in public mass-audience discourse (print, radio, television). Both tendencies can be linked to a spread of conversational discourse from the private domain of the lifeworld into institutional domains. These social and discursive tendencies are established through struggle, and they are furthermore established with only a limited stability, with the prospect that their own heterogeneous elements will be experienced as contradictory and lead to further struggle and change.

One aspect of the openness of orders of discourse to struggle is that the elements of an order of discourse do not have ideological values or modes of ideological investment of a fixed sort. Consider counselling, for example, the apparently non-directive, non-judgemental, empathizing way of talking to people about themselves and their problems in a one-to-one situation. Counselling has its origins in therapy, but it now circulates as a technique across many institutional domains, as an effect of a significant restructuring of the order of discourse. But this development is highly ambivalent ideologically and politically. Most counsellors see themselves as giving space to people as individuals in a world which increasingly treats them as ciphers, which makes counselling look like a counter-hegemonic practice, and its colonization of ever new institutions a liberating change. However, counselling is now used in preference to practices of an overtly disciplinary nature in various institutions, which makes it look like a hegemonic technique for subtly drawing aspects of people's private lives into the domain of power. Hegemonic struggle appears to occur partly through counselling and its expansion, and partly over it. This accords with Foucault's observation: 'Discourses are tactical elements or blocks operating in the field of force relations; there can exist different and even contradictory discourses within the same strategy; they can, on the contrary, circulate without changing their form from one strategy to another, opposing strategy' (1981: 101).

Exploration of tendencies of change within orders of discourse can make a significant contribution to current debates on social change. Processes of marketization, the extension of market models to new spheres, can, for example, be investigated through the recent extensive colonization of orders of discourse by advertising and other discourse types (see Fairclough 1989a, and chapter 7 below). While democratization of discourse and synthetic personalization can be linked to substantive democratization in society, they are also arguably connected with marketization, and specifically with the apparent shift in power away from producers to consumers which has been associated with consumerism and the new hegemonies it entails. There could also usefully be a discursive dimension in debates on modernity and postmodernity. For example, can democratization and synthetic personalization and the spread of conversation to institutional domains be seen as aspects of a 'dedifferentiation' of public and private domains (Jameson 1984), or a fragmentation of hitherto structured professional practices? (See chapter 7 for a fuller discussion.)

Conclusion

The approach to discourse and discourse analysis which I have set out in this chapter attempts to integrate a variety of theoretical perspectives and methods into what is, I hope, a powerful resource for studying discursive dimensions of social and cultural change. I have tried to combine aspects of a Foucaultian view of discourse and a Bakhtinian emphasis on intertextuality: the former includes the vital emphasis upon the socially constructive properties of discourse, the latter emphasizes the 'texture' (Halliday and Hasan 1976) of texts and their composition from snatches of other texts, and both point to the way in which orders of discourse structure and are restructured by discourse practice. I have also tried to locate the dynamic view of discursive practice and of its relationship with social practice that emerges from this conjuncture within a Gramscian conceptualization of power and power struggle in terms of hegemony. At the same time, I have drawn upon other traditions in linguistics, text-based discourse analysis, and ethnomethodological conversation analysis for the textual analysis. The resulting framework does, I believe, allow one to combine social relevance and textual specificity in doing discourse analysis, and to come to grips with change.

4

Intertextuality

I introduced the concept of intertextuality in chapter 3 (p. 84 above), and pointed to its compatibility with the primacy I have ascribed to change in discourse, and the structuring and restructuring of orders of discourse. The concept of intertextuality was also referred to in chapter 2 as a significant element in Foucault's analyses of discourse. Recall his statement that 'there can be no statement that in one way or another does not reactualize others' (1972: 98). My aim in this chapter is firstly to make the concept of intertextuality somewhat more concrete by using it to analyse texts, and secondly to set out rather more systematically the potential of the concept for discourse analysis, as a part of the development of an analytic framework.

The term 'intertextuality' was coined by Kristeva in the late 1960s in the context of her influential accounts for western audiences of the work of Bakhtin (see Kristeva 1986a, actually written in 1966). Although the term is not Bakhtin's, the development of an intertextual (or in his own terms 'translinguistic') approach to analysis of texts was a major theme of his work throughout his academic career, and was closely linked to other important issues including his theory of genre (see Bakhtin 1986, a paper he wrote in the early 1950s).

Bakhtin points to the relative neglect of the communicative functions of language within mainstream linguistics, and more specifically to the neglect of ways in which texts and utterances are shaped by prior texts that they are 'responding' to, and by subsequent texts that they 'anticipate'. For Bakhtin, all utterances, both spoken and written, from the briefest of turns in a conversation to a scientific paper or a novel, are demarcated by a change of speaker (or writer), and are oriented retrospectively to the utterances of previous speakers (be they turns, scientific articles, or novels) and prospectively to the anticipated utterances of the next speakers. Thus 'each utterance is a link in the chain of speech communication.' All utterances are populated, and indeed constituted, by snatches of others' utterances, more or less explicit or complete: 'our speech...is filled with others' words, varying degrees of otherness and varying degrees of "our-own-ness", varying degrees of awareness and detachment. These words of others carry with them their own expression, their own evaluative tone, which we assimilate, rework, and reaccentuate' (Bakhtin 1986: 89). That is, utterances – 'texts' in my terms – are inherently intertextual, constituted by elements of other texts. Foucault adds the refinement of distinguishing within the intertextual aura of a text different 'fields' of 'presence', 'concomitance', and 'memory' (see pp. 46–7 above).

I indicated in chapter 3 that the salience of the concept of intertextuality in the framework I am developing accords with my focus upon discourse in social change. Kristeva observes that intertextuality implies 'the insertion of history (society) into a text and of this text into history' (1986a: 39). By 'the insertion of history into a text', she means that the text absorbs and is built out of texts from the past (texts being the major artefacts that constitute history). By 'the insertion of the text into history', she means that the text responds to, reaccentuates, and reworks past texts, and in so doing helps to make history and contributes to wider processes of change, as well as anticipating and trying to shape subsequent texts. This inherent historicity of texts enables them to take on the major roles they have in contemporary society at the leading edge of social and cultural change (see the discussion in chapters 3 and 7). The rapid transformation and restructuring of textual traditions and orders of discourse is a striking contemporary phenomenon, which suggests that intertextuality ought to be a major focus in discourse analysis.

The relationship between intertextuality and hegemony is important. The concept of intertextuality points to the productivity of texts, to how texts can transform prior texts and restructure existing conventions (genres, discourses) to generate new ones.

But this productivity is not in practice available to people as a limitless space for textual innovation and play: it is socially limited and constrained, and conditional upon relations of power. The theory of intertextuality cannot itself account for these social limitations, so it needs to be combined with a theory of power relations and how they shape (and are shaped by) social structures and practices. The combination of hegemony theory (described above pp. 91–6) with intertextuality is particularly fruitful. Not only can one chart the possibilities and limitations for intertextual processes within particular hegemonies and states of hegemonic struggle, one can also conceptualize intertextual processes and processes of contesting and restructuring orders of discourse as processes of hegemonic struggle in the sphere of discourse, which have effects upon, as well as being affected by, hegemonic struggle in the wider sense.

Bakhtin distinguishes what Kristeva calls 'horizontal' and 'vertical' dimensions of intertextuality (or relationships in intertextual 'space': see Kristeva 1986a: 36). On the one hand there are 'horizontal' intertextual relations of a 'dialogical' sort (though what are usually seen as monologues are, in my view, dialogical in this sense) between a text and those which preceed and follow it in the chain of texts. The most obvious case is how speaking turns in a conversation incorporate and respond to turns which preceed them, and anticipate those which follow; but a letter is also related intertextually to earlier and subsequent letters within the correspondence. On the other hand, there are 'vertical' intertextual relations between a text and other texts which constitute its more or less immediate or distant contexts: texts it is historically linked with in various time-scales and along various parameters, including texts which are more or less contemporary with it.

In addition to incorporating or otherwise responding to other texts, the intertextuality of a text can be seen as incorporating the potentially complex relationships it has with the conventions (genres, discourses, styles, activity types – see below) which are structured together to constitute an order of discourse. Bakhtin, discussing genre, notes that texts may not only draw upon such conventions in a relatively straightforward way, but may also 'reaccentuate' them by, for example, using them ironically, parodically, or reverently, or may 'mix' them in various ways (1986: 79–80). The distinction between intertextual relations of texts to specific other texts, and intertextual relations of texts to conventions, is linked to another distinction used by French discourse analysts: 'manifest' as opposed to 'constitutive' intertextuality (Authier-Révuz 1982; Maingueneau 1987). In manifest intertextuality, other texts are explicitly present in the text under analysis; they are 'manifestly' marked or cued by features on the surface of the text, such as quotation marks. Note, however, that a text may 'incorporate' another text without the latter being explicitly cued: one can respond to another text in the way one words one's own text, for example. The constitutive intertextuality of a text, however, is the configuration of discourse conventions that go into its production. The primacy I have given to orders of discourse highlights constitutive intertextuality (see pp. 68–9 above). I shall use intertextuality as a general term for both manifest and constitutive intertextuality when the distinction is not at issue, but introduce the new term 'interdiscursivity' rather than constitutive intertextuality when the distinction is needed, to underline that the focus is on discourse conventions rather than other texts as constitutive.

Intertextuality entails an emphasis upon the heterogeneity of texts, and a mode of analysis which highlights the diverse and often contradictory elements and threads which go to make up a text. Having said that, texts vary a great deal in their degrees of heterogeneity, depending upon whether their intertextual relations are complex or simple. Texts also differ in the extent to which their heterogeneous elements are integrated, and so in the extent to which their heterogeneity is evident on the surface of the text. For example, the text of another may be clearly set off from the rest of the text by quotation marks and a reporting verb, or it can be unmarked and integrated structurally and stylistically, perhaps through a rewording of the original, in the surrounding text (see the discussion of discourse representation below, pp. 118–20). Again, texts may or may not be 'reaccentuated'; they may or may not be drawn into the prevailing key or tone (e.g. ironic or sentimental) of the surrounding text. Or again, the texts of others may or may not be merged into unattributed background assumptions of the text by being presupposed (see below, pp. 120–1 for a discussion of presupposition). So a heterogeneous text may have an uneven and 'bumpy' textual surface, or a relatively smooth one.

Intertextuality is the source of much of the ambivalence of texts. If the surface of a text may be multiply determined by the various other texts which go into its composition, then elements of that textual surface may not be clearly placed in relation to the text's intertextual network, and their meaning may be ambivalent; different meanings may coexist, and it may not be possible to determine 'the' meaning. The speech of another may be represented in what is traditionally called 'indirect speech' (for example, 'The students say how much they like the flexibility and range of course choice'), in which case there is always an ambivalence about whether the actual wording is attributable to the person whose speech is represented, or to the author of the main text. Is the claim here that students actually say 'I like the flexibility and range of course choice', or words to that effect? Whose 'voice' is this, the students' or that of the university administration? And as I noted above (p. 79), elements of a text may be designed to be interpreted in different ways by different readerships or audiences, which is another, anticipatory, intertextual source of ambivalence.

In the remaining part of this chapter, I shall analyse two sample texts to illustrate some of the analytical potential of the concept of intertextuality; on the basis of these examples, I shall discuss those dimensions of intertextuality which are important in building up a framework for discourse analysis: manifest intertextuality, interdiscursivity, textual 'transformations', and how texts constitute social identities.

Sample 1: News Report

The first sample is an article which appeared in a British national newspaper, *The Sun*, in 1985 (see Fairclough 1988b for a more detailed analysis). It is a report about an official document produced by a House of Commons committee entitled *Hard Drug Abuse: Prevention and Control*.

I shall focus upon the article's speech 'reportage' or 'representation' (for a good standard account, see Leech and Short 1981). I shall in fact use a different term, for reasons I go into later: 'discourse representation'. Discourse representation is a

Britain faces a war to stop pedlars, warn MPs

CALL UP FORCES IN DRUG BATTLE!

By DAVID KEMP

THE armed forces should be called up to fight off a massive invasion by drug pushers, MPs demanded yesterday.

Cocaine pedlars are the greatest threat ever faced by Britain in peacetime — and could destroy the country's way of life, they said.

The MPs want Ministers to consider ordering the Navy and the RAF to track suspected drug - running ships approaching our coasts.

On shore there should be intensified law enforcement by Customs, police and security services.

Profits

The all-party Home Affairs Committee visited America and were deeply shocked by what they saw.

In one of the hardest-hitting Commons reports for years, the committee — chaired by Tory lawyer MP Sir Edward Gardner — warned gravely:

Western society is faced by a warlike threat from the hard-drugs industry.

The traffickers amass princely incomes from the exploitation of human weakness, boredom and misery.

They must be made to lose everything — their homes, their money and all they possess which can be attributed to their profits from selling drugs.

Sir Edward said yesterday: "We believe that trafficking in drugs is tantamount to murder, and punishment ought to reflect this."

The Government is expected to bring in clampdown laws in the autumn.

form of intertextuality in which parts of other texts are incorporated into a text and usually explicitly marked as such, with devices such as quotation marks and reporting clauses (e.g. 'she said' or 'Mary claimed'). Discourse representation is obviously a major part of the news: representations of what newsworthy people have said. But it is also extremely important in other types of discourse, for instance, in evidence in courts of law, in political rhetoric, and in everyday conversation, in which people endlessly report what others have said. In fact, it has not generally been appreciated just how important discourse representation is, both as an element of language texts and as a dimension of social practice.

I have chosen this particular article because we have available information which readers usually do not have: the document which is being reported (HMSO 1985); we can therefore compare report and original and focus upon how discourse is being represented.

Accounts usually draw a basic distinction between 'direct' and 'indirect' discourse representation. 'Mrs Thatcher warned Cabinet colleagues: "I will not stand for any backsliding now"' is an example of direct discourse, and 'Mrs Thatcher warned Cabinet colleagues that she would not stand for any backsliding then' is an example of indirect discourse. Both consist of a reporting clause ('Mrs Thatcher warned Cabinet colleagues') followed by a representation of discourse. In the case of direct discourse, the words represented are in quotation marks and the tense and deictics – words which relate to the time and place of utterance such as 'now' in this example – are those of the 'original'. There is an explicit boundary between the 'voice' of the person being reported and the 'voice' of the reporter, and direct discourse is often said to use the exact words of the person being reported. In indirect discourse, the quotation marks disappear and the represented discourse takes the form of a clause grammatically subordinated to the reporting clause, a relationship marked by the conjunction 'that'. Tense and deictics are shifted to incorporate the perspective of the reporter, for example 'now' becomes 'then'. The voices of reporter and reported are less clearly demarcated, and the words used to represent the latter's discourse may be those of the reporter rather than those of the reported.

Such standard 'grammar book' accounts typically understate

the complexity of what actually happens in texts. Let us focus on the headlines. The main headline ('Call up Forces in Drug Battle!') has none of the formal markers of discourse representation – no reporting clause, no quotation marks – yet it is an imperative clause in its grammatical form, and the exclamation mark indicates that it is to be taken as a demand. But who is demanding? There is nothing formally to mark this as other than the 'voice' of *The Sun* itself, but newpaper articles traditionally report the demands of others, rather than make their own demands (except in editorials), which suggests that perhaps this is a peculiar form of discourse representation after all. On the other hand, the distinction between 'report' and 'opinion' in the tabloid press is less clear than this analysis suggests, so perhaps this *is* the voice of *The Sun*. Yet in the opening paragraph of the report, the demand of the headline is attributed to 'MPs'. We are faced with an ambivalence of voice, a headline whose ambiguous linguistic form makes it 'double-voiced' (Bakhtin 1981). *The Sun* appears to be blending the voice of the HMSO document with its own voice. This conclusion is supported by the preceding sub-headline ('Britain faces a war to stop pedlars, warn MPs'). In this case there is a reporting clause, but it is backgrounded by being placed after the reported discourse, and the latter again lacks quotation marks even though it is direct discourse. These formal properties again contribute to an ambivalence of voice.

Next, compare these headlines and the opening paragraph with their original in the HMSO document:

> The Government should consider the use of the Royal Navy and the Royal Air Force for radar, airborne or ship surveillance duties. We recommend, therefore, that there should be intensified law enforcement against drug traffickers by H. M. Customs, the police, the security services and possibly the armed forces.

In blending the voice of the document into its own voice, *The Sun* is also translating the former into the terms of the latter. This is partly a matter of vocabulary: 'call up', 'battle', 'fight off', 'massive', 'invasion', 'pushers' and 'pedlars' are not used in the HMSO document. It is also a question of metaphor: *The Sun* is picking up a metaphor – dealing with drug traffickers as fighting a war – which is in fact used at one point in the HMSO document, and is transposing the voice of the document into its frame. The headline contains an elaboration of this metaphor wholly absent from the HMSO document – mobilization ('call up') of armed forces – and the same is true of the representation of drug trafficking as an 'invasion'. Finally it is also a question of translating the cautious recommendations of the report into a set of 'demands'.

What we find in the discourse representation of *The Sun*, then, is (i) ambiguity of linguistic form, which means that it is often unclear whether something is represented discourse or not (further examples are the two paragraphs immediately before and after the sub-head 'Profits'; and (ii) a merging of the voice of *The Sun* with the voice of the HMSO document, which involves *The Sun* representing the recommendations of the document as if they were its own, but at the same time translating the document into its own language.

Is it, however, simply 'its own language'? The process of translation involves shifts away from the legitimate terminology of written language towards a spoken language vocabulary ('traffickers' becoming 'pedlars' and 'pushers', 'forces' occurring without 'armed' as a modifier), from written monologue towards conversational dialogue (the demand in the headline is implicitly dialogic), drawing upon a metaphor (mobilization for war) which has resonances in popular experience and mythology. The shift, in short, is from official document to popular speech, or rather to 'the newspaper's own version of the language of the public to whom it is principally addressed' (Hall et al. 1978: 61). This is associated with a tendency for the providers of news to act as 'mediators', figures who cultivate 'characteristics which are taken to be typical of the "target" audience' and a relationship of solidarity with that assumed audience, and who can mediate newsworthy events to the audience in its own 'common sense' terms, or in a stereotypical version thereof (Hartley 1982: 87).

News media have been broadly shifting in this direction, and one needs to consider why. On one level, it reflects what has been identified as an important dimension of consumerism: a shift, or apparent shift, in power from producers to consumers. News media are in the competitive business of 'recruiting' readers, viewers and listeners in a market context in which their sales or ratings are decisive for their survival. The linguistic tendencies I have noted can be interpreted as one realization of a wider tendency for producers to market their commodities in ways that maximize their fit with the life styles and aspired-to life styles of consumers (though I would add that they are in the business of constructing people as consumers and the life styles they aspire to).

However, the process is more complex than that. Newsworthy events originate from the contracted set of people who have privileged access to the media, who are treated by journalists as reliable sources, and whose voices are the ones which are most widely represented in media discourse. In some news media, these external voices tend to be explicitly identified and demarcated, a point I return to below. When, however, they are translated into a newspaper's version of popular language, as in this case, there is a degree of mystification about whose voices and positions are being represented. If the voices of powerful people and groups in politics, industry, etc. are represented in a version of everyday speech (even a simulated and partially unreal one), then social identities, relationships and distances are collapsed. Powerful groups are represented as speaking in a language which readers themselves might have used, which makes it so much easier to go along with their meanings. The news media can be regarded as effecting the ideological work of transmitting the voices of power in a disguised and covert form.

Translating the language of official written documents into a version of popular speech is one instance of a more general translation of public language – be it written or spoken – into private language: a linguistic shift which is itself part of the rearticulating of the relationship between the public domain of political (economic, religious) events and social agents, and the private domain, the domain of the 'lifeworld', of common experience. There has been a tendency for 'private' events and individuals (for example, the grief of relatives of accident victims) to become newsworthy in at least some of the media, and this tendency is beginning to move out from the tabloid press into, for example, television news. Conversely, people and events in the public domain have come to be depicted in private terms. Here is an example from the British press (*Sunday Mirror* 28 March 1980):

Di's butler bows out...in sneakers!

PRINCE CHARLES'S butler is quitting his job.

And yesterday he revealed that sometimes he carried out his royal duties in *sneakers*.

Mr Alan Fisher usually wore the traditional Jeeves-style dark jacket and striped trousers at Charles' and Diana's Kensington Palace home.

The battered sneakers, he admitted, were a legacy from his service with Bing Crosby.

Mr Fisher, who leaves in six weeks, says the royal couple "are the most charming nice and ordinary of people. The Princess is terribly down to earth and natural."

The 54-year-old butler, who also worked for the Duke and Duchess of Windsor in Paris, has no job lined up but hopes to return to America.

"There was something about the informality of life over there that I missed," he said.

"There is a certain formality about working in a royal household, but I am a great lover of the Royal Family."

Would he be writing his memoirs about the Royal couple?

"If you don't like the people you work for then perhaps," he said. "But I have really enjoyed working here."

A Buckingham Palace spokesman said last night the Prince and Princess had received Mr Fisher's resignation "with regret".

(*Daily Mirror* 17 May 1984)

A butler in a royal household would traditionally be seen as a public figure, if a marginal one, in terms of role and function rather than as an individual. The voice of the royal butler in this case, however, is a popular speech voice, both in the direct discourse representation at the end of the article, and in the attributed use of 'sneakers'. This translation into the private domain of ordinary lives is underlined by the butler 'quitting his job' rather than, for instance, resigning his post. At the same time, the more significant shift of members of the royal family themselves into the private domain is evident: Diana is referred to universally in the tabloid press with the reduced form of her first name ('Di'), generally used in everyday experience only among family and friends, which implies that the royal family is like the rest of us in using such reduced forms, and that 'we' (journalists, readers) can refer to Diana as 'Di' as if we were on similar intimate terms with her. What is implicit in this universal use of 'Di' is made explicit in this report in words attributed to the butler: she is 'nice', 'ordinary', 'down to earth' and 'natural'.

Kress (1986) notices a similar restructuring of the boundary between public and private in the Australian press. He contrasts the coverage in two Australian newspapers of the 'deregistration' of the Builders Labourers' Federation (BLF), that is, the removal of its trade union immunities. One newspaper treats the event in public terms, focusing upon the legal process, whereas the other treats it in private terms, focusing upon the person and personality of BLF leader Norm Gallagher. The contrast is clear in the opening paragraphs of the two articles:

Full bench announces decision on BLF today

A FULL Bench of the Arbitration Commission will this morning bring down its decision in the deregistration case against the Builders Labourers' Federation.

(Sydney Morning Herald 4 April 1986)

Too busy for court, says Norm

NORM GALLAGHER will not attend an Arbitration Commission sitting today to hear its decision in the deregistration case against his union.

'I've got work to do,' the general secretary of the Builders Labourers' Federation said last night.

(Daily Telegraph 4 April 1986)

Again, the restructuring of the public/private boundary involves style as well as subject-matter, for example the use of first name and present tense in the headline, and the blunt comment quoted from Gallagher.

The media have an important hegemonic role in not only reproducing but also restructuring the relationship between the public and private domains, and the tendency I have identified here involves a fragmentation of the distinction, so that public and private life are reduced to a model of individual action and motivation, and of relationships based in presumed popular experience of private life. This is effected largely through restructuring within the order of discourse of relationships between 'popular speech' and various other public types of discourse.

I began this discussion by focusing upon discourse representation as a mode of intertextuality – how a text incorporates parts of other texts – but it has now broadened to a question of how the media discourse of newspapers such as *The Sun* is constituted through a particular articulation of discourse types, and particular processes of translation between them: what we can can call the 'interdiscursivity' or 'constitutive intertextuality' of media discourse (see below, pp. 124–30). In the text on drug abuse, translations into popular speech coexist with direct quotations from the HMSO document, though the former are foregrounded in the headlines and opening paragraph. Although the media are diverse and include various practices of discourse representation and various patterns of interdiscursivity, the dominant tendency is to combine public and private discourse types in this way.

Sample 2: 'A Cardholder's Guide to Barclaycard'

The second sample taken from Fairclough (1988a) is the language content of 'A Cardholder's Guide to Barclaycard'. The text occupies the top third of a double page, the rest being taken up by a photograph of a smiling Japanese receptionist offering a (non-represented) customer a pen, presumably to sign the voucher referred to in the text. (The numbering of sentences is my addition.)

Using it's simple you don't even have to speak the language

Wherever you see a Visa sign you can present your Barclaycard when you wish to pay [1]. The sales assistant will put your Card and sales voucher through an imprinter to record your name and account number [2].

He will then complete the voucher and after ensuring that the details are correct, you just sign it [3].

You'll receive a copy of the voucher, which you should keep for checking against your statement, and the goods are yours [4].

That's all there is to it [5].

You may use your Barclaycard as much as you wish, provided your payments are up to date and you keep within your available credit limit (this is printed on the folder containing your Barclaycard) [6].

Occasionally the shop may have to make a telephone call to Barclaycard to obtain our authorisation for a transaction [7]. This is a routine requirement of our procedure, and we just make sure that everything is in order before giving the go-ahead [8].

In an effort to deal more quickly with these calls, Barclaycard is introducing a new automated system [9].

This will save time for you, but *please note that any transactions which could take a Barclaycard account over its credit limit could well be declined* [10].

It is important to ensure that your credit limit is sufficient to cover all your purchases and Cash Advances [11].

When you wish to take advantage of a mail order offer it's so much easier to give your Barclaycard number rather than sending cheques or postal orders [12].

Just write your card number in the space provided on the order form, sign it and send it off [13].

Or if you want to book theatre tickets, make travel reservations or even make a purchase by telephone, just quote your card number and the cost can be charged to your Barclaycard account [14].

You'll find Barclaycard can make life a whole lot easier [15].

My focus for this sample is upon interdiscursivity (constitutive intertextuality) within a framework of hegemonic struggle and change, upon the social conditions and mechanisms for the emergence of a new discourse type which is constituted through a novel configuration of existing types, and specifically the emergence of hybrid information-and-publicity (or 'telling-and-selling') discourse. The particular mix in this sample is of financial regulations and advertising: the text sets out the conditions of use of the Barclaycard service, and at the same time tries to 'sell' it. The text producers are functioning in two situations and two sets of subject positions at the same time, and also positioning readers in contradictory ways. The central contradiction is the authority relation between bank and public: the bank is on the one hand the 'authoritor' communicating regulations to an 'authoritee', and on the other hand a producer (authoritee) trying to sell to a consumer (authoritor). Also at issue are interpersonal meanings in Halliday's sense (see pp. 64–5 above).

The text manifests a pattern of alternation at the level of the sentence between the discourse types of financial regulation and advertising, such that certain sentences are fairly clearly attributable to one discourse type or another. For example, the headline looks like advertising, and sentence (6) looks like financial regulation. Others, such as (12) and (14), are more ambivalent. But even sentences which generally belong to one discourse type often contain some trace of the other. For instance, in sentence (6) and throughout the text, the reader is directly addressed (as 'you'). Direct address is conventionally used as a marker of informality in modern advertising. There is one page in the guide headed 'Conditions of Use' which makes an interesting comparison. It lists thirteen conditions in very small print. There is no mixing of discourse types, and no direct address. Here is one of the conditions:

2. The card must be signed by the cardholder and may only be used (i) by that cardholder, (ii) subject to the terms of the Barclaycard Conditions of Use which are current at the time of use, (iii) within the credit limit from time to time notified to the principal cardholder by the Bank, and (iv) to obtain the facilities from time to time made available by the Bank in respect of the card.

The word 'just' as it is used in the text (sentences (3), (8), (13) and (14)) belongs to advertising. It minimizes impositions on the client, and thus mitigates the authority of the text producer with a shift towards the meaning of consumer authority. It communicates the core advertising meaning of simplicity: 'it's easy'. A rather different case is the avoidance of meanings which would be problematic within this mix of telling-and-selling. For instance, one would expect in financial regulations that what is required from the client would be made explicit, as it is in the extract from the 'Conditions of Use' quoted above. Yet although the text refers to ten actions required of the client, obligation is explicitly expressed in only one case ('which you should keep for checking'), and even then the meaning is a weak obligation ('you ought to' rather than 'you must'). (See the discussion of 'modality' below, pp. 158–62).

The italicized portion of the text – sentences (10) and (11) – is the most clearly regulatory, yet even here there is a lot of toning down. The meaning expressed in (10) is potentially offensive to the client, but it is toned down through hypothetical meaning ('could take', 'could be declined'), the 'hedging' of 'could be declined' with 'well', and the use here of a passive without an agent, which leaves unspecified who might do the 'declining' – it can easily be inferred from the rest of the text that it is the bank, but the text does not foreground it. In (11), the cardholder's obligation is put in impersonal terms ('it is important to ensure' rather than 'you must ensure'), and oddly transformed into a requirement to control the credit limit, which the bank in fact controls, rather than stay within it.

This mix of information about financial regulations and advertising can be interpreted as a way of reacting to a dilemma which institutions such as banking face in the modern market. Sectors of the economy outside commodity production are increasingly being drawn into the commodity model and the matrix of consumerism, and are under pressure to 'package' their activities as commodities and 'sell' them to 'consumers'. This creates a particular difficulty for banks: to emulate consumer goods their services must bow to the power of the consumer and be made attractive, simple and maximally unconstrained; yet the peculiar nature of the 'goods' on offer makes it imperative that consumers' access to them be controlled by rules and safeguards. This dilemma is not unique to banking. It arises in a rather different form in education, where pressure to 'sell the product' is offset by pressure to protect it from the adulterating effects of the market. The dilemma is manifest in the 'mode' of intertextual relation between the financial information and advertising elements of the text, and specifically the fact mentioned above that the text alternates between sentences which are primarily one rather than another. This gives the sense of the two discourse types trying uneasily to coexist in the text, rather than being more fully integrated. (On modes of intertextual relations see the beginning of the next section.)

Texts of the information-and-publicity or telling-and-selling sort are common in various institutional orders of discourse within contemporary society. They testify to a colonizing movement of advertising from the domain of commodity marketing in a narrow sense to a variety of other domains. One can relate this to a current surge (associated in Britain with 'enterprise culture') in the long-term process of commodification, the incorporation of new domains into the market, and a spread of consumerism. Consumerism has been seen as entailing a shift in the relative power of producer and consumer in favour of the latter, though it is arguable to what extent this shift in power is substantive or cosmetic.

Commodification, spreading consumerism, and marketization are having widespread effects upon orders of discourse, ranging from a pervasive restructuring of institutional orders of discourse under the impact of the colonizing movement of advertising, marketing and managerial discourse, to the ubiquitous 'rewording' (see, p. 194 below) of publics, clients, students and so forth as 'consumers' or 'customers'. These tendencies give rise to resistance, to hegemonic struggle over the structuring of orders of discourse, and to dilemmas for text producers and interpreters trying to work out ways of accommodating, containing or subverting colonization (see chapter 7 below).

Manifest Intertextuality

In what follows, I shall work with the distinction already alluded to above between 'manifest intertextuality' and 'interdiscursivity' ('constitutive intertextuality'). Manifest intertextuality is the case where specific other texts are overtly drawn upon within a text, whereas interdiscursivity is a matter of how a discourse type is constituted through a combination of elements of orders of discourse. The principle of interdiscursivity, though not the term, was discussed in connection with orders of discourse in chapter 3 above. It is also useful to bear in mind typological distinctions between different 'modes' of intertextual relations which have already emerged in my discussion of the samples. One can distinguish between:

'sequential' intertextuality, where different texts or discourse types alternate within a text, as is partly the case in sample 2;

'embedded intertextuality', where one text or discourse type is clearly contained within the matrix of another. This is the relationship between the 'styles' distinguished by Labov and Fanshel for therapeutic discourse (see the discussion in chapter 2);

'mixed intertextuality', where texts or discourse types are merged in a more complex and less easily separable way.

I shall discuss manifest intertextuality in relation to: discourse representation, presupposition, negation, metadiscourse, and irony. (I have found Maingueneau 1987 a particularly useful source for this discussion.)

Discourse Representation

I use the term 'discourse representation' in preference to the traditional term 'speech reportage' because (i) it better captures the idea that when one 'reports' discourse one necessarily chooses to represent it in one way rather than another; and (ii) what is represented is not just speech, but also writing, and not just their grammatical features but also their discursive organization, as well as various other aspects of the discursive event – its circumstances, the tone in which things were said, etc. (See Fairclough 1988b for more detail.)

Discourse types differ not only in the way in which they represent discourse, but also in the types of discourse they represent and the functions of discourse in the representing text. Thus there are differences in what is quoted when, how, and why, between sermons, scientific papers, and conversation. A major variable in how discourse is represented is whether representation goes beyond ideational or 'message' content to include aspects of the style and context of represented utterances. Volosinov (1973: 119–20) suggests that some cultures are more exclusively message-oriented than others, and the same is true of some discourse practices within any particular culture, and within our culture.

Volosinov (perhaps a *nom de plume* used by Bakhtin) highlights a dynamic interplay between the 'voices' of represented and representing discourse. Sample 1, for example, has illustrated how voices can be merged. Again there is considerable variation between discourse types, which can be explained in terms of two overlapping scales: (i) to what extent the boundaries between representing and represented discourse are explicitly and clearly marked; and (ii) to what extent represented discourse is translated into the voice of the representing discourse.

The degree of 'boundary maintenance' is partly a matter of the choice between direct and indirect discourse representation. The former purports at least to reproduce the exact words used in the represented discourse, although, as sample 1 showed, this is not always the case. Indirect discourse, by contrast, is ambivalent: one cannot be sure whether the words of the original are reproduced or not. Many accounts (see, for example, Leech and Short 1981) also distinguish a category of 'free indirect discourse', which lacks a reporting clause and is 'double-voiced', mixing the voices of representing and represented discourse, for instance the headline in sample 1 ('Call up Forces in Drug Battle!').

Another claim in Volosinov's account is that the meaning of represented discourse cannot be determined without reference to how it functions and is contextualized in the representing discourse. A good example of this is the use of 'scare quotes' – placing single words or short expressions in quotation marks – such as the journalistic examples 'probe into "girlie" spy plot', 'a "final" pay offer'. Expressions in scare quotes are simultaneously used and referred to: scare quotes establish them as belonging to an outside voice. Beyond that, they can have various more specific functions, such as distancing oneself from the outside voice, using its authority to support one's position, showing a usage to ᴅᴇ new or tentative, or introducing a new word. Similarly, one may use direct discourse to build up or show up represented discourse.

Contextualization of represented discourse takes many forms. This is from sample 1: 'In one of the hardest-hitting Commons reports for years, the committee – chaired by Tory lawyer MP Sir Edward Gardner – warned gravely: "Western society is faced..."'. The specification of the context of the represented discourse, of the prestigious status of its chairman, and of its 'grave' tone, all underscore the weightiness and importance of it. Notice also 'warned' (selected in preference to 'said', 'made out', or 'pointed out'). The choice of representing verb, or 'speech act' verb, is always significant. As in this case, it often marks the illocutionary force of the represented discourse (the nature of the action performed in the uttering of a particular form of words), which is a matter of imposing an interpretation upon the represented discourse.

Presupposition

Presuppositions are propositions which are taken by the producer of the text as already established or 'given' (though there is the question of for whom they are given, as I argue below), and there are various formal cues in the surface organization of the text to show this. For example, the proposition in a clause introduced by the conjunction 'that' is presupposed following verbs such as 'forget', 'regret', and 'realize' (e.g. 'I'd forgotten that your mother had remarried'); and definite articles cue propositions which have 'existential' meanings (e.g. 'the Soviet threat' presupposes that there is a Soviet threat, 'the rain' that it is/was raining).

Some accounts of presuppositions (see Levinson 1983 chapter 4 for an overview) treat them in a non-intertextual way as merely propositions that are given for, and taken for granted by, text producers. But there are problems with this position: it would entail, for example, that the sentence 'the Soviet threat is a myth' is semantically contradictory, because the text producer would be simultaneously taking it for granted that there was a Soviet threat, and asserting that there was no such threat. If, on the other hand, we take an intertextual view of presupposition, and assume that presupposed propositions are a way of incorporating the texts of others, there is no contradiction in this case: the expression 'the Soviet threat' and the presupposition it cues come from another ('alien', as Bakhtin puts it) text which is here contested. It should be added that in many cases of presupposition the 'other text' is not an individual specified or identifiable other text, but a more nebulous 'text' corresponding to general opinion (what people tend to say, accumulated textual experience). The expression 'the Soviet threat' in this case, for example, is one that we can all recognize as a widely-used formula, in Pêcheux's terms a 'preconstructed' expression, which circulates in a ready-made form.

Within an intertextual account of presupposition, the case where the presupposed proposition does constitute something taken for granted by the text producer can be interpreted in terms of intertextual relations with previous texts of the text producer. A special case of this is where a proposition is asserted and established in one part of a text, and then presupposed in the rest of it.

It should be noted that presuppositions, whether they are based upon prior texts of the text producer or upon others' texts, may be manipulative as well as sincere. That is, the text producer may present a proposition as given for another or established by himself dishonestly, insincerely, and with manipulative intent. Presuppositions are effective ways to manipulate people, because they are often difficult to challenge. An interviewee in a media interview who challenges a presupposition in a question from the interviewer can easily appear to be dodging the issue. Manipulative presuppositions also postulate interpreting subjects with particular prior textual experiences and assumptions, and in so doing they contribute to the ideological constitution of subjects.

Negation

Negative sentences are often used for polemical purposes. For instance, a newspaper headline in *The Sun* reads 'I Didn't Murder Squealer! Robbey Trial Man Hits Out'. This negative first sentence presupposes the proposition, in some other text, that the person quoted here did murder a 'squealer' (police informant). So negative sentences carry special types of presupposition which also work intertextually, incorporating other texts only in order to contest and reject them (see the account of negative sentences in Leech 1983). (Notice that 'the Soviet threat is a myth' works in the same way: although the sentence is not grammatically negative, it is semantically negative, as shown by a paraphrase such as 'the Soviet threat is not a reality'.)

Metadiscourse

Metadiscourse is a peculiar form of manifest intertextuality where the text producer distinguishes different levels within her own text, and distances herself from some level of the text, treating the distanced level as if it were another, external, text (see Maingueneau 1987: 66–9). There are various ways of achieving this. One is the use of 'hedging' (Brown and Levinson 1978) with expressions such as 'sort of', 'kind of', to mark some expression as possibly not quite adequate (e.g. 'he was sort of paternalistic'). Or an expression can be marked as belonging to another text or a particular convention ('as x might have put it', 'in scientific terms'), or as metaphorical ('metaphorically speaking'). Another possibility is to paraphrase or reformulate an expression (on reformulation, see pp. 157–8 below); for example a government minister may offer paraphrases of the key term 'enterprise' in the course of a speech dealing with 'enterprise culture': 'Early in life we have an abundance of enterprise, initiative, the ability to spot an opportunity and take rapid advantage of it.'

Metadiscourse implies that the speaker is situated above or outside her own discourse, and is in a position to control and manipulate it. This has interesting implications for the relationship between discourse and identity (subjectivity): it seems to go against the view that one's social identity is a matter of how one is positioned in particular types of discourse. There are two sides to this. On the one hand, the possibility of a metadiscursive distance from one's own discourse can support the illusion that one is always fully in control of it, that one's discourse is an effect of one's subjectivity rather than vice-versa. It is interesting in this regard that metadiscourse seems to be common in discourse types where there is a premium upon displaying oneself as in control, such as literary criticism or other forms of academic analysis in the humanities. On the other hand, I have emphasized a dialectical view of the relationship of discourse and subjectivity: subjects are in part positioned and constituted in discourse, but they also engage in practice which contests and restructures the discursive structures (orders of discourse) which position them. This includes restructurings which are motivated by polemical considerations and manipulative objectives: the paraphrases offered by the government minister above constitute 'semantic enginering' (Leech 1981: 48–52). What may appear as an innocent clarification of the meaning of 'enterprise' can be interpreted rather as a politically and ideologically motivated definition (for further discussion, see Fairclough 1990a and pp. 187–90 below).

Irony

Traditional accounts of irony describe it in terms of 'saying one thing and meaning another'. Such an explanation is of limited utility, because what it misses is the intertextual nature of irony: the fact that an ironic utterance 'echoes' someone else's utterance (Sperber and Wilson 1986: 237–43). For example, suppose you say 'It's a lovely day for a picnic'. We go for a picnic, it rains, and I then say 'It's a lovely day for a picnic'. My utterance would be ironic: it echoes your utterance, but there is disparity between the meaning I am giving voice to, so to speak, in echoing your utterance, and the real function of my utterance which is to express some sort of negative attitude towards your utterance, or indeed you – be it anger, sarcasm, or whatever. Notice that irony depends upon interpreters being able to recognize that the meaning of an echoed text is not the text producer's meaning. That recognition may be based upon various factors: a blatant mismatch between apparent meaning and situational context (in the above example, rain), cues in a speaker's tone of voice or in a written text (e.g. putting words between scare quotes), or interpreters' assumptions about the beliefs or values of the text producer ('we are all fully aware of the economic achievements of communism' will easily be recognized as ironic by regular readers of *The Daily Telegraph* in Britain, or in a speech by the president of the United states of America).

Interdiscursivity

In chapter 3 (p. 68 above) I asserted, in different terms, the principle of interdiscursivity (or constitutive intertextuality) by suggesting that orders of discourse have primacy over particular types of discourse, and that the latter are constituted as configurations of diverse elements of orders of discourse. I also suggested that the principle of interdiscursivity applies at various levels: the societal order of discourse, the institutional order of discourse, the discourse type, and even the elements which constitute discourse types. Furthermore, the adoption of a hegemonic model points in the same direction, leading to a view of orders of discourse as unstable equilibria, consisting of elements which are internally heterogeneous – or intertextual in their constitution – the boundaries between which are constantly open to being redrawn as orders of discourse are disarticulated and rearticulated in the course of hegemonic struggle.

In this section I want to take up the question of what sort of elements are combined in the constitution of discourse types. In the earlier discussion I stressed their diversity, and the variability of their scale: they range from turn-taking systems to vocabularies, scripts for genres such as crime reports, sets of politeness conventions, and so forth. But it is possible to classify the elements which make up orders of discourse, and which are open to articulation in discourse types, in terms of a small number of major types, of which particular vocabularies, turn-taking systems and so forth are properties. Widely-used terms for these types include 'genre', 'style', 'register', and 'discourse'. Thus one can talk of 'interview genre', 'conversational style', 'the register of cookery books', or 'scientific medical discourse'.

The advantage of using such terms is that they enable us to pick out in our analyses major differences of type between the elements of orders of discourse which we might otherwise lose sight of, and in so doing make clear the sense in which discursive practice is constrained by conventions. It is also easier to use an analytical framework with a small number of fairly well-differentiated categories, and some of the terms are widely used by social scientists in, for example, the analysis of popular culture

(Bennett and Woollacott 1987); using them in discourse analysis helps to make its value as a method more immediately obvious to social scientists. This is true of 'genre', and of 'discourse' used to refer to a particular type of convention ('a discourse', 'these discourses'), rather than in a general way to language use as a mode of social practice (as I have mainly used it so far: recall the discussion of 'discourse' in the Introduction). But there are disadvantages. The elements of orders of discourse are extremely diverse, and it is by no means always easy to decide whether one is dealing with genres, styles, discourses, or whatever. Too rigid an analytical framework can lead one to lose sight of the complexities of discourse. So we should use these terms cautiously, recognizing that each is bound to cover a diverse and heterogeneous domain, that it will sometimes be difficult to use them in well-motivated ways, and that we may have to resort to vaguer terms such as 'discourse type' (which I have used hitherto for any type of convention). We should also recognize that there is not, and could not be, a determinate list of genres, styles or discourses, and that we are constantly faced with what often appear to be rather arbitrary decisions (influenced by the point of departure of one's analysis) about whether something is or is not a separate instance of one of these types.

With these provisos in mind, let us come to a discussion of types. The terms I shall use are 'genre', 'activity type', 'style', and 'discourse'. Although these different types of element have a certain autonomy with respect to each other, they are not strictly equal. In particular, genre overarches the other types, in the sense that genres correspond closely to types of social practice (see below), and the system of genres which obtains in a particular society at a particular time determines which combinations and configurations the other types occur in. Moreover, the other elements differ in their degree of autonomy in relation to genre, that is, the extent to which they are freely combinable with a variety of genres and with other types of element. They rank on a scale from least to most autonomous: activity type, style, discourse. From the perspective of this book, it is change in the system of genres and its effects upon configurations of other elements that is of particular interest. However, one strength of the (essentially Bakhtinian) view of genre I am adopting here is that it allows us to give due weight to both the way in which social practice is constrained by conventions, and the potentiality for change and creativity.

I shall use the term 'genre' for a relatively stable set of conventions that is associated with, and partly enacts, a socially ratified type of activity, such as informal chat, buying goods in a shop, a job interview, a television documentary, a poem, or a scientific article. A genre implies not only a particular text type, but also particular processes of producing, distributing and consuming texts. For example, not only are newspaper articles and poems typically quite different sorts of text, but they are also produced in quite different ways (e.g. one is a collective product, one an individual product), have quite different sorts of distribution, and are consumed quite differently – the latter including quite different protocols for reading and interpreting them. So genre cuts across the distinction between 'description' and 'interpretation' which I introduced in chapter 3.

According to Bakhtin (1986: 65), genres are 'the drive belts from the history of society to the history of language'. Changes in social practice are both manifested on the plane of language in changes in the system of genres, and in part brought about through such changes. In referring to a system of genres, I am applying here the principle of the primacy of orders of discourse introduced in chapter 3: a society, or a particular institution or domain within it, has a particular configuration of genres in particular relationships to each other, constituting a system. And, of course, the configuration and system are open to change.

Focusing upon genre as text type, a particular genre is associated with a particular 'compositional structure', as Bakhtin calls it (1986: 60), or, in the terminology I shall use, a particular 'activity type' (a category I am adapting from Levinson 1979). An activity type can be specified in terms of the structured sequence of actions of which it is composed, and in terms of the participants involved in the activity – that is, the set of subject positions which are socially constituted and recognized in connection with the activity type. For example, the activity of buying goods from a greengrocer's shop involves 'customer' and 'shop assistant' as designated subject types, and a sequence of actions, some of which may be optional or repeated, along these lines: customer enters shop and awaits turn; shop assistant greets customer (customer returns greeting, they exchange social pleasantries) and solicits purchase request; customer makes purchase request (possibly preceded by a pre-request sequence such as 'What are the apples like this week?' – 'Well, the Coxes are nice'); shop assistant gets (weighs out, packages, etc.) goods and gives them to customer (customer and shop assistant possibly negotiate on whether the goods are acceptable, whether variations in the requested weight are acceptable, etc.); customer thanks shop assistant; shop assistant informs customer of the cost; customer pays; shop assistant gives change and thanks customer; customer thanks shop assistant and gives a farewell greeting; shop assistant returns farewell greeting. As this example shows, an activity type often delimits a range of options rather than specifying a single rigid pattern. See Hasan's contributions in Halliday and Hasan (1985) for a view of genre which emphasizes such properties of compositional structure.

A genre tends to be associated with a particular style, though genres may often be compatible with alternative styles, for example interviews may be 'formal' or 'informal'. Style, like the other terms I am using, is difficult to pin down, and has been used in various ways. We can think of styles as varying along three main parameters, according to the 'tenor', 'mode' and 'rhetorical mode' of the text, to use the terminology of systemic linguistics (Halliday 1978). Firstly, styles vary according to tenor, that is, according to the sort of relationship that obtains between participants in an interaction. So we can classify styles with such terms as 'formal', 'informal', 'official', 'intimate', 'casual', and so on. Secondly, styles vary according to mode, according to whether texts are written or spoken or some combination of the two (e.g. written-to-be-spoken, written-as-if-spoken, spoken-as-if-written). So we can classify styles as spoken, written, spoken-as-if-written, and so forth. We can also use terms which in part reflect mode but in part reflect tenor, or genre, or discourse, such as 'conversational', 'formal written', 'informal written', 'academic', 'journalistic', and so forth. Thirdly, styles vary according to rhetorical mode, and can be classified with terms such as 'argumentative', 'descriptive', and 'expository'.

The most autonomous of the types of element (other than genre) is 'discourse' (see Kress 1988; Kress and Threadgold 1988 on the relationship between 'genre' and 'discourse'). Discourses correspond roughly to dimensions of texts which have traditionally been discussed in terms of 'content', 'ideational meanings', 'topic', 'subject matter', and so forth. There is a good reason for using 'discourse' rather than these traditional terms: a discourse is a particular way of constructing a subject-matter, and the concept differs from its predecessors in emphasizing that contents or subject-matters – areas of knowledge – only enter texts in the mediated form of particular constructions of them. It is helpful in this regard to choose terms for particular discourses which designate both the relevant area of knowledge, and the particular way it is constituted, for example 'techno-scientific medical discourse' (i.e. medicine as an area of knowledge constructed from a technological and scientific perspective, in contrast with the discourses associated with various 'alternative' medicines), or 'feminist discourses of sexuality' (i.e. sexuality as an area of knowledge constructed from feminist points of view). Discourses in this sense are a major concern of Foucault's (see chapter 2 above). As I indicated above, discourses are more autonomous than the other types of element. That is, although there are still important constraints and rules of compatibility between particular genres and particular discourses, a discourse such as techno-scientific medical discourse is standardly associated with a range of genres (scientific articles, lectures, consultations, and so forth) and can show up in all sorts of other genres (conversations, television chat shows, or indeed poems).

Particular genres are associated with particular 'modes of (manifest) intertextuality'. For example, the frequency, modes and functions of discourse representation are quite different in a news report, a chat, and a scientific article. Contrasting modes and practices of discourse representation develop in connection with different sorts of social activity, according to the different significance and values the discourse of others comes to have. For example, a verbatim report of a conversation produced in a conversation, or even in a court of law, is not necessarily expected to be word-perfect, whereas a quotation from one scientific paper in another would be. Or again, while representations of the speech of others in conversation often attempt to capture aspects of the style in which things were said, this is rarely so in news reports. In more general terms, the extent to which other texts figure in a text depends upon the genre, as do the forms of manifest intertextuality which are used, and the ways in which other text function within a text.

Let me now try to illustrate this set of types of element with reference to sample 1 above. The genre is news report, and perhaps a sub-genre of tabloid news report which involves configuration with different styles from other sub-genres (see below). The activity type sets up subject positions for a news giver (a fictive individual author of the report, given that such reports are collectively produced), and a news receiver (the reader). It involves the following sequential structure: headlines (two in this case), which give the gist of the story; summary (two initial paragraphs), which gives a slightly fuller version of the gist; elaboration (two further paragraphs); development (all except the final paragraph under the sub-head 'Profits'), which gives further detail on the story; outcome (the final paragraph), which indicates what action is to be taken. (On the structure of news articles, see van Dijk 1988.) It is also worth noting that the story has a crisis–resolution structure: the headline and much of the body of the report sets out the crisis, while the short final paragraph sets out the resolution.

The report is rather complex in terms of style. Let us begin with the rhetorical mode, which is giving information. More precisely, the news giver is here constructed as the source of knowledge and information, and the reader as a passive recipient of it, and report consists of the authoritative categorical assertions which newspapers typically make about events, despite the fact that such events are usually of an uncertain character and open to various interpretations. What is interesting in this case is how the rhetorical mode combines with tenor-based and mode-based dimensions of style. The style is vernacular in tenor: as I suggested earlier, the writers simulate popular speech, as if the relationship between news givers and readers were a symmetrical one, and a 'lifeworld' one (in the sense of Habermas 1984). And the style is spoken and conversational in mode. This stylistic configuration appears to be contradictory, because the rhetorical mode sets up asymmetrical subject positions, and implies the written formality of public institutions, which are at odds with the informal, conversational, lifeworld elements of the style.

There is one discourse whose presence in the report is particularly striking: what we might call a militarized discourse of crimi-
nality, built around the metaphor of criminals being 'at war' with
society, and society having to 'mobilize its forces' to 'fight them
off'. In this report, however, the discourse and the metaphor are
articulated with an appeal for mobilization in a literal sense, for
the armed forces to be used against drug dealers, which leads to a
certain ambivalence in the opening sentence: is *The Sun* projecting
some sort of real battle here?

Intertextuality and Transformations

Particular practices within and across institutions have associated
with them particular 'intertextual chains', series of types of texts
which are transformationally related to each other in the sense that
each member of the series is transformed into one or more of the
others in regular and predictable ways. (On transformation see
Kristeva 1986a; Hodge and Kress 1988; and the discussion of
Critical linguistics in chapter 1 above.) These chains are sequential
or syntagmatic, in contrast to the paradigmatic intertextual relations discussed in the previous section under the heading of
interdiscursivity. Specifying the intertextual chains into which a
particular type of discourse enters is a way of specifying its
'distribution': recall the discussion above (pp. 78–80) of the
production, distribution and consumption of texts. A simple example would be the chain which links medical consultations with
medical records: doctors routinely transform the former into the
latter. Given the considerable number and range of different types
of text, there could in principle be a huge and indeed indeter-
minable number of intertextual chains between them. However,
the number of actual chains is probably quite limited: social institutions and practices are articulated in particular ways, and
this aspect of social structuring constrains the development of
intertextual chains. (Indeed, the study of actual intertextual
chains is one way of gaining insight into this dimension of social
structuring.)

Intertextual chains can be quite complex, for example those
that the texts of international diplomacy and arms negotiation

enter into. A major speech by President Gorbachev will be transformed into media texts of various types in every country in the world, into reports, analyses and commentaries by diplomats, into academic books and articles, into other speeches which paraphrase it, elaborate it, answer it, and so on. On the other hand, a contribution to a casual conversation is likely to be transformed only into formulations of it by coparticipants, and perhaps reports of it by others. So different types of texts vary radically in the sort of distributional networks and intertextual chains they enter into, and therefore the sorts of transformation they undergo. Although those designing a speech for Gorbachev can in no way anticipate in detail the many circuits of text production and consumption it will enter, they are likely to try to design it in a way that anticipates the responses of the main types of audience. Such complex anticipation is, as I have already suggested, a source of heterogeneity and ambivalence, and it may well be that texts with complex intertextual chains are more prone to these properties than others.

Transformations between text types in an intertextual chain can be of diverse sorts. They may involve forms of manifest intertextuality, such as discourse representation. They may, on the other hand, have a more diffuse character. What can be interpreted as common elements shared by different text types may be manifested at different levels and in radically different ways – in the vocabulary in one case, in narratives or metaphors in another, or in selections among grammatical options, or in the way dialogue is organized. For example, a theoretical account of non-hierarchical, collaborative classroom practice in a book on educational theory may mainly shape the vocabulary of the book, whereas the 'same' theory may show up in actual classroom practice in the way in which dialogue between teacher and learners is organized, and in the staffroom (or in research interviews) in metaphors the teacher uses in talking about her classes and her relationship with learners (for example, do learners work in 'groups', 'teams', or indeed 'task forces'?).

Let us consider a real example taken from Fairclough (1990a). The speeches of Lord Young as British Secretary of State for Trade and Industry between 1985 and 1988 were a major element in the development of the concept, practices and policies of 'enterprise culture'. It was Lord Young who renamed his department 'the Department of Enterprise'. In his speeches, the word 'enterprise' is subjected to a process of semantic engineering (discussed in more detail below pp. 187–90), which involves articulating around the word a set of qualities associated with entrepreneurship as understood by proponents of enterprise culture, including self-reliance and self-help. There appears to be a relationship between the theoretical construction in these speeches of enterprising subjects, 'the enterprising self', and the publicity put out by the Department of Trade and Industry (DTI) on Young's 'enterprise initiative'. What is contained in the vocabulary of the speeches is transformed here into a particular communicative style.

A DTI brochure on the enterprise initiative contains an article dealing specifically with 'the marketing initiative', which it sums up in these terms: 'The essence of good marketing is to provide your customers with what they want. Not to spend time and money trying to persuade them to take what you've got. So, whether you're selling at home or abroad, it's important to understand both the market and your competitors.' This summary comes in the opening orientation section of the article, and like other orientation sections in the brochure, it consists of categorical, bald assertions about business practice which, like the first sentence in this example, must be truisms for the business audience the brochure is addressed to, or, like the second sentence, may be threatening to some businesses. Notice that it is a negative sentence which presupposes that some businesses do spend time and money trying to persuade people to take what they have to sell. One might therefore expect business readers to find such orientations irritating and/or insulting. But I suspect they will be read quite differently. An enterprising person in Young's sense can talk and can be talked to straight; what these orientations are perhaps attempting to do is both give the DTI an enterprising identity, and offer a model of an enterprising person and enterprising behaviour to businesses. The nature of the 'enterprising self' figures not only in the vocabulary of the speeches, but also in the style of writing (implying a style of speaking) of the brochure.

Intertextual chains may constitute relatively settled transformational relationships between text types (as in the relationship between medical consultation and medical records, or the routines for transforming reports into newspaper articles). But they often become lines of tension and change, the channels through which text types are colonized and invested, and along which relationships between text types are contested. This is the way to interpret intertextual chains associated with 'enterprise culture': texts in health care, education, social services, and the media, as well as official publicity such as the DTI brochure, are being colonized with meanings associated with enterprise culture from centres such as Young's speeches, and invested with ideologies of enterprise and with New Right political strategies. Existing lines and channels within intertextual chains are being used for strategic purposes.

Intertextuality, Coherence and Subjects

Intertextuality has important implications for an issue of major concern in this book: the constitution of subjects through texts, and the contribution of changing discursive practices to changes in social identity (see Kristeva 1986b; Threadgold 1988, and Talbot forthcoming). The intertextuality of texts substantially complicates the processes of text interpretation discussed above (pp. 80–4), for in order to make sense of texts, interpreters have to find ways of fitting the diverse elements of a text into a coherent, though not necessarily unitary, determinate or unambivalent, whole. It is easy to see this as simply an achievement of interpreters, which implicitly places interpreters as discourse subjects above and outside intertextuality, as able to control discursive processes which are exterior to them. Such a view implies social and discursive subjects that mysteriously pre-exist social and discursive practices, and misses the contribution of those practices to the constitution of subjects, and to their transformation over time. The position which I shall adopt here is that intertextuality, and constantly changing intertextual relations in discourse, are central to an understanding of processes of subject constitution. This is so on a biographical time-scale, during the life of an individual, and for the constitution and reconstitution of social groups and communities.

Kress (1987) provides an example which underscores the social significance of such discursive processes. He analyses samples of educational texts of various types, and suggests that their intertextual constitution incorporates elements shared with advertising discourse. For example, advertisements for household cleaning agents share with school textbooks for home management classes the property of distributing agency in cleaning processes between the human cleaner – by implication the reader of the advertisement or the textbook – and the commodity (for example, 'Ajax cleans without rinsing', 'fine powders can absorb liquids'), which suggests in both cases that the human cleaner 'needs' the commodity. School textbooks, and other forms of educational discourse, thus contribute to the constitution of subjects as consumers, and the educational process appears, amongst other things, to be educating readers to read advertisements. As suggested above, examples of this sort are relevant to the constitution of social groups and communities, as well as to the socialization of individuals; such discursive practices simultaneously generate a (consumerist) view of the world, and a community (of consumers) associated with such a view. This accords with a view of the ideological work of discourse as simultaneously generating representations and organizing people into communities (see Debray 1981; Maingueneau 1987: 42).

The concept of 'coherence' is at the centre of most accounts of interpretation. As I have already indicated, coherence is not a property of texts, but a property which interpreters impose upon texts, with different interpreters (including the producer of the text) possibly generating different coherent readings of the same text. Nor should coherence be understood in an absolute, logical sense: a coherent text hangs together sufficiently well for present purposes as far as the interpreter is concerned, which does not preclude indeterminacies and ambivalence.

In chapter 3, I used an example to illustrate the dependence of coherence upon assumptions which interpreters bring to the process of interpretation, including assumptions of an ideological nature. 'She's giving up her job next Wednesday. She's pregnant', for example, makes sense on the assumption that women cease to work when they have (and are expecting) children. I suggested also that producers interpellate interpreting subjects who are 'capable' of making relevant assumptions, and of making the connections which yield coherent readings. This view of coherence and its role in ideological interpellation can be extended to take account of intertextuality. Texts postulate, and implicitly set up interpretative positions for, interpreting subjects who are 'capable' of using assumptions from their prior experience to make connections across the intertextually diverse elements of a text, and to generate coherent interpretations. This should not be taken to imply that interpreters always fully resolve the contradictions of texts; interpreters may generate resistant interpretations (see below), and it is possible for interpreters to arrive at partial reconciliation or patching up of contradictions that is adequate for their immediate purposes. But in so far as interpreters do resolve contradictions interpretatively, they are themselves also being positioned (or having existing positionings reinforced) as complex subjects by texts.

Coherent interpretations across the intertextually diverse elements of a text are generated simultaneously for its various dimensions of meaning, ideational and interpersonal (the latter breaking down into relational and identity meanings: see p. 64 above). For example, both sample 1 and sample 2 above have complex relational meanings associated with the ways in which they mix heterogeneous styles and genres. It is interpreters that find acceptable ways of marrying these diverse relational meanings. In the case of sample 1, marrying relational meanings is a matter of rendering compatible on the one hand the relationship between a source and provider of information and a passive recipient of information, and on the other hand the relationship between co-members of the ordinary lifeworld. In the case of sample 2, it is the advertiser–consumer relationship, and the relationship between institution as rule-giver and member of the public as subject (e.g. bank and customer), that need to be married. An example of a text with complex identical meanings is the radio interview with Margaret Thatcher which I analyse in Fairclough (1989a). A complex subject position for the reader is constituted from a diverse range of elements (including the British patriot, the careful housekeeper, the worried parent, the entrepreneur), and it is again up to the interpreter to marry these contradictory identities into a coherent whole. Hall (1988) gives an account of Thatcher's discourse in similar terms, the concept of 'condensation' in Laclau (1977) addresses the process of interpretatively marrying elements in terms of its ideological effects, and both embed these issues within a theory of hegemony. What is missing in their account, however, is the specificity of actual texts.

What I have said so far implies interpreters that are compliant, in the sense of fitting in with the positions set up for them in texts. But not all interpreters are compliant: some are to a greater or lesser extent, and more or less explicitly, resistant. Interpreters are, of course, more than discourse subjects in particular discourse processes; they are also social subjects with particular accumulated social experiences, and with resources variously oriented to the multiple dimensions of social life, and these variables affect the ways they go about interpreting particular texts. Other variables are the particular interpretative protocols which are available to them, and drawn upon by them, in that particular domain of discourse practice: the capacity for critical reading, for example, is not distributed equally among all interpreters in all interpretative environments.

Resistant readings may disarticulate to one extent or another the intertextual articulation of a text. For example, an interpreter may react against the advertising elements in sample 2, reading them in terms of Barclaycard 'trying to sell me something'. As part of this process, the interpreter adds a further dimension of intertextuality to the text by bringing other texts to bear interpretatively – in this case sociological analyses or political critiques of consumerism. Resistant interpretations are one mode of hegemonic struggle over the articulation of intertextual elements. While they typically lead to processes of text production which project the hegemonic struggle into more explicit forms, this is not necessarily the case, and it is important to take account of the ways in which interpreters interpret texts if one is properly to assess their political and ideological effectiveness. (Recall my criticism of Critical linguistics along similar lines in chapter 1 above, though see the use of the concept of 'resistant readers/readings' in Kress (1988).)

5

Text Analysis: Constructing Social Relations and 'the Self'

Chapters 5 and 6 focus upon text analysis, and associated 'micro' aspects of discourse practice, developing very selectively the analytical categories introduced in chapter 3 (with the exception of intertextuality, which has been dealt with in chapter 4): vocabulary, grammar, cohesion, text structure, force and coherence. The difference between chapters 5 and 6 is one of emphasis. Chapter 5 concentrates mainly upon analytical properties of texts which are particularly connected to the interpersonal function of language and interpersonal meanings, while chapter 6 deals mainly with aspects of text analysis which are particularly connected to ideational function and ideational meanings.

I suggested in chapter 3 that the interpersonal function could be split into two component functions, which I called the 'relational' and 'identity' functions. These have to do with the ways in which social relations are exercised and social identities are manifested in discourse, but also, of course, with how social relations and identities are constructed (reproduced, contested, restructured) in discourse. I want to focus in this chapter on the construction of social identities, or the construction of 'the self' in discourse, and more particularly on the ways in which discourse contributes to processes of cultural change, in which the social identities or 'selves' associated with specific domains and institutions are redefined and reconstituted. I want to place the emphasis here because it is a very important discursive aspect of cultural and social change, but an aspect which has tended until recently to receive less attention than it should in discourse analysis.

I shall focus upon the following analytical properties of texts: interactional control (including turn-taking, exchange structure, topic control, control of agendas, formulation), modality, politeness, and ethos. In terms of the analytical categories of chapter 3 above, interactional control is a dimension of text structure, modality a dimension of grammar (though a conception of grammar which is very much oriented to meaning, such as that of Halliday 1985), and politeness an aspect of what I called 'force'. Ethos transcends the categories, as I shall explain below, and is motivated by the focus on the self. The selection of these particular topics for attention is not an arbitrary one: each of them is a rich basis for insight into socially and culturally significant aspects of change in the relational and identity functions of discourse.

As in chapter 4, I begin with a discussion of particular discourse samples. Two of the samples are taken from the same broad discourse type, medical interviews, because they show contrasting ways in which doctor-patient relations and the social identity of the doctor, 'the medical self', are constructed in contemporary society. The third sample is from informal conversation, and it has been included to underline another contrast between the first two which takes us back to the last chapter: differences in modes of intertextuality.

Sample 1: 'Standard' Medical Interview

My first sample is an extract from an interview between a male doctor and a female patient, which I have taken from a study of medical interviews recorded in the USA by Mishler (1984). Silences are marked by sequences of full stops, each representing one tenth of a second; colons mark prolongation of a syllable; interruptions and overlaps are marked by square brackets; material in round brackets is unclear speech. The roman numerals divide the sample into 'cycles', corresponding roughly to 'exchanges' in the Sinclair and Coulthard system (see p. 13 above),

```
DOCTOR:  ⌈Hm hm...Now what do you mean by a sour stomach?
PATIENT: |..........What's a sour stomach? A heartburn
      I  ⌊like a heartburn or someth⌈ing.
   D:                               ⌊Does it burn over here?
 5 P:   II ⌈                                        Yea:h.
```

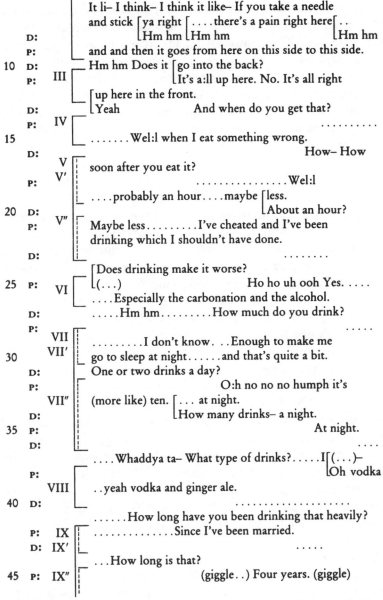

I shall begin by focusing upon a range of what I shall call 'interactional control features', which broadly have to do with ensuring that the interaction works smoothly at an organizational level: that turns at talking are smoothly distributed, that topics are selected and changed, questions are answered, and so forth.

An obvious starting point is the way in which the interaction is organized around questions from the doctor, which are answered by the patient. The transcription incorporates Mishler's analysis of the data into nine cycles, each of which is initiated by a question from the doctor. The division of cycles V, VII and IX (the last of which I have curtailed) into sub-cycles shows that they also involve 'follow-up' questions from the doctor which solicit elaborations of the patient's answers. In some cases (lines 10, 13, and 27), the doctor's question is preceded by an element which overtly acknowledges or accepts the patient's previous answer. I shall call it an 'acceptance'. Even when this is absent, the fact that the doctor proceeds to a next question, rather than asking a follow-up question, may be taken as implicitly accepting the patient's previous answer. That is why the doctor's questions are shown as between the cycles: they terminate one cycle by implicitly accepting the patient's answer, as well as initiating the next. We may say, therefore, following Mishler, that these cycles have a basic three-part structure: a question from the doctor, a response from the patient, and an implicit or explicit acceptance of that response by the doctor.

The doctor, then, is closely controlling the basic organization of the interaction by opening and closing each cycle and accepting/acknowledging the patient's responses. One corollary of this is that the doctor is controlling the turn-taking system, the way talking turns are distributed between participants in the interaction (on turn-taking see Sacks, Schegloff and Jefferson 1973; Schenkein 1978). The patient only takes turns when offered them by the doctor, which means when the doctor directs a question at her. The doctor, on the other hand, is not offered turns but takes them when the patient has finished her response, or when he decides the patient has said enough for his purposes (see below).

A further corollary of this basic organization is to do with 'topic control'. It is mainly the doctor who introduces new topics through his questions, for example when he shifts in lines 1–13 from what is meant by 'sour stomach', to where 'it burns', to whether the pain 'goes into the back', to when the patient gets the pain. Notice, however, that the patient does introduce a topic in ll. 21–22 – drinking – which the doctor takes up in l. 024. I return to this exception below.

The selective way in which the doctor takes up the responses of the patient to previous questions is another aspect of his topic control. For example, in the sequence at ll. 21–4 to which I have just referred, the patient acknowledges having done wrong by drinking, but the doctor does not pursue this admission. He seems concerned only with the effect of alcohol on the patient's medical condition. Similarly, the patient's responses in ll. 29–30 and 42 signal problems on the patient's part which the doctor ignores in favour of the narrowly medical detail. One has the sense of the doctor shifting and constraining topic in accordance with a pre-set agenda, which the patient is not being allowed to disturb.

Another aspect of the doctor's control is the nature of the questions he asks. They are not open questions, giving the patient the floor (as 'Tell me how you've been' would be), but more or less closed questions which set relatively tight limits on the content of the patient's answers. Some are 'yes/no' questions, which require a 'yes' or 'no' answer confirming or disconfirming some proposition (e.g. 'Does it burn over here?'). Others are so-called 'wh-questions' beginning with 'what', 'when', 'how', which elicit specific details of time, and quantity and type of alcohol.

It is also instructive to look closely at the relationship between the doctor's questions and the patient's answers. In l. 4, the doctor begins his question before the patient has finished speaking, and there is an overlap. Similarly in ll. 20 and 34, though in those cases there is a pause in the patient's turn which the doctor perhaps takes as indicating completion. In other cases, the doctor's turn follows immediately on from the patient's without a pause, either with an assessment followed at once by a question (ll. 10, 13) or with just a question (l. 16). The pattern is different in l. 23 for reasons suggested below. This reinforces the impression that the doctor is working through a pre-set agenda or routine, shifting from one stage of it to another as soon as he has what he regards as enough information, even if that means cutting short the patient's turn. Looked at from the patient's point of view, this routine can come across as a series of disconnected and unpredictable questions, which is perhaps why the patient's answers, in contrast to the doctor's questions in the first part of the extract, are preceded by hesitations (ll. 15, 18, 29, and 42).

The overall picture, then, with respect to interactional control features, is that through the question-response-assessment cycles the doctor pursues a pre-set agenda, in accordance with which he controls the taking, content and length of patient turns, and the introduction and shift of topics. Let me now add some brief comments on three other aspects of the sample which are treated more fully later in the chapter: modality, politeness, and ethos.

Modality concerns the extent to which producers commit themselves to, or conversely distance themselves from, propositions: their degree of 'affinity' with the proposition, as Hodge and Kress (1988) call it. As Hodge and Kress point out, however, the affinity a producer shows with a representation of the world is inseparable from the relationship (and 'affinity') between the producer and other participants in the discourse. In ll. 2–3, for example, the patient defines a 'sour stomach' as 'a heartburn like a heartburn or something'. The patient first glosses it with a 'folk medicine' term, then distances herself from the gloss by demoting it into a simile ('like' a heartburn), and then further distances herself from it by hedging' it (Brown and Levinson 1978) with 'or something'. This is low affinity modality. But it is difficult to disentangle factors of propositional truth and social relations in the patient's motivation for it: does she select low modality because she is not sure how accurate the gloss is, or because she is reluctant to claim anything resembling medical knowledge in an interaction with a legitimized medical expert? Propositional truth and social relations, knowledge and power, seem to be intricately linked in such cases.

Let me turn to politeness. The patient introduces the presumably difficult and potentially embarrassing issue of her drinking in ll. 21–2, as an addition tagged on to the answer to one of the doctor's questions. According to Mishler (1984: 86), she speaks at this point in a 'teasing', 'flirtatious' or 'childish' tone, which may be interpreted as a way of mitigating the threat to her self-esteem, her 'face' (see Brown and Levinson 1978, and the section on politeness later in this chapter), of her admission. By contrast, the doctor's questions about the patient's drinking are unmitigated, bald, and even rather brutal (l. 41): he formulates the patient's situation as 'heavy drinking' without diplomacy or mitigation (on formulation, see pp. 157–8 below). The doctor's questions are low in politeness, using the term in the broad way it is used in the pragmatics literature (for instance, Leech 1983; Brown and Levinson 1978) for orientation and sensitivity to the 'face' of participants, their self-esteem, their privacy and autonomy.

The absence of politeness can be linked to the more general concept of ethos – how the total comportment of a participant, of which her verbal (spoken or written) style and tone are a part, express the sort of person she is, and signal her social identity and subjectivity (Maingueneau 1987: 31–5). Doctors in standard medical practice manifest what one might call a scientific ethos (modern medicine prides itself on being 'medical science') which is variously realized in the ways in which they touch and look at patients when they examine them, the way in which they filter patients' contributions in terms of topic, and the absence of niceties of interpersonal meaning such as politeness, which would suggest an orientation to the patient as a person rather than a scientific orientation to the patient as a case. (See Emerson 1970 for a study of gynaecological examinations along these lines, and Fairclough 1989a: 59–62 for a discussion of it).

The account of sample 1 so far has been very one-sided in its focus upon control over the interaction by the doctor. Mishler points out that there are ways of analysing the interview which are more oriented to the perspective of the patient. They also turn out to be more interesting in terms of intertextuality. I have already pointed to evidence of a mismatch between the medical perspective and the perspective of ordinary experience in the way in which the doctor filters out parts of the patient's turns which, for him, are off topic. Whereas the doctor consistently manifests the 'voice' of medicine, the patient's contributions mix the voice of medicine with the voice of 'the lifeworld', or ordinary experience (these terms are Mishler's, following Habermas). The alternative analysis suggested by Mishler focuses upon the dialectic, conflict and struggle within the interaction between these two voices. This suggests a way of extending what I have said so far about intertextuality, to allow for the possibility, in explicit dialogue, of an intertextual relation between different voices brought to the interaction by different participants.

Seen in these terms, the interaction appears to be rather more fragmented and rather less well ordered than if one views it as a manifestation of doctor control. The voices of medicine (M) and the lifeworld (L) interrupt one another repeatedly: L interrupts M in l. 21 (from 'I've cheated'), M interrupts L in l. 24 ('Does drinking make it worse?'), L interrupts M in l. 29 ('Enough to make me go to sleep') and vice-versa in l. 31 ('One or two drinks a day?'), L interrupts M in l. 42 ('Since I've been married') and vice-versa in 44 ('How long is that?'). The patient continues the turn initiated in l. 45 with a lengthy account of why she needs alchohol, and why she uses alchohol rather than just pills, which is again followed by an M question ('How often do you take them?', i.e. the pills) from the doctor. In this part of the interview, M and L are in contestation. The doctor repeatedly uses his control of questions to reassert M. Nevertheless, the repeated incursions of L appear to disturb the doctor's agenda: notice the hesitations which begin to appear before the doctor's questions (ll. 23–4, 27, 37, 41, and 44). Whereas the doctor rarely draws upon L, the patient uses M extensively, and is far more accommodating to the doctor in that sense than vice-versa. The voices evidently contrast in their content: M embodies a technological rationality which treats illness in terms of context-free clusters of physical symptoms, whereas L embodies a 'common sense' rationality which places illness in the context of other aspects of the patient's life. Mishler points out (1984: 122) that the contrast seems to correspond to the distinction made by Schutz (1962) between the 'scientific attitude' and the 'natural attitude'.

Both analysis in terms of the doctor's control of the interaction, and analysis in terms of a dialectic of voices, are ways of gaining insight into standard medical practice at a micro-analytical level, and into medicine as a mode of professionalism. However, medicine like other professions is undergoing rather dramatic changes in contemporary society. Perhaps what discourse analysis can contribute most is a means of investigating what these changes amount to 'on the ground', in the ways in which doctors and patients really interact.

Sample 2: 'Alternative' Medical Interview

My second sample is designed to address such issues of change in medical practice. It is also a medical interview, though of a radically different sort. Short pauses are marked with full stops; longer pauses with dashes; square brackets show overlap; and unclear material is in round brackets.

PATIENT: but she really has been very unfair to me . got ⌈no
DOCTOR: ⌊hm
   P: respect for me at ⌈all and I think. that's one of the reasons
   D: ⌊hm
5 P: why I drank s⌈o much you ⌈know – a⌈nd em
   D: ⌊hm   ⌊hm   hm⌊hm   are you
            you back are you back on it have you started drinking
            ⌈again
   P: ⌊no
10 D: oh you haven't (uncle⌈ar...)
   P: ⌊no . but em one thing that the
            lady on the Tuesday said to me was that . if my mother
            did turn me out of the ⌈house which she thinks she
   D: ⌊yes   hm
15 P: may do . coz . she doesn't like the way I've been she has
            turned me o⌈ut befo⌈re . and em . she said that .
   D: ⌊hm   ⌊hm
   P: I could she thought that it might be possible to me for
            me to go to a council ⌈flat
20 D: ⌊right yes ⌈yeah
   P: ⌊but she
            said it's a very em she wasn't ⌈pushing it because . my
   D: ⌊hm
   P: mother's got to sign a whole ⌈lot of ⌈things and
25 D: ⌊hm   ⌊ hm
   P: e: . she said it's difficult ⌈and em . there's no rush over
   D: ⌊hm
   P: it . I I don't know whether . I mean one thing they say in
            AA is that you shouldn't change anything . for a year
30 D: hm
   D: hm   yes I think I think that's wise . I think that's wise
            (5 second pause) well look I'd like to keep you know seeing
            you keep . you know hearing how things are going from
            time to time if that's possible

The doctor in this case belongs to a minority group within the British National Health Service which is open to 'alternative' (such as homeopathic) medicine, and treatment of the 'whole person', which accords well with the use of counselling techniques. This sample lacks the overt structures of doctor control of sample 1, as well the manifest discrepancy and conflict of different voices.

The most striking difference between the two samples in terms of interactional control features is that the question-response-assessment cycle is missing from sample 2, which is structured around a lengthy account by the patient, with the doctor giving a great deal of feedback in the form of minimum response tokens ('hm', 'no', 'yes', 'right'), asking a question which is topically linked to the patient's account (ll. 6–7), giving an assessment not of the patient's answers to questions, as in sample 1, but of a course of action recommended by a third party (l. 29), and suggesting a further interview (30–2).

Turn-taking is collaboratively managed rather than being asymmetrically controlled by the doctor. There is evidence of the negotiated nature of turn distribution in the doctor's question (ll. 6–7), which is articulated rapidly and quietly as an aside, showing the doctor's sensitivity to the way he is 'intruding' onto the patient's 'floor'. The question is so treated by the patient, who answers it briefly, then immediately resumes her account. Further evidence is the long pause by the doctor in l. 30 after his assessment, which appears to be making the 'floor' available again to the patient to continue her account if she wishes to, before the doctor moves towards terminating the interview.

Control over the introduction and change of topics, that was exercized mainly by the doctor in sample 1, is here exercized by the patient. The mode of topical development is that of conversation and of the 'lifeworld': the patient is 'talking topically' without sticking to a single topic, but shifting across a series of interconnected topics – her mother's unfairness, her drinking, possible alternatives to living with her mother, and so forth. In so doing, she is elaborating in ways which are quite relevant by conversational standards but probably not medically relevant from the perspective of conventional medicine. Throughout, the doctor's attentive feedback implies acceptance of this conversational mode of topical development.

Yet one cannot simply conclude that the doctor is surrendering interactional control to the patient. Notice that the initiative for yielding a measure of control to the patient in medical interviews of this sort invariably comes from the doctor, which suggests that doctors do still exercise control at some level, even if in the paradoxical form of ceding control. In fact, however, there remain manifest control features even here: the fact that the doctor does ask the medically important question about the patient's drinking, does offer an assessment, and does control the initiation and termination of the interview (not evident from this sample) and future action.

He does so, however, with a reticence which is uncharacteristic of traditional medical practice and traditional doctor–patient relations, which brings us to modality, politeness and ethos. The assessment in l. 29 has an explicit 'subjective' modality marker ('I think'), which makes it clear that the assessment is just the doctor's opinion, and tones down its authoritativeness (see the section on modality below): 'that's wise' on its own would imply access on the doctor's part to implicit, and mystified, sources of professional judgement. The one question is, as I have already pointed out, produced as an aside, and it consists of a vague and disfluent initial formulation ('are you you back are you back on it') followed by a more explicit formulation ('have you started drinking again'). These features of the question minimize its face-threatening potential and in that sense heighten its politeness. The suggestion of further interviews is also polite in that sense. It is very indirect: presumably the doctor is asking the patient to make further appointments, but what he actually says, tentatively ('I'd like...if that's possible'), is that he wants to see her again. He also formulates the purpose of further interviews as if they were social visits ('to see how things are going'). And he hedges his suggestion twice with 'you know' and hesitates ('keep . you know hearing'), again giving a sense of disfluency.

These comments can be linked to the notion of ethos. Whereas in sample 1, the doctor's style of speaking accords with a scientific ethos, in this sample the doctor's reticence, tentativeness, and apparent disfluency accord with a lifeworld ethos: doctors in this sort of medical interview appear to be rejecting the elitism, formality, and distance of the medical scientist figure in favour of a (frequently simulated) 'nice', 'ordinary' person, a 'good listener'. This accords with general shifts is dominant cultural values in our society, which devalue professional elitism and set a high value of informality, naturalness, and normalness.

Sample 2 also differs from sample 1 in terms of its intertextuality. There is nothing analogous to the dialectic of the voices of medicine and the lifeworld that I noted in the latter. Rather, the doctor appears himself to be drawing upon the voice of the lifeworld – for example, in portraying future interviews in terms of 'hearing how things are going' – and endorsing the patient's recourse to it by giving her space to give her account in her own words, and encouraging her with extensive feedback.

Nevertheless, the doctor does exercise control, even if in an uncharacteristic manner. We can see this fact in terms of interdiscursivity (constitutive intertextuality), by postulating a convergence of standard medical interview genre with other genres, such that some of the interactional control features of the former are maintained, but realized in an indirect and mitigated form under the influence of the latter. The acts themselves emanate from one genre, their realizations from others. What are these other genres? I have referred already to conversation, but conversation is present here as a constitutive element of another genre, counselling. The primary interdiscursive relation in this type of medical interview seems to be between standard medical interview genre and counselling, or what ten Have (1989; see also Jefferson and Lee 1981), in an analysis along the same lines, calls 'therapy talk'. Counselling emphasizes giving patients (or clients) the space to talk, empathizing with their accounts (with the counsellor often echoing them or formulating them in the voice of the patient), and being non-directive. The search for models for counselling has not surprisingly led outside institutional discourse to conversational discourse, where such values (manifest here in the doctor's reticence and mitigation) are widely realized, for instance in the lifeworld figure of the 'good listener'.

Different varieties of medical interview do not simply coexist: they enter into relations of contestation and struggle, as a part of the more general struggle over the nature of medical practice. Medical interviews like sample 2 are transparently linked to values such as treating the patient as a person rather than just a case, encouraging the patient to take some responsibility for treatment, and so forth. In struggles between varieties of medical interview, it is boundaries within orders of discourse, such as the boundary between counselling and medical interview, and the interdiscursive articulation of elements within orders of discourse, that are at issue.

The primary direction of change within contemporary medicine would seem to be towards interviews which are more like sample 2. This is a particular manifestation of shifts in cultural values and social relations that I have already referred to – shifts in the construction of the 'medical self' away from overt authority and expertise, shifts in power away from the producers of goods and services towards the consumers or clients, away from formality towards informality, and so forth. Change is not smooth, however. For one thing, there are divergent and contradictory tendencies at work. Secondly, tendencies in cultural change can harmonize with tendencies at other levels, or come into conflict with them. For example, transformation of medical practice in the direction of sample 2 is economically costly. A doctor can 'process' patients far more 'efficiently' and speedily through a pre-set routine like that of sample 1, than with techniques which give patients the time they feel they need to talk. There are currently in Britain and elsewhere huge pressures on doctors and other professionals to increase their 'efficiency', and these pressures conflict with dominant tendencies at the cultural level. (For further discussion of contemporary tendencies in discursive change see chapter 7 below.)

Sample 3: Conversational Narrative

The third sample illustrates a further dimension of intertextuality. It is an extract from an account by a married couple to another couple of a close encounter with Customs and Excise on returning from a holiday abroad. The transcription is organized in four-line 'staves', with a line for each participant; after the first, staves include lines only for participants who speak. Overlap is shown as simultaneous speech on two or more lines; pauses are shown as full stops; an equals sign shows one utterance following immediately on from another; and capital letters show loud speech.

```
HUSBAND 1:  Silvie'd got some plants under the seat which were illegal to bring
HUSBAND 2:
WIFE 1:                                        oh gosh        yeh
WIFE 2:


H1:      in anyway            colorado beetle
H2:            plants                      oh good grief
W1:      really illegal . plants oh yes        mm      and rabies


H1:      an er an er–
H2:            rabies
W1:                  yeh cos if an animal that has rabies spits on the
```

H2:   good
W1:   leaves lying on the floor some other animal could catch it

H1:   and er . Silvie's mother'd
H2:   grief
W1:   so heh heh plants are really out heh
W2:   heh heh

H1:   bought me this telescope for a . birthday present yeh well was
H2:   oh yeh

H1:   combined birthday and christmas present
W1:   no   combined birthday and

H1:   and that also ought to have been declared   = well
H2:   . why =
W1:   christmas present

H1:   they're cheaper over there than it's like when you buy watches or

H1:   optical instruments   you've got to declare it because you pay
H2:   good grief

H1:   import duty on it. erm so w we got got quite a lot of gear   it's
H2:   mm

H1:   all small stuff   but cu cumulative   and my air of innocence
H2:   mm   yeheh

H1:   would have been stretching its cred credulity somewhat   I'd got er
H2:   mm

H1:   . a bought er . a pack of 250 grams of tobacco yknow . for you and

H1:   Martin, and Mary of course yknow heh   and er–   yeh
H2:   heh was that over as well

H1:   well– . no that was within the limit . but I forgot . that I'd also
·W1:   no that–

H1:   got a couple of packets of Gitanes which I'd been smoking myself=
H1:   over but one pack I WISH YOU'D STOP INTERRUPTin
W1:   =yeh but they were open

H1:   me   there's one packet which er was unopened (tape continues)
H2:   hmhm

In the penultimate stave, H1 asks W1 to stop interrupting him. Whether one regards what W1 is doing during the account as 'interrupting H1' depends upon one's assumptions about the precise nature of the activity here. There are various 'sub-genres' of narrative or story-telling, and one important way in which they differ is in whether they have single or multiple narrators. Jointly developed narratives on the part of two or even more persons 'whose story it is' are not uncommon in conversational story-telling. Perhaps in this case H1 is working on the assumption that he is producing a single-narrator story, whereas W1 (as well as H2) assumes that they are jointly producing a story, though she may see her own role as a 'supporting' one. W1 and H2 also appear to be working on the model of an interactively produced story, in the additional sense of a story produced partly through dialogue between narrators and audience. This situation of different participants working to different generic models can be seen as another mode of intertextuality, rather like the situation of sample 1 where the different participants are oriented to different voices (recall the differentiation of modes of intertextuality at the beginning of chapter 4 above).

The two sub-genres of narrative I am postulating will, of course, differ in their systems for turn-taking and topic control. Single-narrator story-telling ascribes rights to the 'floor' for the duration of the story to the one narrator, which implies that other participants have no right to take substantive turns, though they will still be expected to give feedback in the form of minimal responses, and therefore no rights to control topic. The jointly-produced story, however, implies a shared floor, shared rights in turn-taking and topic introduction and shift. H1's attempt to 'police' his right to the floor comes across as heavy-handed because of its insensitivity to the orientation of W1 and H2 to jointly-developed narrative.

To what extent is the issue of gender relevant here? The fact that H2 shares with W1 an orientation to jointly-produced narrative is itself evidence against any straightforward equation of the latter with women speakers, and single-narrator genre with male speakers, even if that were not implausible on other grounds. Nevertheless, this sample does approximate to what my experience tells me is a widespread pattern in story-telling by married couples: the husband tells the story (and steals the limelight) while the wife acts in a supporting role, interpellating comments which support the husband's account and elaborate it in a minor way, without attempting to share control of the topic. In terms of this pattern W1 has overstepped this limitation in introducing topics and engaging in dialogue with H2. Notice the similarity of this second, husband-oriented analysis to the analysis of sample 1 in terms of doctor control.

I move now from the discourse samples to a more systematic discussion of the types of analysis to which they give rise.

Interactional Control Features

Interactional control features ensure smooth interactional organization – the distribution of turns, selection and change of topics, opening and closing of interactions, and so forth. Interactional control is always exercized to some extent collaboratively by participants, but there may be asymmetry between participants in the degree of control. The interactional control conventions of a genre embody specific claims about social and power relations between participants. The investigation of interactional control is therefore a means of explicating the concrete enactment and negotiation of social relations in social practice.

Turn-taking

Genres differ in their turn-taking systems. Ethnomethodological conversation analysis (see Sacks, Schegloff and Jefferson 1974; Schenkein 1978; and my discussion of Conversation analysis in chapter 1 above) has produced influential accounts of turn-taking in conversation as a collaborative organizational achievement of participants, based upon a simple set of ordered rules: (i) the current speaker may select the next speaker, by addressing her, naming her, etc.; (ii) if that does not happen, any participant may 'select herself' as next speaker; and (iii) if that does not happen, the current speaker may continue. These ordered options are equally available to all participants. They apply at possible points of completion in the current speaker's turn, for instance when she comes to the end of a grammatical unit (a sentence, clause, phrase, or even word) with a closing intonation pattern.

As sample 1 has shown, however, turn-taking systems are not always built around equal rights and obligations for all participants. The turn-taking system of sample 1 is typical of systems one finds in a variety of institutions where professionals, 'insiders', or 'gatekeepers' interact with 'the public', 'clients', outsiders, or learners. In these cases, the following sort of distribution of rights and obligations between powerful (P) and non-powerful (N-P) participants is common: (i) P may select N-P, but not vice-versa; (ii) P may self-select, but N-P may not; or (iii) P's turn may be extended across any number of points of possible completion.

Conversation analysis set out to explain the remarkable fluency of ordinary conversation, the fact that people generally manage to speak without extensive overlapping and without major gaps in the flow of talk. Another feature of asymmetrical turn-taking systems is that both overlaps and gaps may be available as devices for P: P may have the right to interrupt N-P when the latter becomes 'irrelevant', according to criteria of relevance controlled by P, and P but not N-P may have the right to 'hold the floor' without actually speaking, for example to remain silent as a way of reasserting one's control, or as a way of implicitly criticizing others.

Exchange Structure

The question–response–assessment cycles identified in sample 1 manifest one type of exchange, in the sense of a recurrent patterning of the turns of different participants. I referred in chapter 1 above to the pioneering work of Sinclair and Coulthard (1975) on exchanges in classroom discourse: they isolated an 'initiation-response–feedback' structure which is similar to the exchange structure of sample 1. We can also include here the less elaborate and less specific type of structure which the conversation analysts have called an 'adjacency pair' (Schegloff and Sacks 1973). Adjacency pairs are a general structural type rather than a particular sort of exchange. They involve two ordered categories of speech act, such that the occurrence of the first predicts the occurrence of the second, but that particular pairings are quite diverse: question–answer, greeting–greeting, complaint–apology, invitation–acceptance, invitation–rejection, and so on. And as the last two examples indicate, there is not always a one-to-one relationship between the first and second parts of adjacency pairs: an invitation may be followed by either an acceptance or a rejection, though there are various ways in which the latter might be marked as a 'dispreferred' option (Schegloff, Jefferson and Sacks 1977; Pomerantz 1978; Levinson 1983: 332–45). The question–answer adjacency pair is central to many exchange types. In some genres, one finds sequences of question–answer exhanges constituting higher-level structures, which we might call (after Sinclair and Coulthard 1975) 'transactions' or 'episodes'. This is so in classrooms where parts of lessons may be constituted as question–answer sequences on particular topics, usually with an opening and closing of the transaction by the teacher; it also applies, but in a different way, to legal cross-examination, where counsel may use such sequences to build up a case against a witness (Atkinson and Drew 1979).

The nature of the exchange system is relevant not only to turn-taking, but also to the sort of things people can say. For example, in initiating an exchange, teachers can give pupils information, ask them questions, set out agendas for the class, or control pupils' behaviour. Pupils, on the other hand, are far more constrained in what they can say or do: they mainly answer questions and perform certain tasks in response to requests, with the requirement that they do so within limits of what is judged relevant. Many questions in the classroom are 'closed', requiring 'yes' or 'no' answers or minimal elaboration.

Topic Control

Harvey Sacks (1968) points out that '"talking topically" doesn't consist of blocks of talk about "a topic". And when one presents a topic, except under rather special circumstances, one may be assured that others will try to talk topically with what you've talked about, but you can't be assured that the topic you intended was the topic they will talk to.' There are always a great many diverse topics which can be construed as relevant to, and a development of, any topic one happens to introduce, and Sacks is pointing out that one cannot predict in conversation which will be opted for. The topics of conversation, and the ways in which people do in fact chain topics together in talking topically, can give a lot of insight into the preoccupations of ordinary life and the common sense structuring of the lifeworld. Also interesting are the mechanisms through which conversational topics are established (Button and Casey 1984): topics are typically offered by one participant, accepted (or rejected) by another, and then elaborated by the first participant. For example (Button and Casey 1984: 167):

A: Whaddiyoh kno:w
B: hh Jis' got down last night.
A: Oh you *di:d*?

B offers the topic, A accepts it, and B goes on (later) to develop it. Research on domestic interaction between female and male partners for example has shown an asymmetry in the take-up of topics: women offer more topics than men, but men's topics are more often accepted by women than vice-versa (Fishman 1983).

Ethnomethodological research on topics is, however, based on conversation, and on an assumption of equal rights and obligations between participants. Sack's account of talking topically, and the unpredictability of how other participants will develop one's topics, is hardly relevant to the talk of patients in a standard medical interview, or pupils in a classroom. In such interactions, as I suggested in analysing sample 1, topics are introduced and changed only by the dominant participant, often according to a pre-set agenda or routine, which may or may not be overtly set in the discourse.

Setting and Policing Agendas

The setting and policing of agendas is an important element in interactional control. Agendas are often explicitly set at the beginning of an interaction by P. Teachers do so at the beginnings of lessons, or of transactions within lessons, and a disciplinary interview will often begin with the interviewer spelling out to the interviewee 'why you're here' (see Thomas 1988 for an example). Setting agendas is one aspect of the general control by P over the initiation and termination of an interaction, and its structuring into transactions or episodes.

Both explicit and implicit agendas are also 'policed', in the sense that P keeps other participants to their agendas in various ways during an interaction. Sample 1 contained one manifestation of policing: the doctor cut short the patient's turns, when he apparently decided that the patient had given the information relevant at that stage of the agenda. Another manifestation is illustrated by this extract from a school lesson (transcribed from Barnes 1976) in which teacher is getting her pupils to talk about problems of urban overcrowding:

PUPIL: the exhaust fumes will cause pollution
TEACHER: pollution good word Maurice something more about
          the traffic
P: the pavements would get ⌈(unclear)
T: ⌊no I'm thinking of some
          different form of traffic can anybody. Philip
P: e:m ⌈(unclear)
T: ⌊I'm on traffic . I'm on traffic David
P: the trains ⌈(unclear)
T: ⌊trains yes

The second pupil turn is rejected by T despite being perfectly relevant to the general topic, on the apparent grounds that it does not fit in with the order of development of the topic specified in the agenda that the teacher is implicitly following: she is eliciting the name of another form of traffic. The rejection is achieved by the teacher specifying 'where she is' in the agenda, but notice that she also appears to interrupt the pupil before he has finished his utterance. As the first two turns suggest, the agenda is designed to elicit not only particular information from pupils, but also key words such as 'pollution'.

One striking aspect of interaction between teachers and pupils is that the former typically evaluate the utterances of the latter. In this case, for example, the teacher in her first turn positively evaluates Maurice's use of the word 'pollution'. The 'initiation-response–feedback' exchange structure suggested for classroom discourse by Sinclair and Coulthard (1975) incorporates this evaluation element in the 'feedback'. Such systematic evaluation of the utterances of others is a powerful way of policing agendas. Its use in the classroom not only underlines the power of teachers over pupils, but also shows the extent to which routine classroom practice places pupils in a test or examination situation: in this form of classroom discourse, virtually everything they say is verbally 'marked'.

There are various other ways in which one participant in an interaction may police the contributions of others. One that Thomas (1988) has described is forcing explicitness. Being ambivalent and/or being silent are classic defence mechanisms on the part of N-P in unequal encounters, which may be countered by formulations on the part of P designed to force N-P to be explicit, or insistence by P that N-P acknowledge what has been said (e.g. 'You understand that, don't you?').

Formulation

Formulation is another aspect of interactional control that has received most attention from conversation analysts (see Heritage and Watson 1979). Sacks describes formulating as follows: 'A member may treat some part of the conversation as an occasion to describe that conversation, to explain it, to characterize it, to explicate, or translate, or summarize, or furnish the gist of it, or take note of its accordance with rules, or remark on its departure from rules' (1972: 338). Apart from the last two clauses, which associate with formulation policing mechanisms such as those described in the previous section, formulation in Sacks's account looks like a particular form of discourse representation where the discourse is part of the ongoing interaction rather than a prior one. The boundary between current and prior interactions is in any case not as clear as one might think: is the conversation we had before the interruption of a phone call, or before lunch, or last week, part of our current conversation or a different conversation? There is no simple answer.

As Sacks's final two clauses may imply, formulating is often a form of policing. An effective way of forcing one's interlocutor out of ambivalence is to offer a formulation of what he has been saying. Here is an example taken from a disciplinary interview between a policeman (P) and a senior police officer (O) (Thomas 1988):

O: you say that you're working to er er er the proper standards is that right
P: well I've never had any comment other than that
O: are you saying that nobody's brought your shortcomings to your notice

Both of O's turns formulate P's contributions, and both (as is clear in the second case from the extract above) substantially reword what P has actually said, and are manifestly designed to get P to make more explicit what he 'is saying'.

Even when formulating is not specifically to do with policing, it often still has a major interactional control function, in attempts by some participants to win acceptance from others for their versions of what has been said, or what has transpired in an interaction, which may then restrict the latter's options in ways which are advantageous to the former. One finds formulations functioning in this way not only in police interviews and interrogations, but also in radio interviews (Heritage 1985).

Modality

Given some proposition about the world such as 'the earth is flat', one may categorically assert it ('the earth is flat') or deny it ('the earth is not flat'), but there are also available various less categorical and less determinate degrees of commitment to it or against it: 'the earth may be/is probably/is possibly/is sort of flat', for example. This is the sphere of modality, the dimension of the grammar of the clause which corresponds to the 'interpersonal' function of language (see p. 65 above). In any propositional utterance, the producer must indicate what Hodge and Kress (1988: 123) call a degree of 'affinity' with the proposition, so any such utterance has the property of modality, or is 'modalized'.

Modality in grammar was traditionally associated with the

'modal auxiliary verbs' ('must', 'may', 'can', 'should', and so forth), which are an important means of realizing modality. However, the 'systemic' approach to grammar which Hodge and Kress (1988) draw upon has stressed that modal auxiliaries are only one modality feature among many (see Halliday 1985: 85–9). Tense is another one: as the example in the last paragraph shows, simple present tense ('is') realizes a categorical modality. Another is the set of modal adverbs such as 'probably', 'possibly', 'obviously', and 'definitely', with their equivalent adjectives (for example, 'it's likely/probable/possible that the earth is flat'). Beyond these possibilities, there is a further somewhat diffuse range of ways of manifesting various degrees of affinity: hedges such as 'sort of', 'a bit', 'or something', intonation patterns, speaking hesitantly, and so forth. There was an example of hedging in sample 1, when the patient glossed 'sour stomach' as 'heartburn like a heartburn or something'.

Modality may be 'subjective', in the sense that the subjective basis for the selected degree of affinity with a proposition may be made explicit: 'I think/suspect/doubt that the earth is flat' (recall also 'I think that's wise' in sample 2). Or modality may be 'objective', where this subjective basis is left implicit: 'the earth may be/is probably flat.' In the case of subjective modality, it is clear that the speaker's own degree of affinity with a proposition is being expressed, whereas in the case of objective modality, it may not be clear whose perspective is being represented – whether, for example, the speaker is projecting her own perspective as a universal one, or acting as a vehicle for the perspective of some other individual or group. The use of objective modality often implies some form of power.

It is common for modality to be realized in multiple features of a single utterance or sentence. For example, in 'I think she was a bit drunk, wasn't she?', low affinity is expressed in the subjective modality marker ('I think'), hedging ('a bit'), and the addition of a 'tag question' to the assertion ('wasn't she?')

But there is more to modality than speaker or writer commitment to propositions. Producers indicate commitment to propositions in the course of interactions with other people, and the affinity they express with propositions is often difficult to disentangle from their sense of affinity, or solidarity, with interactants. For example, 'isn't she beautiful!' or 'she's beautiful, isn't she!'

are ways of expressing high affinity with the proposition 'she is beautiful', but also ways of expressing solidarity with whoever one is talking to. Questions of this type (a negative question, and a positive assertion with a negative tag question, both of which anticipate a positive answer) presuppose that high affinity with the proposition is shared between speaker and addressee, and (given that the latter's answers are known in advance) such questions are asked to demonstrate this affinity and solidarity rather than to get information. So expressing high affinity may have little to do with one's commitment to a proposition, but a lot to do with a desire to show solidarity (Hodge and Kress 1988: 123). Conversely, the example from sample 1 just alluded to ('heartburn like a heartburn or something') shows that low affinity with a proposition may express lack of power, rather than lack of conviction or knowledge, and that what can be claimed as knowledge (and so the expression of high affinity with a proposition) depends upon relations of power. Modality, then, is a point of intersection in discourse between the signification of reality and the enactment of social relations – or in the terms of systemic linguistics, between the ideational and interpersonal functions of language.

Modality is a major dimension of discourse, and more central and pervasive than it has traditionally been taken to be. One measure of its social importance is the extent to which the modality of propositions is contested and open to struggle and transformation. Transformations of modality are, for intance, widespread in media reporting. Hodge and Kress (1988: 148–9) give the example of a highly modalized low affinity statement by Michael Foot as leader of the British Labour Party ('in general I do think that one factor that influenced the election was some of the affairs that have happened at the Greater London Council'), which gets transformed into the categorical newspaper headline 'Foot Blasts Red Ken over Poll Trouncing'. ('Red Ken' is Ken Livingstone, leader of a controversial Labour administration in London in the early 1980s.)

Beyond particular instances, there are more general properties associated with modality in the practices of the media. The media generally purport to deal in fact, truth and matters of knowledge. They systematically transform into 'facts' what can often be no more than interpretations of complex and confusing sets of events. In terms of modality, this involves a predilection for categorical modalities, positive and negative assertions, as the example in the last paragraph illustrates, and therefore relatively little in the way of modalizing elements (modal verbs, adverbs, adjectives, hedges, and so forth). It is also a predilection for objective modalities, which allow partial perspectives to be universalized.

Let us take a specific example. The NATO summit of 30 May 1989 dealt with the contentious issue of what NATO's stance should be on negotiating a reduction in short-range nuclear missiles sited in Europe. It was variously credited with resolving or covering up disagreements, and was in some cases construed as a victory for Britain's (Thatcher's) hard-line position. Here are some of the headlines: NATO Summit Ends in Uneasy Compromise (*Guardian*), Maggie's Nuclear Victory in the Battle of Brussels (*Mail*), Bush Hails NATO Unity as Missiles Row is Settled (*Daily Telegraph*). Each gives a different reading of the summit, yet each uses categorical modality. Notice that the *Mail* headline actually 'presupposes' (see, pp. 120–1 above) that 'Maggie' won a nuclear victory in the battle of Brussels, rather than asserting it: we might view presupposition as taking categorical modality one stage further, taking factuality for granted. An objection might be made to these examples on the grounds that categorical modality is imposed by the abbreviating and summarizing nature of headlines, not by media discourse *per se*. Surely, though, headlines are merely a particularly obvious instance of a general tendency in media discourse. Newspapers tend to offer sometimes contending (though often harmonizing) versions of the truth, each of which is based upon the implicit and indefensible claim that events can be transparently and categorically represented, and perspective can be universalized. This myth underpins the ideological work of the media: offering images of and categories for reality, positioning and shaping social subjects, and contributing for the most part to social control and reproduction.

What the media discourse example indicates is that modality is not simply a set of choices available to the speaker or writer for registering degrees of affinity. What such a choice-oriented perspective on its own misses is the variability of modality practices as between discourse types, and the extent to which particular modality practices are imposed upon those who draw upon particular discourse types. Another example is academic writing: in a familiar and still influential (though widely criticized) tradition of academic writing, avoidance of categorical modality is a fundamental principle. This is arguably for rhetorical reasons, motivated by the projection of an approved cautious and circumspect subjectivity and ethos for 'the scholar', rather than because of low affinity with propositions. (On the rhetoric of academic and especially scientific writing, see *Economy and Society* 1989.)

Politeness

Politeness in language has been a major concern of Anglo-American pragmatics in the 1970s and 1980s (Brown and Levinson 1978; Leech 1983; Leech and Thomas 1989). The most influential account is that of Brown and Levinson. They assume a universal set of human 'face wants': people have 'positive face' – they want to be liked, understood, admired, etc. – and 'negative face' – they do not want to be impinged upon or impeded by others. It is generally in everyone's interests that face should be protected. They see politeness in terms of sets of strategies on the part of discourse participants for mitigating speech acts which are potentially threatening to their own 'face' or that of an interlocutor. This account is typical of pragmatics in seeing language use as shaped by the intentions of individuals.

What is missing is a sense of the variability of politeness practices across different discourse types within a culture, of links between variable politeness practices and variable social relations, or of producers being constrained by politeness practices. Bourdieu (1977: 95, 218) suggests a view of politeness which is very different from that of Brown and Levinson, claiming that 'the concessions of politeness are always political concessions.' He elaborates as follows: 'practical mastery of what are called the rules of politeness, and in particular the art of adjusting each of the available formulae... to the different classes of possible addressees, presupposes the implicit mastery, hence the recognition, of a set of oppositions constituting the implicit axiomatics of a determinate political order.' In other words, particular politeness conventions embody, and their use implicitly acknowledges, particular social and power relations (see Kress and Hodge 1979), and in so far as they are drawn upon they must contribute to reproducing those relations. A corollary is that investigating the politeness conventions of a given genre or discourse type is one way of gaining insight into social relations within the practices and institutional domains with which it is associated. This is not to exchange Brown and Levinson's voluntaristic account (1978) of politeness strategies for a structuralist account of politeness conventions: my position is a dialectical one, recognizing the constraints of conventions, but also the possibility, under certain conditions, of creatively rearticulating and so transforming them (see p. 65 above).

Locke 2004, 47.

Brown and Levinson's work does, however, incorporate an excellent account of politeness phenomena, which can be appropriated within a different theoretical framework. Figure 5.1 summarizes major parts of their framework, in which they differentiate five general strategies for doing 'face-threatening acts' (FTAs: Brown and Levinson 1987: 60):

seeking compensation or attempting to restore balance.

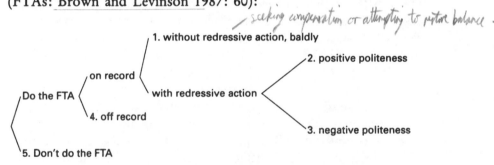

Figure 5.1   Strategies for doing 'face-threatening acts'

Let us take requesting help with a punctured tyre as an example. A request is potentially damaging to the negative face of an addressee (A)–as well as to the face of the speaker–in that it puts pressure upon A to act in a certain way. The request may be made 'baldly' (strategy 1) without attempting to mitigate it, i.e. without 'redressive action' ('Help me fix this tyre'); it may be made with 'positive politeness' (strategy 2), in which case it is mitigated, or redressed, for instance by showing liking or sympathy for, or solidarity with, A ('Give us a hand to fix this tyre, mate'); it may be made with 'negative politeness' (strategy 3), in which case it is mitigated by showing respect for A's privacy, or his wish not be disturbed or imposed upon, etc. ('Sorry to bother you but could you help me with this tyre?'); it may be made 'off record' (strategy 4), so that it has to be inferred, and what is said is open to alternative interpretations ('Now how on earth am I going to fix that?', or hinting, 'Did you notice I've got a flat tyre?'). Notice that the example of negative politeness uses the verb form 'could (you) help', rather than simply 'help'. This is an indirect way of making a request – it apparently asks about A's hypothetical ability to help – and it shares the property of indirectness with the 'off record' strategy. Saying things indirectly – using 'indirect speech acts' – is an important part of being polite. But while the indirectness of the off-record examples may call for some working out by A of the meaning, the indirectness of 'could (you) help' has become conventionalized, and poses no interpretative problems.

One dimension of the shift that, as I have suggested, is taking place in the nature of medical interviews, seems to be a shift in politeness conventions, some indication of which is present in samples 1 and 2. The low affinity modality, achieved through hedging, of the patient's gloss on 'sour stomach' ('a heartburn like a heartburn or something'), may be explicable, as I suggested earlier, as a reluctance to appear to be too certain given the power and expertise of the doctor. This modality feature is also a negative politeness feature: it avoids impinging upon the doctor's domain of authority. The patient's shifts into the voice of the lifeworld in ll. 21–2, 29–30 and 42 can also be seen in terms of politeness. They can be taken as off-record hints to the doctor about a set of problems additional to and underlying the problem in focus. Being off record, they protect the positive face of the patient, who comes across as being reticent about raising what are often dismissed as 'personal' problems. They are perhaps also oriented to the negative face of the doctor: in conventional medical interviews, 'non-medical' problems are often seen as not strictly the doctor's business, and raising them may therefore be construed as imposing upon the doctor beyond the usual call of duty.

The doctor in sample 1 is neither negatively nor positively

polite. Questioning is an act which is potentially threatening to the negative face of the addressee, and some of the doctor's questions are also potentially threatening to the patient's positive face, in being possibly embarrassing or demeaning (most obviously, 'How long have you been drinking that heavily?'). Yet the doctor does not mitigate these questions, and is consistently bald on record.

In sample 2, the politeness conventions appear to be reversed: it is the doctor who shows both positive and negative politeness to the patient. He shows positive politeness in himself entering the voice of the lifeworld, both productively (future consultations are for 'hearing how things are going') and receptively (in his feedback to the patient's lifeworld account). He shows negative politeness in the reticent and mitigated forms of his question, assessment, and suggestion for further visits. The patient shows no negative politeness; in fact, she baldly interrupts the doctor's move towards a close with a resumption of her account (this is not included in my sample). She does, however, show positive politeness in the very fact of talking to the doctor in the voice of the lifeworld, which implicitly claims common ground with the doctor.

In summary, sample 1 shows negative politeness for the patient, but neither negative not positive politeness for the doctor, whereas sample 2 shows negative and positive politeness for the doctor, and positive politeness for the patient. These differences accord with the contrasting social relations of standard and 'alternative' medical practice. In standard medical practice, there is marked asymmetry of knowledge and authority between doctor and patient, which implies deference, and negative politeness, from patient to doctor. The relationship between doctor and patient is a formal and socially distanced one, which is inimical to positive politeness. And the patient is treated not as a person but as the bearer of a problem: this justifies an absence of negative politeness on the doctor's part, which is often criticized precisely as insensitivity to the patient as a person. In alternative medical practice, the doctor simulates symmetry, informality, and social closeness, which militate against negative politeness on the patient's part, and favour mutual positive politeness. The patient is treated as a person, which means that the potentially face-threatening acts, which are inseparable from the doctor's treatment of the patient, will tend to be mitigated by negative politeness.

Ethos

I referred, in discussing the two medical samples, to differences in 'ethos', in the sorts of social identity the doctors implicitly signal through their verbal and non-verbal comportment. The question of ethos is an intertextual one: what models from other genres and discourse types are deployed to constitute the subjectivity (social identity, 'self') of participants in interactions? In the case of sample 1, the models were taken from scientific discourse; in the case of sample 2, from discourses of the lifeworld.

Ethos can, however, be seen as part of a wider process of 'modelling', wherein the place and time of an interaction and its set of participants, as well as participant ethos, are constituted by the projection of linkages in certain intertextual directions rather than others. Maingueneau (1987: 31–5) gives the example of the discourse (political speeches, for instance) of the French Revolution, which was modelled on the republican discourse of ancient Rome in terms of place, time, and 'scene' (in the sense of overall circumstances of discourse), as well as participants and participant ethos.

Sample 2 is a less historically extended case. 'Alternative' medicine of this sort constitutes the discourse of medical practice on the model of lifeworld 'troubles talk' (Jefferson and Lee 1981; ten Have 1989), between a person with a problem and a sympathetic listener. It makes sense to assume that this model is made available to medical discourse via the discourse of counselling, which is itself built upon it. Participants are constructed in a relationship of solidarity and common experience, if not friendship, and the scene is constructed as unburdening oneself of one's troubles. While the place is still clearly medical – a doctor's office – it is common for doctors within alternative medicine (as well as teachers and other professionals adopting parallel positions) to be concerned with issues such as the positioning of items of furniture or decor, attempting to change institutional locations to make people feel at ease or 'at home'. And the ethos signalled by the doctor's talk, and more generally by the way doctors behave in this sort of interview, is that of the caring and sympathetic friend, the 'good listener'.

Ethos, then, is manifested by the whole body, and not just the voice. Bourdieu (1984: chapter 3) has suggested that language be seen as 'a dimension of bodily hexis in which one's whole relationship to the social world is expressed'. For example, the 'articulatory style of the popular classes' is 'inseparable from an overall relationship to one's body dominated by the rejection of "mannerisms" or "chichis" and the valorisation of virility'. It is not just the way in which doctors talk that signals ethos; it is the cumulative effect of their total bodily disposition – the way they sit, their facial expression, their movements, their ways of responding physically to what is said, their proxemic behaviour (whether they get close to, or even touch, their patients, or keep their distance).

Conclusion

The concept of ethos constitutes a point at which we can pull together the diverse features, not only of discourse but of behaviour more generally, that go towards constructing a particular version of the self. Within that configuration, the aspects of text analysis I have concentrated upon in this chapter – interactional control, modality and politeness – all play a part. In fact, most if not all analytically separable dimensions of discourse and text have some implications, direct or indirect, for the construction of the self.

Yet, as I said at the beginning of this chapter, this is a neglected issue in language studies and discourse analysis. Most of the attention that is usually given to the self in discourse is focused upon the concept of 'expression': it is common to distinguish an 'expressive' or 'emotive' function of language, which has to do with how people word things in ways that show their feelings about them, or attitudes towards them, and there is a widely used concept of 'emotive meaning' for 'expressive' aspects of the meaning of words. Jakobson's influential account of language functions, for example, distinguishes as 'emotive' or 'expressive' a function which 'aims at direct expression of the speaker's attitude toward what he is speaking about' (1961: 354). What this leaves out is the crucial perspective of construction: the role of discourse in constituting or constructing selves. When one emphasizes construction, the identity function of language begins to assume great importance, because the ways in which societies categorize and build identities for their members is a fundamental aspect of how they work, how power relations are imposed and exercized, how societies are reproduced and changed. Focusing on expression, on the other hand, has completely marginalized the identity function into a minor aspect of the interpersonal function. This is why I have distinguished the identity function in my modification of Halliday's account (1978) of the functions of language (see p. 64 above). Nevertheless, a more technical and detailed case remains to be made for distinguishing a separate identity function: for Halliday, to identify a separate function one would need to show that there is a relatively discrete area of grammatical organization corresponding to it.

6

Text Analysis:
Constructing Social Reality

The main focus in this chapter is upon those aspects of text analysis that relate to the ideational function of language and to ideational meanings – to 'constructing social reality' as I have put it in the title. The emphasis is, therefore, upon the role of discourse in signification and reference (see p. 60 above for the distinction), where the former comprises the role of discourse in constituting, reproducing, challenging and restructuring systems of knowledge and belief. But it is no more than a question of emphasis: inevitably there will be overlap with the relational and identity functions that were my concern in chapter 5.

The two main discourse samples I discuss are an extract on antenatal care from a booklet for expectant parents, and the set of speeches I have already briefly alluded to by a British Cabinet Minister, Lord Young, on 'enterprise culture'. The particular analytical topics I cover are: connectives and argumentation, transitivity and theme, word meaning, wording, and metaphor. In terms of the analytical categories of chapter 3, the last three topics fall under the general heading of vocabulary, the first appertains to cohesion, and the second to grammar.

Connectives and Argumentation

The following sample is part of a section on antenatal care from *The Baby Book* (Morris 1986), a booklet issued to expectant parents by hospitals. I shall also introduce during the analysis contrasting extracts from *Pregnancy Book* (Health Education Council 1984), a similar publication produced by the Health Education Council. (I have omitted a subsection entitled 'Length of pregnancy', which occurs in the original before the subsection headed 'Examination'.)

Antenatal care

The essential aim of antenatal care is to ensure that you go through pregnancy and labour in the peak of condition. Inevitably, therefore, it involves a series of examinations and tests throughout the course of your pregnancy. As mentioned above, antenatal care will be provided either by your local hospital or by your general practitioner, frequently working in cooperation with the hospital.

It is important to attend for your first examination as early as possible, since there may be minor disorders that the doctor can correct which will benefit the rest of your pregnancy. More particularly, having seen your doctor and booked in at a local hospital, you will usually receive the assurance that everything is proceeding normally.

The first visit

Your first visit involves a comprehensive review of your health through childhood and also right up to the time you became pregnant. Just occassionally women may suffer from certain medical disorders of which they are unaware — such as high blood pressure, diabetes and kidney disease. It is important for these problems to be identified at an early stage since they may seriously influence the course of the pregnancy.

The doctor and midwife will also want to know about all your previous health problems, as well as discussing your social circumstances. We do know that social conditions can influence the outcome of the pregnancy. For this reason, they will ask you details about your housing, as well as your present job. In addition they will need to know if you smoke, drink alcohol or if you are taking any drugs which have been prescribed by your doctor or chemists. All of these substances can sometimes affect the development of a baby.

Examination

You will be weighed so that your subsequent weight gain can be assessed. Your height will be measured, since small women on the whole have a slightly smaller pelvis than tall women – which is not surprising. A complete physical examination will then be carried out which will include checking your breasts, heart, lungs, blood pressure, abdomen and pelvis.

The purpose of this is to identify any abnormalities which might be present, but which so far have not caused you any problems. A vaginal examination will enable the pelvis to be assessed in order to check the condition of the uterus, cervix and the vagina. A cervical smear is also often taken at this time to exclude any early pre-cancerous change which rarely may be present.

We will begin by analysing certain aspects of text cohesion and sentence structure in this sample; this will provide a way into looking at the sort of argumentation that is used, and the sort of standards of rationality it presupposes; this in turn will give some insight into the sorts of social identity that are constructed in the text, in particular the medico-scientific voice and ethos that it contains.

Let us begin with the way in which sentences are constructed in the section headed 'Examination', which consists of two paragraphs, each of three sentences. With the exception of the last sentence of the first paragraph and the first sentence of the second paragraph, each sentence consists of two clauses (i.e. they are simple sentences: see p. 75 above) linked with a conjunction which marks purpose or reason. Schematically,

Clause 1 so that/since/in order to/to Clause 2

Even the two exceptions fit partially into this pattern, because the connection between them is one of purpose: the first sentence of the second paragraph begins 'The purpose of this is to', where 'this' refers back to the last sentence of the first paragraph. In fact the pattern of sentences being linked in terms of purpose or reason, as well as clauses within sentences, is repeated throughout the sample. The message that comes across is one of reassurance:

everything that happens during antenatal care is there for a good reason. It is clear who is being reassured, but what is less clear is precisely who is doing the reassuring.

Let us try to establish this by looking at the participants: those who are participating in this as a piece of discourse practice, and those who participate in the processes of antenatal care that are being depicted. The former are (i) readers of the text, who in most cases will be subject to (as pregnant women) or closely involved in (as partners) antenatal care; and (ii) the producers of the text: no author is identified, but an editor (a professor of obstetrics and gynaecology) and editorial team are named. The participants in antenatal care are (i) pregnant women, and (ii) medical staff. The relationship between readers as discourse participants and women as participants in antenatal care is obvious: most of the former are about to become the latter. The relationship between the producers of the text and participants in antenatal care is rather less obvious; in principle, the text producers could adopt the perspective of the pregnant women, or of the medical staff, or indeed of neither.

In this case, the text producers are clearly identified with the medical staff. The most explicit evidence for this is in the second paragraph of the section headed 'The first visit'. The first and third sentences of that paragraph predict what the medical staff will 'want to know' and 'ask'. The second sentence is an explanation of why they ask, but the scientific knowledge that medical staff ground their practices in is significantly worded as what 'we' know: the 'we' marks a slippage between text producers as participants in the discourse process, and medical staff as participants in the antenatal care process.

There is, however, one instance of distancing between the two, the second sentence in the first paragraph under 'Examination': the tagged-on comment 'which is not surprising' comes across as the lifeworld voice of the prospective patient, or indeed of the medical staff in their non-professional capacities (recall Mishler's discussion of lifeworld voices in his analysis of the sample of medical discourse discussed above, p. 143). But notice the contrast in voices between this and the second clause of the sentence ('since small women on the whole have a slightly smaller pelvis than tall women'), which is a reason clause. This is in the medical voice: 'pelvis' is a medical term, the clause consists of an author-itative assertion, which we take to be grounded in medico-scientific evidence. It is also far more typical of the extract as a whole: most reason clauses are in the medical voice. The hedging of the assertion ('on the whole') is interesting: on the one hand its vagueness suggests a shift into the voice of the lifeworld, while on the other it marks the cautious and circumspect ethos we associate with scientific medicine.

Clearly, those doing the reassuring are the medical staff. The clauses of reason or purpose, consistently cast in the voice of medicine, give the sort of rationalization and argumentation one would expect from medical staff, which contributes to the con-struction of medico-scientific ethos (see p. 143 above) in the ex-tract. Compare the following extract from the *Pregnancy Book*: 'Throughout your pregnancy you will have regular check-ups ...This is *to make sure that both you and the baby are fit and well, to check that the baby is developing properly*, and, *as far as possible to prevent anything going wrong*...' (my italics). The italicized expressions are evidently closer to the voice of the lifeworld than equivalent ones in *The Baby Book*, but I feel nevertheless that there is an ambivalence of voice in the *Pregnancy Book*. The reason for this is that medical staff often do shift partly into a lifeworld voice when talking to patients (recall sample 2 above, pp. 144–9), and the italicized expressions *could* be used by medical staff. It therefore remains unclear whether the producer of the *Pregnancy Book* is writing from the patient's perspective, or from that of (a 'modernizing' position among) medical staff.

Further evidence of a merging of text producers with medical staff in *The Baby Book* extract comes from its modality (see pp. 158–62 above). In the first paragraph of the section headed 'Examination', all three sentences are modalized with 'will', which gives a meaning of categorical prediction – 'this is what will happen' – and suggests that the text producer is writing from a position of insider knowledge. Similarly with 'can' (e.g. 'these substances can sometimes affect...') and 'may' ('any early pre-cancerous change which rarely may be present'), where the text producer makes expert assertions about medical possibilities. The frequency adverbials ('sometimes', 'rarely'), if anything, add to the authoritativeness of these assertions. Notice also 'it is important to' (opening sentence in the second paragraph) and 'inevitably' (second sentence of the first paragraph). Use of technical medical vocabulary (e.g. 'pre-cancerous') strengthens the 'insider' effect.

To sum up, an analysis of cohesion in this sample provides a way into its mode of argumentation and mode of rationality, and so into the medico-scientific voice and ethos that are constructed in it. Generalizing from this example, text types differ in the sorts of relation that are set up between their clauses, and in the sorts of cohesion they favour, and such differences may be of cultural or ideological significance. These differences in cohesion combine with others to give differences in the overall 'texture' (Halliday 1985: 313–18) of text types – in the overall mode of structuring clauses into a text. Other dimensions of variation include theme, discussed in the next section, ways in which 'given information' (presented by the text producer as already known or established) is distinguished from 'new information' (Halliday 1985: 271–86; Quirk et al. 1972: 237–43), and ways of foregrounding or backgrounding particular parts of the text (Hoey 1983). One aspect of discursive change which is perhaps less obvious than others, but may prove to be worth investigating, is changes in texture and cohesion: is it the case, for example, that types of public information colonized by advertising (e.g. government publicity on issues like AIDS) manifest changes in these respects, and if so how might such changes link to changes in modes of rationality and ethos?

In a passage already quoted, Foucault refers to 'various rhetorical schemata according to which groups of statements may be combined (how descriptions, deductions, definitions, whose succession characterizes the architecture of a text, are linked together)' (1972: 57). At one level, analysis of cohesion focuses upon functional relations between clauses, and can be used to investigate such 'rhetorical schemata' in various types of text. For example, in *The Baby Book* extract a predominant pattern is a description (of what will happen to the pregnant woman) followed by an explanation (of the medical reasons for this). The following extract, the opening of a magazine advertisement, is quite differently structured:

Consider for a moment why diplomats and company directors the world over choose to travel S-class. Perhaps it's because the Mercedes-Benz flagship conveys presence without courting ostentation. Its styling complements the demeanour of those who have nothing to prove.

(*Sunday Times Magazine*, 21 January 1990)

This advertisement opens with a question – answer sequence, or more precisely an indirect question (a request to the reader to consider a question) followed by a (two-sentence) suggested possible answer; this is a rhetorical schema widely used in advertising. It is likely that different rhetorical modes, such as types of narrative, are distinctive in the schemata they use.

Halliday (1985: 202–27) provides a detailed framework for analysing some major types of functional relationship between clauses (see also Hoey 1983), though it does not include the question-answer relation in the last extract. A version of the same framework can be used for functional relations between whole sentences (pp. 303–9). In broad outline Halliday distinguishes the three main types of relation between clauses as 'elaboration', 'extension' and 'enhancement'. In elaboration, one clause (sentence) 'elaborates on the meaning of another by further specifying or describing it', that is, by rewording it, exemplifying it, or clarifying it. An example of the latter is the last sentence of the second paragraph of the antenatal care text, beginning More particularly'. In extension, one clause (sentence) 'extends the meaning of another by adding something new to it'. This may be a matter of straight addition (marked with 'and', 'moreover', etc.), an adversative relation (marked with 'but', 'yet', 'however', etc.), or variation (marked with 'or', 'alternatively', 'instead' etc.). In enhancement, one clause (sentence) 'enhances the meaning of another by qualifying it in a number of possible ways: by reference to time, place, manner, cause or condition'. The main relations between clauses and sentences here are temporal relations (A then B, A after B, A when B, A while B, etc. – taking A and B be to clauses or sentences); causal relations (such as the relations of reason and purpose identified in the analysis of *The Baby Book*); conditional relations (if A then B); spatial relations (A where B); and comparisons (A like B, A similarly B).

An important variable between text types is the extent to which relations between clauses and sentences are explicitly marked. One difference between *The Baby Book* and the *Pregnancy Book* is that causal relations (reasons and purposes) are generally more explicitly marked in the former – there are, for example, more conjunctives like 'so that', 'since' – and this explicitness seems to contribute to the clear dominance in the former of the medico-scientific voice and ethos.

This variability in explicitness also points to the need to distinguish two levels in analysis of cohesion: the analysis of cohesive functional relations, such as those described above, and the analysis of explicit cohesive markers on the surface of the text, such as the conjunctives just referred to. The latter are also worthy of attention, not only to determine to what extent functional relations are explicitly marked, but also because there are significant differences between text types in the types of markers they tend to favour. Halliday (1985: 288–9) distinguishes four main types of surface cohesive marking: 'reference', 'ellipsis', 'conjunction', and 'lexical cohesion'. Again, I can give only a broad sketch of these here. Reference is a matter of referring back to an earlier part of a text, forward to a part of the text that is coming, or outwards to the situation or wider cultural context of the text, using items such as personal pronouns, demonstratives, and the definite article. Ellipsis leaves out material that is recoverable from another part of the text, or replaces it with a substitute word, and so makes a cohesive link between the two parts of the text (for example, the ellipsis of 'spades' in the second part of this exchange: 'Why didn't you lead a spade?' – 'I hadn't got any'). Conjunction has already been quite extensively referred to: it is cohesion with conjunctive words and expressions, including what are traditionally called 'conjunctions' ('since', 'if', 'and' etc.) as well 'conjunctive adjuncts' (Halliday 1985: 303) or 'conjuncts' (Quirk et al. 1972: 520–32) such as 'therefore', 'in addition', 'in other words'. Lexical cohesion is cohesion through the repitition of words, the linking of words and expressions in meaning relations (see Leech 1981) such as synonymy (sameness of meaning) or hyponymy (where the meaning of one 'includes' the meaning of the other), or the linking of words and expressions which 'collocate' (Halliday 1966), that is, belong to the same semantic domain and tend to co-occur (for example, 'pipe', 'smoke', 'tobacco').

It would be misleading to regard these types of surface cohesive marking as simply objective properties of texts. Cohesive markers have to be interpreted by text interpreters as part of the process of constructing coherent readings of texts (see above, pp. 83–4); cohesion is one factor in coherence. For example, one cannot specify which lexical items in a text collocate, without considering interpreters' interpretations of texts in this regard, that is, which items interpreters actually discern relations between. Yet cohesive markers also need to be seen dynamically from the perspective of the text producer: text producers actively set up cohesive relations of particular sorts in the process of positioning the interpreter as subject. Consequently, cohesion seen in these dynamic terms may turn out to be a significant mode of ideological 'work' going on in a text.

The magazine advertisement given earlier (p. 175 above) illustrates these points. A coherent interpretation of this passage depends on a lot of inferential work, which centres upon reconstructing the collocational cohesive links set up by the text producer – between 'diplomats and company directors', 'conveys presence without courting ostentation', and 'the demeanour of those who have nothing to prove'. That is, one can make sense of the text by assuming that conveying presence without courting ostentation is a characteristic of diplomats and company directors (transferred here to the car), and that diplomats and company directors possess 'demeanour', and have nothing to prove. Notice that these collocational relationships are not ones you would find in a dictionary (unlike, for example, the relationship between 'dog and 'bark'); they are set up in this text by the text producer. In setting them up, the producer is also assuming an interpreter who is 'capable' of picking up these collocational relationships; and in so far as interpreters are successfully placed in that position, the text succeeds in doing ideological work in constructing subjects for whom these connections are common sense (see the discussions of subjection above, pp. 90–1 and 133–6).

Transitivity and Theme

The ideational dimension of the grammar of the clause (see p. 70 above) is usually referred to in systemic linguistics as 'transitivity'

(Halliday 1985: chapter 5), and deals with the types of process which are coded in clauses, and the types of participant involved in them ('participant' here means elements in clauses). As I indicated in chapter 1 above, it has received a great deal of attention in analyses within Critical linguistics (see Fowler et al. 1979; Kress and Hodge 1979; Kress 1988; Hodge and Kress 1988). Two main types of process are 'relational' processes, where the verb marks a relationship (being, having, becoming, etc.) between participants, and 'action' processes, where an agent acts upon a goal. I shall also say a little in this section about 'theme', a textual dimension of the grammar of the clause concerned with the ways in which clause elements are positioned according to their informational prominence.

One thing to notice about the action type of process in the extract from the antenatal care booklet, is that pregnant women are rarely referred to as agents. Agents in action processes are often the medical staff (in many cases implicitly so, because the clause is passive and the agent is 'deleted', e.g. 'you will be weighed'), or non-human entities (e.g. 'social conditions' and 'substances' in the second paragraph under the heading 'Your first visit'). Conversely, pregnant women or their physical characteristics ('you', 'your height') quite often occur as goals in action clauses. It is also the case that 'you' (referring to pregnant women) rarely occurs in the informationally-important initial position of a clause, as its 'theme' (see further below).

The *Pregnancy Book* is different in these respects. It contains a lot of action processes with 'you' as agent, and many of its clauses have 'you' as theme. For example:

> You will probably want to ask a lot of questions yourself – about antenatal care, about the hospital, about your pregnancy. You may also want to say something about what you hope for in pregnancy and at the birth. Tell the midwife anything that **you** feel is important. Write down in advance the things you want to ask or say.

'You' is the agent of 'want', 'ask questions', 'say', and implicitly of 'tell' and 'write down'; and 'you' is theme in five clauses (including dependent clauses, such as 'what you hope for in pregnancy and at the birth'). We might say it is also an implicit theme in the imperatives 'tell' and 'write down'. The instance of 'you' in bold print underlines the 'you-centredness' of the *Preg-*

nancy Book, in contrast to the decentering of the women in *The Baby Book*. In the latter, the relatively high proportion of agent-less passives, where the implicit agent is a member of the medical staff, combined with the categorically predictive modalities I referred to in the last section ('you will be weighed' combines the two features), give the sense of pregnant women being subjected to anonymous and invariant procedures. The thematization of 'you' in the *Pregnancy Book* shows again that it adopts (if ambivalently, as I suggested in the last section) the perspective of the pregnant women, whereas the perspective in *The Baby Book* is firmly that of the medical staff.

A final transitivity feature is the degree of 'nominalization' in the sample. Nominalization is the conversion of processes into nominals, which has the effect of backgrounding the process itself – its tense and modality are not indicated – and usually not specifying its participants, so that who is doing what to whom is left implicit. Medical and other scientific and technical language favours nominalization, but it can be abstract, threatening and mystifying for 'lay' people such as the readers of this sample. There are a lot of nominalizations in *The Baby Book*; some examples in the subsection 'The first visit' are 'a comprehensive review of your health', 'medical disorders', 'kidney disease', 'your previous health problems', 'the outcome of the pregnancy', 'the development of a baby'. The high frequency of nominalizations is another indication of the orientation of this text to a medical voice.

I now discuss the issues raised by this example in more general terms, beginning with transitivity, then going on to voice (active versus passive), nominalization, and theme.

There are processes and participants – animate and inanimate – in reality, and there are processes and participants in language, but we cannot simply extrapolate from the nature of a real process to the way it is signified linguistically. On the contrary, a real process may be signified linguistically in a variety of ways, according to the perspective from which it is interpreted. A language differentiates a small number of process types and associated participant types, and the signification of a real process is a matter of assimilating it to one of these. A social motivation for analysing transitivity is to try to way to work out what social, cultural, ideological, political or theoretical factors determine how a process is signified in a particular type of discourse (and in different discourses), or in a particular text.

The main process types in English are: 'action', 'event', 'relational', and 'mental' processes. I have already referred to action and relational processes above. Two types of action processes can be distinguished: 'directed' and 'non-directed' action. Directed action is the type I have identified in *The Baby Book*, where an agent is acting upon a goal. It is generally realized – manifested on the surface of the text – as a transitive (subject – verb – object) clause, for example 'the police shot 100 demonstrators'. Non-directed action involves an agent and an action but no (explicit) goal, and it is usually realized as an intransitive (subject – verb) clause such as 'the police were shooting'. Event processes involve an event and a goal, and are also generally realized as intransitive clauses, such as '100 demonstrators died'. Non-directed action and event clauses are not always sharply distinguished, but they do differ in terms of how they are most naturally questioned: non-directed action is most naturally linked to the question form 'What did x (= the agent) do?', and events with the question form 'What happened to x (= the goal)?' Relational processes involve relations of being, becoming, or having (possession) between entities, for example '100 demonstrators are dead'. Finally, mental processes include cognition (verbs such as 'know', 'think'), perception ('hear', 'notice'), and affection ('like', 'fear'). They are generally realized as transitive clauses (for example 'the demonstrators feared the police'), and involve what Halliday calls a 'senser' ('the demonstrators' in this case – the entity that experiences the mental process), and a 'phenomenon' ('the police' in this case – the target or source of that experience).

Which process type is chosen to signify a real process may be of cultural, political or ideological significance, as I suggested above. Halliday provides a literary example of its cultural significance in a study of William Golding's *The Inheritors* (Halliday 1971). He shows how the perspective of Lok (Neanderthal man) is signified in the novel with event processes, with the consequence that 'directed action' and the relations of agency and causality associated with it cannot be represented. This registers the cultural primitiveness of Lok, and his inability to make sense of the actions of The People (Homo sapiens).

Some of the illustrative examples I used above ('the police shot 100 demonstrators', '100 demonstrators died', '100 demonstrators

are dead') suggest the possible political and ideological significance of choice of process type. For example, an issue which is
always important is whether agency, causality and responsibility
are made explicit or left vague in media accounts of important
events. The examples above evoke one category of events where
this issue constantly arises: violence and violent death. Thus Trew
(1979) shows that the political orientation of a newspaper determines choice of process types to signify deaths in the course of
political demonstrations in South Africa, and thus determines
whether responsibility for the deaths is explicitly attributed, and
to whom. Similarly, wars, unemployment, industrial decline, and
industrial accidents are sometimes signified as events that just
happen, and sometimes signified in terms of actions with responsible agents. These alternatives can be a focus of political and
ideological struggle. The same is true of the signification of processes of antenatal care in the example earlier, and the question of
whether pregnant women are represented as agents of actions, or
only goals of actions.

The grammatical form of a clause is not always a straightforward guide to its process type; there are, for example, cases
of what Halliday calls 'grammatical metaphor' (1985: chapter 10),
where one process type takes on the typical grammatical realization of another. These are some extracts from a report in the
British Communist newspaper *The Morning Star*: 'Big Demos
Boost Health Service Fight' (headline); 'health workers and colleagues demonstrated and rallied, marched and picketed, leafleted
and petitioned'; 'Parliament was hit by hundreds of northerners'.
These are apparently action clauses which give a strong impression of purposeful activity. The first and third are transitive
(subject–verb–object) clauses, the typical realization of directed
action, but one might see them as metaphorical alternatives to, for
example, 'many people have demonstrated and this has helped
those fighting for the health services', and 'hundreds of northerners conducted a lobby of Parliament.' The second consists of a
series of apparently non-directed action clauses, which again can
be seen as metaphors (for 'took part in demonstrations', 'held
rallies', etc.). In this case, there is a clear motivation for the
grammatical metaphor in the political position of the newspaper.

An additional variable with directed action clauses is 'voice',
which can be either active or passive (Quirk et al. 1972: 801–11;
Halliday 1985: chapter 5). In a passive clause, the goal is subject

and the agent is either 'passive agent' (a phrase beginning with 'by'), or omitted altogether (examples with and without agent from *The Baby Book* are 'antenatal care will be provided either by your local hospital or by your general practitioner', and 'your height will be measured'). Active is the 'unmarked' choice, the form selected when there are no specific reasons for chosing the passive. And motivations for choosing the passive are various. One is that it allows for the omission of the agent, though this may itself be variously motivated by the fact that the agent is self-evident, irrelevant or unknown. Another political or ideological reason for an agentless passive may be to obfuscate agency, and hence causality and responsibility (compare 'police shot 100 demonstrators' with '100 demonstrators were killed'). Passives are also motivated by considerations relating to the textual function of the clause. A passive shifts the goal into initial 'theme' position, which usually means presenting it as 'given' or already known information; it also shifts the agent, if it is not omitted, into the prominent position at the end of a clause where we usually find new information. For example, in 'antenatal care will be provided either by your local hospital or by your general practitioner', 'antenatal care' is a given – it is what the whole extract is about – and the new information is who provides it, with the agent (actually two alternative ones) in the new information position. For more on theme, see below.

Nominalization shares with the passive the potentiality of omitting the agent, and the variety of motivations for doing so. The two work in the same direction in 'a complete physical examination will then be carried out': as I noted earlier, the combination here of agentless passive and categorical predictive modality reinforce the medico-scientific voice in the booklet by giving the sense of women being subject to anonymous and invariant procedures, and the nominalization here ('a complete physical examination') – without an identified agent – strengthens this. Nominalizations can also involve omission of participants other than agents; for example, both agent and goal are omitted from 'examinations' and 'tests' in 'it involves a series of examinations and tests throughout the course of your pregnancy.'

Nominalization turns processes and activities into states and objects, and concretes into abstracts. For example, it is one thing to refer to concrete processes in pregnancy which may not be developing normally; it is another to refer to identifying 'any abnormalities which may be present', which creates a new category of abstract entities. The creation of new entities is a feature of nominalization which is of considerable cultural and ideological importance. For instance, an advertisement for cosmetic surgery has the headline 'Good looks can last you a lifetime!'; 'good looks' is a nominalization (from concrete relational processes such as 'you look good!') which entifies a local and temporary condition into an inherent state or property, which can then itself become the focus of cultural attention and manipulation (good looks can, for example, be cultivated, enhanced, looked after; they can be said to bring people good fortune, make them happy, give them trouble). Accordingly, one finds nominalizations themselves taking on the roles of goals and even agents of processes. (For further discussion of the properties of nominalization, see Kress and Hodge 1979: chapter 2.)

I have referred already to 'theme' in discussing the motivations for choosing passive clauses. The theme is the initial part of the clause, the rest of it being sometimes, referred to as the 'rheme' (Quirk et al. 1972: 945–55; Halliday 1985, chapter 3). Analysing clauses in these terms means looking at their textual functions (p. 76 above), and how they structure 'information' in a broad sense. The theme is the text producer's point of departure in a clause, and generally corresponds to what is taken to be (which does not mean it actually is) 'given' information, that is, information already known or established for text producers and interpreters.

Looking at what tends to be selected as theme in different types of text can give insight into commonsense assumptions about the social order, and rhetorical strategies. Consider, first, commonsense assumptions. The 'unmarked' choice of theme in a declarative clause (a statement) is the subject of the clause; this is the choice made if there is no special reason for choosing something else. In the subsection of the *Baby Book* extract headed 'Examination', for instance, we have a sequence of themes (a 'thematic structure') in the main clauses of the sentences, which shows the agenda the medical staff are working to ('your height', 'a complete physical examination', 'a vaginal examination', 'a cervical smear'), and indicates their commonsense assumptions about examination routines. The first clause of the second paragraph, with the theme 'the purpose of this', is rather different, and shows anothers aspect of the potential of theme: the existence of grammatical constructions which allow particular elements to be 'thematized'. In this case, it is the explanation itself that is thematized.

Marked choices of theme are often interesting in what they show, not only about commonsense assumptions but also about rhetorical strategies. The second sentence of the *Baby Book* extract, beginning 'Inevitably, therefore, it involves...', is an example. 'Inevitably' and 'therefore' are adjuncts (Quirk et al. 1972: 420–506) functioning as marked themes. Making elements marked themes is a way of foregrounding them, and what is foregrounded here is the rationality of antenatal care; as I showed in the last section, this is a preoccupation which also makes sense of cohesion in the extract. A rather different case is the second sentence of the subsection headed 'A first visit'. The theme here is 'Just occasionally', and its foregrounding is an illustration of a major preoccupation in antenatal care with anticipating and allaying fears, which often comes across as patronizing.

To sum up, then, it is always worth attending to what is placed initially in clauses and sentences, because that can give insight into assumptions and strategies which may at no point be made explicit.

I conclude this section with an analysis of a short sample which shows how selection of process types, nominalization, and theme interact in texts. The following is extracted from a British Nuclear Forum advertisement:

Can we Seriously Meet our Energy Demands without Nuclear Power?

ENERGY consumption worldwide has grown some twenty fold since 1850. There is a view that energy demand for the industrial nations could even treble in the next 30 years.

(*The Guardian*, 14 August 1990)

The first clause (the headline) can be seen as a grammatical metaphor: it is transitive, and looks like a directed action clause ('we' as agent, 'our energy demands' as goal), but can be regarded as a metaphorical wording of something like 'can we seriously produce as much energy as we want to use without nuclear power?' In the metaphorical version, we have a nominalization ('our energy demands') as goal, which treats as a presupposed entity what one might contentiously word as an assertion (such as 'we keep wanting more energy'). While such an assertion is open to debate, the presupposition is not. Similar things happen in the next two sentences, except that here the presupposed entities are also themes ('energy consumption worldwide', 'energy demand for the industrial nations' – the latter is theme of the subordinate clause introduced by 'that'), which strengthens their status as 'given information', information that can be taken for granted. So grammatical metaphor, nominalization, and theme conspire, as it were, to background the issue of whether we really need so much energy.

Word Meaning

As a producer or interpreter of language texts, one is always confronted with what Raymond Williams calls 'clusters' of words and meanings (Williams 1976: 19), rather than words or meanings in isolation, though it is sometimes useful for analytical purposes to focus upon a single word, as I do below. The relationship of words to meanings is many-to-one rather than one-to-one, in both directions: words typically have various meanings, and meanings are typically 'worded' in various ways (though this is rather misleading, because different wordings change meaning: see the next section). This means that as producers we are always faced with choices about how to use a word and how to word a meaning, and as interpreters we are always faced with decisions about how to interpret the choices producers have made (what values to place upon them). These choices and decisions are not of a purely individual nature: the meanings of words and the wording of meanings are matters which are socially variable and socially contested, and facets of wider social and cultural processes.

My focus here will be on the meanings of words rather than the wording of meanings, but vice-versa in the next two sections. As Williams points out, there are certain culturally salient 'keywords' which are worth focusing on in social research; I shall discuss a current example, 'enterprise'. I shall use the term 'meaning potential' for the range of meanings conventionally associated with a word, which a dictionary will try to represent. Dictionaries usually set out entries for words in ways which imply the following view of meaning potential: (i) meaning potential is stable; (ii) meaning potential is universal, in the sense of being common to all members of a speech community; (iii) meanings within a word's meaning potential are discrete, that is, clearly demarcated from each other; and (iv) meanings within a word's meaning potential are in a complementary 'either/or' relationship to each other, and are mutually exclusive.

While (i)–(iv) work quite well in some cases, they are very misleading in others, and especially where words and meanings are implicated in processes of social or cultural contestation and change. In such cases, the word-meaning relation may change rapidly, so that meaning potentials are unstable, and this may involve struggle between conflicting ascriptions of meanings and meaning potentials to words. (As Pêcheux argued (see p. 31 above), semantic variation is a facet of and factor in ideological conflict.) Moreover, change and contestation of meaning result in changes in the strength and clarity of boundaries between meanings within a word's meaning potential, and indeed contestation may revolve around such boundaries. It may also revolve around the nature of the relationship between meanings within a word's meaning potential, around whether the relationship is indeed one of complementarity or, rather, a hierarchical one, and, if the latter, around specific relations of dominance and subordination between meanings. I shall illustrate some of these possibilities below.

Evidence for these alternative models of meaning potential comes from texts. The dictionary model accords with texts which are produced and interpreted with a normative orientation to meaning potential, which treats it as a code to follow or select within. Papers or essays written by pupils and students in the sciences may be good examples. The alternative model I have suggested finds support in texts with a creative orientation to meaning potential, which treats it as an exploitable and change-able resource, such as the example below. Creative texts are characterized by ambiguities and ambivalences of meaning, and by rhetorical play with the meaning potentials of words. Creative texts necessarily use meaning potentials as a resource, but they contribute to destructuring and restructuring them, including the shifting of boundaries and relations between meanings.

I now examine how the word 'enterprise' is used in the speeches of Lord Young, Secretary of State for Trade and Industry in the Thatcher government (1985–8), and a key figure in its projection of an 'enterprise culture' (see Fairclough 1990a for details of the speeches and further analysis). I have already referred to this example in chapter 4 to illustrate intertextual transformations; I am concerned with it here specifically as an example of features of word meaning. It illustrates how a meaning potential may be ideologically and politically invested in the course of the discursive constitution of a key cultural concept.

The following observations relate to 'enterprise' as a 'mass' or 'noncount' noun, the sort of noun that occurs only in a singular form, and not with an indefinite article (Quirk et al. 1972: 130). 'Enterprise' can also be used as a count noun (e.g. 'an enterprise', 'enterprises'). According to the OED, 'enterprise' as a noncount noun has three senses, which I refer to as the 'activity', 'quality' and 'business' senses:

1   activity: 'engagement in bold, arduous or momentous under-takings';
2   quality: 'disposition or readiness to engage in undertakings of difficulty, risk or danger; daring spirit';
3   business: when modified by 'private' or 'free', 'private busi-ness'.

I refer to these senses collectively as the meaning potential of 'enterprise'. There is also a contrast, in case of the quality sense, between qualities specifically related to business activity (e.g. the ability exploit a market opportunity) and more general personal qualities (e.g. willingness to take risks).

In Young's speeches, 'enterprise' in its business sense is gener-ally used without the modifiers 'private' or 'free'. This increases

the potential ambivalence 'enterprise': in principle, any occurrence of the word is open to being interpreted in any of the three
senses, or any combination of them. However, while most
occurrences of 'enterprise' are indeed ambivalent and involve
some combination of the three senses, this potential ambivalence
is reduced by the context, including the more or less immediate
verbal context in which the word occurs. Verbal context has two
sorts of effect. First, it may eliminate one or more of the senses.
Second, it may give relative salience to one of the senses without
eliminating the others. Examples will be given below.

The meaning potential of 'enterprise', and its potential for
ambivalence, constitute a resource which is strategically exploited
in the Young speeches. Different speeches highlight different
senses, not by promoting one sense to the exclusion of the others,
but by establishing particular configurations of meanings, particular hierarchies of salience relationships among the senses
of 'enterprise', which can be seen to be suited to wider strategic
objectives, notably in contributing to the revaluation of a somewhat discredited private business sector by associating private
enterprise with culturally valued qualities of 'enterprisingness'.
This is an exercise in strategic interdiscursivity, in so far as different elements of the meaning potential of the word are highlighted in different types of discourse.

Here is an example from a speech given in March 1985: 'The
task of government (is) to produce a climate in which prosperity
is created by enterprise'. It occurs immediately after a paragraph
referring to private business, which gives the business sense
salience without, however, excluding the other senses: one could
replace 'enterprise' by any of the expressions 'private enterprise',
'enterprising activity', 'enterprising individuals', without making
the sentence semantically incongruous in its verbal context. In
other cases in the same speech, salience relations are established
through other aspects of verbal context, for instance through the
conjunction of 'enterprise' with other expressions: 'business enterprise and the job of wealth creation' highlights the business
sense, whereas 'individual initiative and enterprise' highlights the
quality sense, though the preceding verbal context places it at the
'business qualities' end of the scale.

A second speech, delivered in July 1985, is concerned with
'entrepreneurs', and this focus is reflected in the way in which the

senses of 'enterprise' are hierarchized, with the quality sense becoming more salient. This relative salience is syntactically marked in some cases through the conjunction of 'enterprise' with expressions which isolate the quality sense: 'harmful to enterprise – and the enterprising instincts of individuals', 'to encourage enterprise and to encourage enterprising individuals'. But it is the business qualities end of the scale which is most prominent, so that, as in the first speech, the structuring of senses of 'enterprise' is business-dominated.

A third speech was delivered in November 1987. What is striking here is the number of instances where the verbal context reduces ambivalence and imposes the quality sense: 'raised the skills and enterprise of individuals', 'recognise the professionalism and enterprise of their managers', 'use the talents and enterprise of people'. In each case, the quality sense is imposed by 'enterprise' being co-ordinated with a noun which signifies personal qualities, and modified by prepositional phrases ('of individuals', etc.) which attribute enterprise – as a quality, of course – to (categories of) persons. Furthermore, the qualities being referred to are more towards the general personal end of the scale than in the two previous speeches. However, this is only a relative shift in salience: a significant proportion of instances remain ambivalent between the three senses, and in some cases the verbal context still highlights the business sense (for example, 'The whole climate for wealth creation and enterprise has changed').

The underlying movement in the speeches is towards a restructuring of the meaning potential of 'enterprise' which elevates the quality sense, and the general personal quality end of the quality scale. This movement is itself a part of the evolution of Tory enterprise strategy over the first ten years of the Thatcher government. In the earlier part of this period, the assumption was that an enterprise culture could be created largely through economic measures (such as privatization, relaxation of regulations affecting industry, reduction of taxation) and political measures (such as reducing the status of local authorities in housing and higher education). Around the mid-eighties, government ministers began to think that what was needed was a set of changes in 'culture and psychology' (in the words of Nigel Lawson). They began to project – through Department of Trade and Industry initiatives, for example, and through 'enterprise' elements in education and training – models for enterprising activity and the enterprising self which were still fundamentally linked to business, but which highlighted sets of enterprising qualities. (See Morris 1990 for detailed analysis of these changes.) The continuing containment of this shift of emphasis within an orientation to business is also reflected in the heterogeneous mixture of senses for 'enterprise' I alluded to above in the third speech.

There is a homology between Young's strategic restructuring of the meaning potential of 'enterprise' and the restructuring of orders of discourse I discussed in chapter 3 (pp. 92–4 above) in terms of a hegemony model. And success in winning acceptance for particular meanings for words, and for a particular structuring of their meaning potential, is indeed interpretable as a matter of achieving hegemony. We might therefore call the model I described at the beginning of this section a 'hegemonic model' of word meaning. It is a model which can be used not only for political speeches, but also for investigating word meaning in education, advertising, and so forth.

Wording

In this section I shift to the second aspect of the many-to-one nature of the word-meaning relation: the multiplicity of ways of 'wording' a meaning (on wording see Mey 1985: 166–8; on 'lexicalization' see Halliday 1978: 164–82). As I suggested above (p. 76), a perspective on vocabulary which focuses upon wording contrasts with a dictionary-based view of vocabulary. Dictionaries are part of the apparatus of standardizing and codifying languages (Leith 1983), and they are always more or less committed to a unitary view of the language of a community and its vocabulary which is implicitly, if not explicitly, normative: they tend to present dominant wordings and word meanings as the only ones.

To talk of 'a multiplicity of ways of wording a meaning', however, misleadingly implies that meanings are given prior to being worded in various ways, and are stable across various wordings. It would be more helpful to say that there are always alternative ways of 'signifying' (Kristeva 1986b) – giving meaning to – particular domains of experience, which entails 'interpreting' in a particular way, from a particular theoretical, cultural or ideological perspective. Different perspectives on domains of experience entail different ways of wording them; it is in these terms that we should view alternative wordings such as the wording of immigration as an 'influx' or 'flood' as opposed to a 'quest' for a new life. In a real sense, then, as one changes the wording one also changes the meaning. (Yet recall my reservations (p. 65 above) about overstating the active process of signifying/constituting reality in a way which ignores the existence, and resistance, of reality as a preconstituted domain of the 'objects' referred to in discourse).

New wordings generate new 'lexical items' (Halliday 1966), a technical term which is sometimes used in preference to 'words' because the latter is used for so many different purposes, and because 'lexical item' captures the idea of expressions which have achieved a degree of fixity and stability. One type of wording which makes this process particularly clear is wording which involves the process of nominalization. For example, the wording of (1) below has become solidified into a new lexical item, 'consciousness-raising', in (2):

1 They held meetings to encourage people to become more conscious of their lives.
2 They held consciousness-raising sessions.

Creating lexical items brings particular perspectives on domains of experience into wider theoretical, scientific, cultural or ideological purview. In cases like this one, it generates new culturally important categories. The effects may be rather more parochial. An advertisement for a cosmetic surgery clinic contains a number of lexical items (such as 'eyebag removal', 'nose refinement', 'wrinkle improvement', and ' "bat ear" correction'), which are ideologically significant in giving cosmetic surgery a 'scientific' vocabulary, and at least the appearance of operating within a complex domain; its implicit claim is thus the prestigious status of scientifically-based therapy.

Multiplicity of wordings can usefully be seen as one aspect of intertextuality. Wording a domain of experience is tantamount, at the level of vocabulary, to constituting a particular configuration of intertextual elements in producing a text. Differences in the vocabulary of *The Baby Book* and the *Pregnancy Book* illustrate this, such as their accounts of the purpose of cervical smears: 'to exclude any pre-cancerous change' (*Baby Book*), 'to detect early changes in the cervix which could later lead to cancer' (*Pregnancy Book*). Both 'pre-cancerous' and 'exclude', in the way they are used here, belong to medical discourse, whereas 'changes ...which could later lead to cancer' belongs to a lifeworld (conversational) discourse. These vocabulary differences are part of differences in the intertextuality of the two booklets. Similar comments apply to news report. In sample 1 of chapter 4 (pp. 105–13 above): the 'translation' in *The Sun* of (drug) 'traffickers' into 'pushers' and 'pedlars' is one dimension of an intertextual configuration which centres around *The Sun*'s simulation of 'the language of ordinary life'.

A further example comes from an article entitled 'Stress and the businessman: stresswise for health success' (Looker and Gregson 1989), which echoes current management wisdom that the key to success in contemporary business is the quality and commitment of the workforce (people as 'human resources', in the wording of the article).

Invest in Stress Management

Stress management facilitates the use of personal skills which in turn improves work performance and leads to the effective operation and management of any organisation. A small investment in stress management courses and programmes can have a major impact on an organisation's profitability. There is no doubt that an organisation's greatest assets is its employees and it is their health and performance that is seen in the balance sheets at the end of the day. So for health and success be wise about stress.

A striking aspect of the intertextual configuration here is the mixture of genres: the genre of the academic article, and the genre of the advertisement (the latter represented in the rhyming slogan at the end). But my main concern is with the configuration of discourses in the extract (see pp. 125–8 above). Firstly, there is, a discourse of accountancy, drawn upon in the wording of employees as 'assets' and 'resources'. Secondly, there is an extension of a discourse of organizational management from the domain of organizations to the domain of the self, in the wording 'stress management'. Thirdly, there is a discourse of personnel management, itself incorporating an application of a discourse of machine technology to human beings (rating people in terms of their 'performance'), which extends the concept of 'skills' from its more traditional use for capacities in manual work, to non-manual but traditionally 'private' capacities ('personal skills').

This extract exemplifies an important shift that is going on in workplaces, a shift linked to technological change and new styles of management. 'Personal' characteristics of employees, which have hitherto been seen as private and outside the legitimate range of intervention of employers, are now being redefined as within that range of intervention. Thus employees' stress problems become a legitimate concern of personnel officers. Extracts of this sort are indicative of attempts to generate a new workplace discourse for such concerns, drawing upon a range of discourses which more traditionally belong in the workplace (those of accountancy, organizational management, machine technology, and personnel management). This configuration of discourses is reflected in the wording of employees, their capacities, and their (health) problems.

It is useful to compare the wording of particular domains from particular perspectives in terms of relative density, that is, in terms of the number of different wordings (including lexical items) that are generated, many of which will be near synonyms. In an important paper, Halliday (1978) uses the term 'overlexicalization' for the dense wording of a domain; I shall use the term 'overwording'. Overwording is a sign of 'intense preoccupation' pointing to 'peculiarities in the ideology' of the group responsible for it (Fowler et al. 1979: 210). An example is the wording of language capacities in the 1988 Kingman Report on the teaching of English in British schools (Department of Education and Science 1988). Wordings include: 'competence', 'effectiveness', 'mastery', 'facility', 'expertise', and 'skill'. This overwording seems to be linked to a preoccupation in the report with the (ideological) projection of a view of language as a set of determinate technical skills that can be taught and acquired in a modular way. It is a view of language that emphasizes conventional and appropriate production, and interpretation of ideational aspects of meaning (see Fairclough and Ivanic 1989).

In addition to overwording, Halliday (1978) distinguishes 're-wording' ('relexicalization' in his terms), that is, generating new wordings which are set up as alternatives to, and in opposition to, existing ones. The term 'rewording' is a useful label for the intertextual and dialogic character of wording. Edelman (1974) highlights the perspective which underlies conventional wordings of the practices of psychiatric treatment, by rewording them in an oppositional and hostile way. The stress management text above involved a rewording of employees and their capacities and problems in order to incorporate them into the sphere of personnel management. In the following example rewording can be seen as part of the marketization of education:

> The vocational preparation product is usually a programme. Its design and implementation are therefore central parts of the marketing process, and should start from the needs of potential customers and clients and the benefits for which they are looking. (Further Education Unit 1987: 51)

Here rewording goes hand in hand with the semantic restructuring I discussed in the previous section. Notice how 'design' is explicitly subordinated to 'marketing' in the second sentence, which is part of a process subsuming the concept of 'course design' into a broader commercially-based sense of 'design'.

Metaphor

Metaphor has traditionally been thought of as a feature of literary language, especially poetry, with little relevance to other sorts of language. Recent work on metaphor has strongly suggested that this is not true (see Lakoff and Johnson 1980). Metaphors are pervasive in all sorts of language and in all sorts of discourse, even the most unpromising cases, such as scientific and technical discourse. Moreover, metaphors are not just superficial stylistic adornments of discourse. When we signify things through one metaphor rather than another, we are constructing our reality in one way rather than another. Metaphors structure the way we think and the way we act, and our systems of knowledge and belief, in a pervasive and fundamental way.

How a particular domain of experience is metaphorized is one of the stakes in the struggle within and over discourse practices. For example, some workers in higher education actively resist commodity and consumer metaphors (such as, 'courses have to be packaged in modules that our consumers want to buy'). And one aspect of discursive change with significant cultural and social implications is change in the metaphorization of reality. To pursue this example, the metaphorical constitution of education and other services as markets is a potent element in the transformation not only of discourse, but also of thinking and practice, in these spheres (see below).

Some metaphors are so profoundly naturalized within a particular culture that people are not only quite unaware of them most of the time, but find it extremely difficult, even when their attention is drawn to them, to escape from them in their discourse, thinking, or action. Lakoff and Johnson discuss the metaphorical construction of argument as war (reflected, for example, in 'your claims are indefensible', 'he attacked every weak point in my argument', 'his criticisms were right on target', and 'I demolished his argument'). They point out that this is not just a superficial matter of wording: 'Many of the things we *do* in arguing are partially structured by the concept of war' (1980: 4). Thus the militarization of discourse is also a militarization of thought and social practice (Chilton 1988), just as the marketization of discourse in education referred to above is also a marketization of thought and practice.

The following example of the militarization of discourse illustrates rather well the effectiveness of metaphors in structuring reality in a particular way. It is taken from a study of the 1987 British General Election, and more specifically of how the issue of defence was handled by the media (Garton, Montgomery and Tolson 1988; Montgomery 1990). The authors note that there is a 'congruence' between the issue of defence itself and the way the media represented it in the campaign: the dominant metaphor for the campaign itself is that of war. The following examples from television and press coverage illustrate the point (my italics):

1 Defence was *the centrepiece of her attack* on Labour and Neil Kinnock. (BBC 1 26 May)

2 Tonight in South Wales the Thatcher *counter-attack* began. (BBC 1 26 May)
3 Mrs Thatcher's *attack* was part of a *two-pronged* Conservative effort to stop Labour. (BBC 2 26 May)
4 The Labour Party *mounted a determined rearguard action* yesterday. (*Financial Times* 27 May)
5 The Conservative and Alliance *pincer movement* against Labour included a bitter *assault* by David Owen. (*Independent* 26 May)

The issue does of course provide the media with a ready-made military metaphor. One practical effect it has, as the authors point out, is to make it extremely difficult for Labour or any other party to promote through the media a defence policy which is not based upon a crude, confrontational view of international relations (cast in terms of 'standing up to bullies', 'deterring', and so forth; see below).

Further, election campaigns are not as a matter of fact conducted as direct, face-to-face confrontations or arguments: this is just the way the media construct them. The media, through the way in which they select, order and represent material, reduce the complexity and confusion of a campaign to a set-piece argument or combat, blow followed by counter-blow. This is then portrayed as a reality that the media merely reflect, thus disguising the constructive effects that the media themselves have upon the reality. Another practical consequence is that media coverage itself comes to be shaped by the metaphor: we may, for example, find a pattern of alternation day by day between the 'attacks' of one party and the 'counter-attacks' of another. And political parties come to adapt their campaigns to fit with the 'reality' of their portrayal in the media. If the opposition is portrayed as having struck a major 'blow' one day, a party needs to produce material in press conferences or speeches which their media advisers tell them can be readily convertible into a 'counter-attack'. In sum, the metaphor has effects upon the coverage of the campaign, and upon the campaign itself.

Garton, Montgomery and Tolson (1988) also point to the ideological potency of 'scripts' in the coverage of the defence issue in the 1987 election. They use the term 'script' as others have used the term 'narrative', for stereotypical scenarios and sequences of events associated with them, which are part of the deeply embedded common sense of a culture. Many scripts have a metaphorical base. For example, Chilton (1988: 64) discusses a British Ministry of Defence leaflet intended to persuade people of the need to increase British nuclear weapons:

HOW TO DEAL WITH A BULLY
PEACE THROUGH DETERRENCE – THE ONLY
ANSWER TO A BULLY'S THREAT

Many of us have had to stand up to a bully at some stage in our lives. The only answer is to say: 'Let me alone – or you'll be sorry.' And to have the strength to back up your words.

Here what Chilton calls the 'bully script' ('Bullies always attack weaker victims: the only way *not* to be attacked is to look strong') is used to metaphorize international relations as relations between individuals, and, archetypically, relations between schoolboys. Garton, Montgomery and Tolson (1988) show that this and other scripts ground the ways in which a key statement on defence by Neil Kinnock, the Labour leader, was transformed and constructed in the media.

The ways in which events which disturb relative social equilibrium (wars, epidemics, ecological disasters, etc.) are metaphorized in the media and elsewhere provides a good insight into the values and preoccupations of a culture. For example, Sontag (1988) has investigated the metaphorization of the disease AIDS. She suggests that the principal metaphor associated with AIDS is that of 'plague'. Like the plague, AIDS has an alien origin, and is linked to foreignness: it is generally seen as originating in Africa, and has a racist aura which feeds upon stereotypical associations of black people with 'animality and sexual licence'. The plague metaphor also connects with a military metaphor: AIDS as an 'invasion', and more specifically an invasion of Europe and America by the Third World. Like the plague, AIDS is construed as a 'judgement on society' for its moral laxity, and the spread of AIDS is used politically and homophobically to push back the 'permissive society'. The metaphor does, however, have contradictory and problematical aspects: no one is immune from plagues, or AIDS, yet this universality puts at risk the ideologically important construction of AIDS as a disease of 'the other': 'their' disease as a threat to 'us'.

Conclusion

This concludes the discussion of analytical properties of texts which has occupied chapters 5 and 6. The topics I have covered will be pulled together in chapter 8 in a summary form as part of the guidelines for doing discourse analysis. It is appropriate to remind readers here of the three-dimensional framework for discourse analysis which I introduced in chapter 3 – analysis of discourse as text, as discourse practice, and as social practice – in order to emphasize that text analysis is not something that should be done in isolation. It is easy to become so involved in the intricacies of texts that text analysis comes to be seen as a laudable end in itself. There are, indeed, some forms of discourse analysis which tend in that direction, such as the forms that Bourdieu had in mind when he described discourse analysis as having 'relapsed into indefensible forms of internal analysis' (1988: xvii). In contrast, I want to insist that analysis cannot consist merely of description of texts carried out in isolation from their interpretation (these terms were distinguished above, p. 73). Thus I have constantly interpreted the texts described in this and the preceding chapter. Interpretation is necessary at two levels. One level is a matter of trying to make sense of the features of texts by seeing them as elements in discourse practice, in particular as 'traces' of the processes of text production (including the intertextual and interdiscursive combination of heterogeneous elements and conventions), and as 'cues' in the processes of text interpretation. There is a similarity here between my account of what the analyst does, and my account in chapter 3 (pp. 78–86 above) of what text interpreters do: analysts too need the resources they have as competent members of communities, even if they use them rather more systematically. The other level of interpretation is a matter of trying to make sense both of the features of texts and of one's interpretation of how they are produced and interpreted, by seeing both as embedded within a wider social practice. In earlier work, I have distinguished these two levels of interpretation respectively as 'interpretation' and 'explanation' (Fairclough 1989a: 140–1).

Description is not as separate from interpretation as it is often assumed to be. As an analyst (and as an ordinary text interpreter) one is inevitably interpreting all the time, and there is no phase of analysis which is pure description. Consequently, one's analysis of the text is shaped and coloured by one's interpretation of its relationship to discourse processes and wider social processes. Even producing a transcription of a spoken text inevitably entails fixing upon an interpretation of it (see p. 229 below), and one's choice of what to describe depends upon prior interpretative conclusions. In addition, what I have called analytical features of texts have in many cases a heavy admixture of interpretation. For example, the patterns of lexical collocation in texts which I analysed as part of the analysis of cohesion are not objectively 'there' in the text; they are, so to speak, 'put there' by the way one interprets a text. So not only are description and interpretation mutually necessary, they also merge into each other.

There are further similarities between analyst and participant. Analysis leads to production of texts which are socially distributed and consumed like other texts, and the discourse of analysis is, like any other discourse, a mode of social practice: it is dialectically related to social structures, it is positioned in relation to hegemonic struggles, and it is open to being ideologically and politically invested. Analysts are not above the social practice they analyse; they are inside it. One might, therefore, expect them to be as self-conscious as possible about the resources they are drawing upon in interpreting discourse, and about the nature of the social practice of analysis itself – the structures which condition it, its orientation to positions in struggle, the outcomes from it and its effects upon struggles and structures.

7

Discourse and Social Change in Contemporary Society

In terms of the double orientation to discursive change I discussed above (pp. 96–9), my concern in this chapter is with ongoing change in orders of discourse rather than change in discursive events. I shall identify certain broad tendencies in discursive change affecting the societal order of discourse, and relate these tendencies to more general directions of social and cultural change. The sort of change I shall be referring to has a partly international or at least transnational character, as I indicated in the Introduction. It is surprising how little attention has been given to such tendencies of change in orders of discourse; the chapter should therefore be seen as an exploratory engagement with a large, and largely neglected, field of research. I shall discuss three major tendencies: 'democratization', 'commodification', and 'technologization' of discourse. The first two relate to substantive changes in discourse practices, whereas the third suggests that conscious intervention in discourse practices is an increasingly important factor in bringing change about. These tendencies are having a pervasive impact upon the contemporary order of discourse, through their impact is uneven, and there are sharp contrasts between local orders of discourse associated with particular institutions or domains.

Focusing upon particular tendencies provides a way into identifying patterns in the complex and contradictory processes of ongoing discursive change, but it is a highly abstract way of looking at change. The final section of the chapter tries to correct this to some extent, by looking at how the tendencies interact with each other, and by considering how the tendencies might figure in the processes of hegemonic struggle over the structuring of orders of discourse. I offer different interpretations of the tendencies in terms of different models of discursive practice, arguing that the hegemonic model I have been advocating gives a more satisfactory account than either a 'code' model or a 'mosaic' (or 'negotiative') model.

Democratization

By 'democratization' of discourse I mean the removal of inequalities and asymmetries in the discursive and linguistic rights, obligations and prestige of groups of people. Democratization in discourse, like democratization more generally, has been a major parameter of change in recent decades, but in both cases the process has been very uneven (in Britain, for example, speakers of Welsh have won far greater rights than speakers of Gujarati), and in both cases there are questions about how real or how cosmetic changes have been. I shall review five areas of discursive democratization: relations between languages and social dialects, access to prestigious discourse types, elimination of overt power markers in institutional discourse types with unequal power relations, a tendency towards informality of language, and changes in gender-related practices in language.

It is broadly the case that languages other than English, social dialects other than standard English, as well as a variety of accents, have become more widely accepted, or tolerated, in a range of public functions since the Second World War than they were before. This is not to claim the dawning of a linguistic utopia. These are achievements of social struggle, and they have been and continue to be resisted. They are, moreover, uneven: the most disadvantaged minorities, such as the various Asian communities in Britain, are subject to racist inequities in this respect as in others. Nevertheless, democratization has been a real force in this regard, and even though much of the debate continues around cases where inequality and bigotry are still flagrant, the level and salience of the debate itself indicates that such issues are really on the agenda. One frequently mentioned example is broadcasting, where people with non-standard dialects and regional accents have had unprecedented access, though still within rather tight limits. For instance, standard English and 'received pronunciation' accents are still *de rigueur* for national newscasters, and although one finds people with other (regional) accents reading, for instance, provincial news on national TV and radio networks, one does not find people with working-class accents. Working-class accents do occur, but in programmes such as quizzes and soap operas. Equally, while there is an extensive Welsh-language broadcasting service, Asian and other minority languages are only marginally catered for. Broadcasting concedes a measure of appropriacy to non-standard varieties and minority languages in the public domain, though in less prestigious areas of it.

These tendencies raise the question of whether the domination of standard English, which has characterized the modern period (Leith 1983), is now coming to an end. Are we living in a 'post-standard' situation (see Jameson 1984)? There is also an international dimension to this question: while the position of English as an unofficial world language continues to strengthen, various 'Englishes' such as Indian English and African English, which have hitherto received little recognition, are beginning to emerge on a more equal footing with British and American English. (Though this should not be overstated: it is still predominantly British and American English that are taught to millions of people in language schools throughout the world.) And if there is a genuine shift away from unitary standards on national and international levels, does this represent a real fracturing of hegemony in the linguistic sphere, or is hegemony merely taking new forms? The discussion below of discursive change in the context of the 'modernism–post-modernism' debate will return to such issues.

Associated with this first mode of democratization is a certain democratization of access to prestigious discourse types, and prestigious and powerful subject positions within them, for speakers of non-standard varieties of English, for women, and for black and Asian people. An example is the increase in the number of women who have gained access to positions in the law (though as magistrates and solicitors, rather than as barristers or high-court judges), or in higher education, or in the media. The main issue here is, of course, access to institutions and to positions within them, and access to discourse is just a part of that. One consequence has been that non-standard dialects and regional accents have come to be accepted to some degree as compatible with discourse practices with which they have hitherto been seen as incompatible. A university lecture can these days be delivered in a Liverpool accent (but that has by no means become an unproblematical thing to do).

Another broadly discernable change, of more central concern to this book, is the elimination of overt markers of hierarchy and power asymmetry in types of institutional discourse where power relations are unequal. The contrast between the standard and alternative medical interview samples above (pp. 138–49) was an example: in the former, the doctor controlled turn-taking and topic through his control of the question–response–assessment cycles, whereas in the latter these overt asymmetries were absent. Similar contrasts could be found between more traditional and more 'modern' practices in interactions between lecturer and student, teacher and pupil, manager and worker, parent and child. Among the many types of marker which may tend to be eliminated are: asymmetrical terms of address; 'bald' (e.g. imperative) directives, in favour of more indirect and 'face'-sensitive forms (Brown and Levinson 1978); asymmetries in rights to make certain sorts of contribution, such as initiating topics, and asking questions; use by powerful participants of specialized vocabulary inaccessible to others. One can, of course, still find all of these features in certain types of interaction.

It is also arguable that as overt markers become less evident, covert markers of power asymmetry become more potent, with the result that power asymmetry becomes more subtle rather than disappearing. For instance, if I am regularly the one who formulates or sums up what we have said in an interaction (and so constantly offer my version of what has gone on), that is a subtler sort of asymmetry than if I am the only person allowed to speak without being invited to do so. Nevertheless, it is still a rather potent asymmetry, and one which can be exploited to control the interaction. Heritage (1985), for example, suggests that radio interviewers use their formulating rights as a way of exercising control, and evaluating what their interviewees say, without contravening their obligation not to express judgements about what is said.

One way of interpreting such cases is that the apparent elimination of overt power markers and asymmetries is really only cosmetic, and that power-holders and 'gatekeepers' of various sorts are merely substituting covert mechanisms of control for overt ones. There is some truth in that, but only a half truth: this mode of democratization is sometimes cosmetic, but it can also be substantive, and there is struggle over its meaning, as I argue below.

The tendency to eliminate overt power markers is closely associated with a tendency towards informality: it is in the more formal types of situation that asymmetries of power and status are sharpest. A central manifestation of increasing informality is the way in which conversational discourse has been and is being projected from its primary domain, in the personal interactions of the private sphere, into the public sphere. Conversation is colonizing the media (Kress 1986; Fowler 1988b), various types of professional/public discourse, education, and so forth: by this, I mean that their discourse is taking on an increasingly conversational character. This is part of a major restructuring of the boundaries between the public and private domains.

One dimension of this manifestation of informality is a shift in the relationship between spoken and written discourse. We had examples of this from newspapers in chapter 4 (pp. 105–13 above): sample I simulates conversational discourse in mediating the doings and sayings of the powerful to the paper's readership, and the headline 'Di's butler bows out...in sneakers!' uses not only conversational vocabulary but also a graphic device – the dots – to simulate 'dramatic' pausing in speech. The division between speech and writing is no longer the commonsense one it may seem to be, in either direction. The expression 'talking like a book' reflects a popular perception of how written language has influenced more formal speech, and one finds the shift towards conversation not only throughout the printed media and advertising, but also in new designs for official forms, such as claim forms for social welfare payments (Fairclough 1989a: 218–22). The shifts of speech towards writing may have had their heyday; contemporary cultural values place a high valuation on informality, and the predominant shift is towards speech-like forms in writing.

But conversation is also a powerful model for other types of spoken discourse. So it is not only the printed media that are becoming more conversational, it is also the broadcast media, radio and television. Tolson (1990) has traced the process of conversationalization of interviews in the media. There is a great deal more conversation to listen to and watch in these media (the 'chat shows', for example), which itself reflects its valuation, but it is also the case that broadcasters extensively 'converse' with their mass audiences, as if they were chatting with individual members of them. And a variety of types of interview, and other sorts of encounter, between professionals and their 'publics' are tending to become more conversational, as I indicated above. As in the case of the elimination of asymmetry markers, there is a question about the extent to which informality is simulated for strategic reasons; I return to this below.

The final domain of democratization I want to refer to is that of gender relations in language, which has been the most publicly salient case of struggle over discursive practices in recent years. The proliferating literature on 'language and gender' contains studies which indicate asymmetries between women and men (in favour of men) in respect of the amount of talk, the take-up of topics, the likelihood of interruption, and so forth (Cameron 1985; Coates 1986; Graddoll and Swann 1989). For example, a study of conversation between young white American professional couples (Fishman 1983) shows that while the women introduced more topics than the men (47 and 29 respectively), nearly all (28) of the men's topics were taken up in the conversation, whereas not much more than a third (17) of the women's topics were taken up. When men introduced topics, the tendency was for women to signal their attention while the topics were being introduced (with 'minimal responses' such as 'yeah' or 'mmhm'), and actively to accept and respond to the topics. In contrast, when topics were introduced by women it was common for men not to signal attention while the women were speaking, and to make just a minimal response to the suggested topic (which does not encourage one to go on with a topic) when the women had finished speaking.

Sexist (and therefore undemocratic) features of language and language use have also been widely documented, such as use of 'he' as if it were a generic pronoun to refer to women as well as men, or the similar use of 'man' and associated terms such as 'chairman' (Graddoll and Swann 1989: 99–110). If 'he' were genuinely generic, we would find it used indifferently to refer to unspecified members of sets of people. Yet there are actually a few cases where 'she' is widely used in this way, for example 'if a secretary starts getting backache, the chances are that her office equipment is at fault.' 'She' is used in this way when the stereotypical member of the set of people at issue is a woman: the typical secretary, or nurse, is a woman. But if the use of 'she' for non-specific reference is based upon such a stereotype, is that not also true of 'he'? If university rules contain things like this: 'If a student wishes to interrupt his course of study for personal or health reasons, he should discuss the matter with his tutor in the first instance,' is not the stereotype of 'the student' here male? For an argument to this effect, see Martyna (1978).

Although most of the debate has again centred upon continuing non-democratic and sexist practices, the context for the debate is a certain opening up and democratization of gender relations which has its discursive facets. Not only self-conscious feminists but many other women, and many men, actively intervene these days to make language practices less sexist, with varying degrees of success. Intervention may take various forms: producing guidelines for non-sexist practice in institutions; inscribing graffiti on billboard advertisements to highlight and challenge sexist discourse; or struggling for women's access to prestigious discursive practices and roles. An important form of intervention is engaging in struggles of a more hegemonic nature, to shift practices in, for example, trade union or academic departmental meetings in directions which make it easier for women to contribute, or to foster collaborative rather than competitive modes of interaction which are often more highly valued by women than men. Nor should 'the language of silence' as a mode of intervention be discounted: people may interpret and react to discourse in oppositional ways even if their opposition is not overtly expressed. Intervention by men is sometimes directed at discursive dimensions of practices of masculinity, for instance at assumptions that 'being a man' entails aggressive and obscene discourse practices. Such practices of intervention are more typical of, and have more impact upon, certain strata within the middle class than elsewhere.

Questions of intervention are a timely reminder that abstract tendencies such as democratization are the summation of contradictory struggles, within which interventions to restructure orders of discourse may be resisted in various ways, and may be subjected to various strategies of containment, in order to preserve existing hegemonies in the sphere of discourse. One such strategy is marginalization, and a notorious example is the title 'Ms'. 'Ms' was originally designed to impose gender symmetry on titles, sharing with 'Mr' the property of leaving marital status open. But 'Ms','Mrs' and 'Miss' are now widely used on official forms as alternatives to chose between. Choosing 'Ms' then becomes a political act, which in most domains may lead to one being marginalized. The struggle over such forms goes on, and although democratization of gender-related discursive practices is anything but a smooth and universal process, gender asymmetries in discourse have been denaturalized and problematized on a significant scale.

Commodification

Commodification is the process whereby social domains and institutions, whose concern is not producing commodities in the narrower economic sense of goods for sale, come nevertheless to be organized and conceptualized in terms of commodity production, distribution and consumption. It is no longer surprising, for example, for sectors of the arts and education such as theatre and English language teaching to be referred to as 'industries' concerned with producing, marketing and selling cultural or educational commodities to their 'clients' or 'consumers'. Commodification is not a particularly new process, but it has recently gained new vigour and intensity as an aspect of the 'enterprise culture' (Keat and Abercrombie 1990). Marx himself noted the effects of commodification on language: referring to people as 'hands' in industrial contexts, for example, is part of seeing them as commodities useful for producing other commodities, as embodied labour power. In terms of orders of discourse, we can conceive of commodification as the colonization of institutional orders of discourse, and more broadly of the societal order of discourse, by discourse types associated with commodity production. I shall refer to examples from education and educational discourse.

A widespread feature of contemporary educational discourse is the wording of courses or programmes of study as commodities or products which are to be marketed to customers. The extract I used in chapter 6 is a typical example:

> The vocational preparation product is usually a programme. Its design and implementation are therefore central parts of the marketing process, and should start from the needs of potential customers and clients and the benefits for which they are looking. (Further Education unit 1987: 51)

The message to course designers and teachers is a more elaborate variant of the marketing maxim 'Give the customers what they want'. Such wordings effect a metaphorical transfer of the vocabulary of commodities and markets into the educational order of discourse. But in contemporary Britain the metaphor is more than just a rhetorical flourish: it is a discursive dimension of an attempt to restructure the practices of education on a market model, which may have (as this extract suggests) tangible effects on the design and teaching of courses, the effort and money put into marketing, and so on.

But commodified educational discourse is commonly more self-contradictory than this might suggest. There is a hint of such contradictions in the conjunction of 'customers' and 'clients' in the extract, which betrays a widespread ambiguity about who educational commodities or 'packages' are being sold to. Is it the learner, or the firms that currently employ or are likely to employ learners? The latter may indeed be 'clients' in the direct sense of paying for the learner to take a course. As a consequence, learners are contradictorily constructed. On the one hand, they are constructed in the active role of discerning customers or consumers aware of their 'needs', and able to select courses which meet their needs. On the other hand, they are constructed in the passive role of elements or instruments in production processes (something like 'hands' in Marx's example), targeted for training in required 'skills' or 'competences', with courses designed around precise 'attainment targets' and culminating in 'profiles' of learners, both of which are specified in terms of quite precise skills. Such a framework and terminology is now widespread, especially in pre-vocational education, but it is also used, for example, in the Cox Report on the teaching of English in schools (Department of Education and Science 1989). The coexistence of these active and passive constructions of the learner facilitates the manipulation of people through education, by overlaying it with what one might call an individualist and consumerist rhetoric.

Commodified educational discourse is dominated by a vocabulary of skills, including not only the word 'skill', and related words like 'competence', but a whole wording (see p. 190 above) of the processes of learning and teaching based upon concepts of skill, skill training, use of skills, transfer of skills, and so forth (see Fairclough forthcoming b). The concept of skill is an important factor in allowing the two contradictory constructions of the learner to coexist without manifest inconsistency, because it seems to fit into either an individualistic and subjectivist view of learning, or an objectivist view of training. This ambivalence is reflected in the history of the concept within liberal humanist and conservative educational discourse, and in the semantic history of the word 'skill'. On the one hand, the concept of skill has active and individualistic implications: skills are prized attributes of individuals, individuals differ in types and degrees of skill, and it is open to each individual to refine skills or add new ones. (Incidentally, the concept is also democratic, implying that everyone has the capacity to learn and develop, given only appropriate training.) On the other hand, the concept of skill has normative, passive and objectifying implications: all individuals acquire elements from a common social repertoire of skills, via normalized training procedures, and skills are assumed to be transferable across contexts, occasions, and users, in a way which leaves little space for individuality.

The vocabulary of skills has a long and respectable pedigree in linguistics and applied linguistics, where the idea that use of language is based upon sets of 'language skills' (writing, reading, speaking, and listening skills) is commonplace. This wording helps to commodify the content of language education, in the sense that it facilitates its division into discrete units, which are in principle separately teachable and assessable, and can be bought and sold as distinct goods in the range of commodities available on the educational market. These units are not only the main skill categories of writing, reading, speaking, and listening, but also more specific parts of each. Speaking skills may be divided into giving information, expressing opinion, and engaging in group discussion, and each of these may be further divided, and so on (see, for example, the list of communication skills for the Youth Training Scheme in Further Education Unit 1987: 38). Depending on which of the contradictory facets of the learner is highlighted, this facilitates either the efficient pin-pointing and correcting of deficiencies, or a provision which is designed to meet consumer needs as specifically as possible. Wording language education in terms of a vocabulary of skills also implies a highly normative view of language, as a determinate set of practices (as I argue in Fairclough forthcoming b).

But commodification of educational discourse is not just a matter of vocabulary; it is also a matter of genre. Education is one of a number of domains whose orders of discourse are being colonized by the advertising genre (Fairclough 1989a: 208–11), and as result there is a proliferation of text types which combine features of advertising with features of other genres. We have already met an example of this in the Barclaycard text (pp. 113–17 above), which mixed advertising with financial regulations. On pp. 212–13 is a rather different example from the educational domain, taken from the University of Lancaster's undergraduate prospectus for 1990. No particular significance should be attached to the choice of the university or the course, as similar tendencies are evident in other entries and other prospectuses.

A common feature of entries in this prospectus is the placing of a photograph near the beginning of the entry, and the 'You Will Need' heading and graphics at the end. The systematic inclusion of photographs in prospectuses is a relatively recent development, which itself reflects the impact of advertising. Contemporary commodity advertising typically consists of a mix of language and visual images, and the trend is for images to become more salient. In part this accords with technological developments in television and printing. But technologies, as I suggested above, are likely to be fully exploited only to the extent that they accord with the thrust of social and cultural change. So, what does advertising gain from visual images? To answer this question, we need to take account of general properties of advertising as a genre.

Advertising is 'strategic' discourse *par excellence*, in the terms of Habermas's distinction between 'strategic' and 'communicative' language (1984). It is in the business of constructing 'images' in the other sense – ways of publicly presenting persons, organizations, and commodities, and the construction of identities or personalities for them. Contemporary market conditions require that numbers of firms market rather similar products; to establish one's own product as different, its identity has to be constructed. At the same time, categories of potential buyers for products are often not specifiable in terms of independently existing types of social membership (class, regional and ethnic group, gender, etc.): they also have to be constructed in the discourse. And so too do the producers and sellers of the product, whose image has to be made to harmonize with the images of the product, and of its potential consumers. Producer, product, and consumer are brought together as co-participants in a life style, a community of consumption (Leiss, Kline and Jhally 1986), which the advertisement constructs and simulates.

What advertisers gain from visual images is their evocative capacity in the simulation of life style, which is generally more powerful and immediate than that of language. A visual image can, if it works, instantaneously create a world which potential consumer, producer and product can jointly inhabit, before a reader gets to read (or a viewer to hear) the language of the advertisement. Thus most of the photographs in this university prospectus represent students doing things (sitting in classes, using equipment, chatting, and so forth), offering potential students a physical and social environment they can imaginatively insert themselves into. The photograph in the example reproduced above does not represent student activity, but it does offer an outstandingly beautiful natural environment for the potential student imaginatively to occupy (spending a year in an American university as part of the degree). The visual image projects an enticing image for the 'product', that is, the degree scheme, and for the potential student as a part of it.

The graphics under the heading 'You Will Need' at the end of the entry do not have the evocative properties of a photograph, but they do, nevertheless, make their own contribution to the co-construction of potential student, university, and course. Graphics of this sort are an effective way of making information available at a glance. The use of graphics implies an institution which is both up to date and sensitive to students' needs especially given the history of informationally complex and 'un-reader-friendly' university prospectuses. It also constructs the potential student as having particular needs and values, such as needing

AMERICAN STUDIES

Enquiries to: Director of Admissions
Teaching staff: members of appropriate departments

Lancaster students have always shown lively interest in American subjects, whether in the English, History, Politics or other departments. Now it is possible to take a specialised degree in American Studies. This degree combines different disciplinary approaches to the study of the United States and offers options covering American history, literature, and politics from the earliest colonial settlements to the present day.

In addition, American Studies majors will spend their second year at an American university, such as the University of Massachusetts at Amherst or another selected American university. Lancaster's close American connections make it possible to integrate the year abroad into the degree, so that, unusually in British universities, the American Studies degree can be completed in *three* years. Special counselling will ensure close integration between the year abroad and the two years at Lancaster.

Degree studies at Lancaster call on specialists in a number of departments, and, as with most Lancaster degrees, students will gain valuable experience in more than one discipline. But a substantial degree of flexibility is maintained, and it is possible for students to concentrate substantially on either history or literature or politics if they so choose.

The first year is largely devoted to providing a disciplinary grounding, and students pursue the normal first year courses in the History, English, and Politics departments, taking American options where they exist. Thereafter the course of study is almost exclusively devoted to American topics, and may include the writing of a dissertation on an American theme.

American Studies graduates pursue careers normally associated with a humanities or social science education: education, business, journalism, publishing, librarianship, and social service, with the wider opportunities which may come from students' transatlantic experience and perspective.

B A Hons **American Studies** Q400

First Year

History (American options)
English
Politics

Second Year

Four of five courses in American subjects taken at a United States university, including at least one interdisciplinary course.

Third Year

Four or five courses, normally from:
History:
The History of the United States of America

Religion in America from Jamestown to Appomatox, 1607–1865
From Puritan to Yankee: New England, 1630–1730
The Great Alliance: Britain, Russia and the United States, 1941–1945
Cold War America: The United States from Truman to Kennedy
English:
American Literature, 1620–1865
American Literature, 1865–1940
American Literature, 1940–1980
Politics:
The Politics of Race
United States Government: The Politics of the Presidency
The American Policy Process
United States Foreign Policy since 1945

Assessment: see under appropriate subjects.

YOU WILL NEED

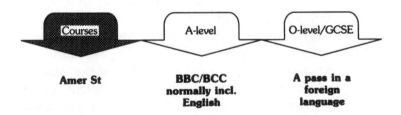

Courses	A-level	O-level/GCSE
Amer St	**BBC/BCC** normally incl. **English**	**A pass in a foreign language**

or other qualifications (IB, EB, Scottish Highers) at a comparable standard.
AS-levels: will be accepted.
Interview policy: special cases only.
Open days: candidates who are offered places will be invited.

practical information in a digestible form, and valuing clarity and efficiency in providing it.

The use of graphics also helps to overcome a contradiction which arises from the colonization of prospectuses by advertising. Universities may set out to sell themselves to students, but they also impose rigid controls and conditions on entry. Consequently, students are positioned on the one hand as powerful consumers with the right to choose, and on the other as powerless applicants. By marginalizing conditions on entry and handling them through graphics, requirements imposed by the university are construed as matters of fact which no one is apparently responsible for. Notice how this also emerges in details of the wording, such as opting for 'you will need' rather than 'we require'.

Let us turn finally to the main body of text. What is striking about it is the blend of information and persuasion, telling potential students about the scheme and selling it to them. This is evident in the ordering of sentences in the first paragraph. The third sentence describes the composition of the scheme, but it is preceded and framed by two sentences which set the scheme in a narrative about American Studies at Lancaster. Is this information, or is it persuasion? It can, of course, be construed as either: the record of the university in American Studies is certainly relevant information for applicants, but innovation is likely to be more attractive if it arises out of past achievement. Prospectuses in the 1980s, compared with the 1970s or earlier, are more concerned to select and order their information on the basis of strategic calculations about persuasive effects. One might reasonably argue that there is nothing new about strategic calculation in information. The real novelty is that information can be manifestly strategic and persuasive without that being regarded as an issue. Under the influence of advertising as a prestigious model, the blending of information and persuasion is becoming naturalized, divisions between them in orders of discourse are being fractured, and as a consequence the nature of 'information' is being radically changed.

The blending of information and persuasion is also evident in the other paragraphs of the text; I shall concentrate on the second. The first sentence looks straightforwardly informational until 'selected' which suggests how solicitous the university is for its students' interests. 'Special' in the third sentence does something very similar. In the second sentence, ordering and framing is again evident: the information about the length of the course is preceded, framed, and in fact causally linked ('so that') to Lancaster's 'close American connections', which are incidentally presupposed, as if applicants ought to know about them. 'Close' hints discreetly at Lancaster's superiority, and is part of an undercurrent of implicit comparison between Lancaster and other universities. The italicization of *three*, and the explicit comparison between Lancaster and other universities, suggest that the shorter length of the course is being projected as a 'selling point'.

Technologization

Modern societies are characterized by a tendency towards increasing control over more and more parts of people's lives. Habermas has described this in terms of the colonization of the 'lifeworld' by the 'systems' of the state and the economy (1984: xl). What I have said above about commodification indicates a discursive aspect of colonization by the economy. Foucault has also addressed this general tendency, cataloguing the 'technologies' and 'techniques' which are at the service of modern 'bio-power' (see p. 50 above).

Foucault's analysis of the technologies of power can be extended to discourse. We can usefully refer to 'discourse technologies' (Fairclough 1989a: 211–23), and to a 'technologization of discourse' (Fairclough 1990b) as characteristics of modern orders of discourse. Examples of discourse technologies are interviewing, teaching, counselling, and advertising. In calling them discourse technologies, I am suggesting that in modern society they have taken on, and are taking on, the character of transcontextual techniques, which are seen as resources or toolkits that can be used to pursue a wide variety of strategies in many diverse contexts. Discourse technologies are coming increasingly to be handled in specific institutional locations by designated social agents. They are coming to have their own specialist technologists: researchers who look into their efficiency, designers who work out refinements in the light of research and changing institutional requirements, and trainers who pass on the techniques.

These technologists include members of university social science departments: a well-established example is research and training in 'social skills' carried out by social psychologists (Argyle 1978). Those who are targeted for training in discourse technologies tend to be teachers, interviewers, advertisers, and other 'gate-keepers' and power-holders, whereas discourse technologies are generally designed to have particular effects upon publics (clients, customers, consumers) who are not trained in them.

Discourse technologies establish a close connection between knowledge about language and discourse, and power. They are designed and refined on the basis of the anticipated effects of even the finest details of linguistic choices in vocabulary, grammar, intonation, organization of dialogue, and so forth, as well as facial expression, gesture, bodily stance, and movements. They bring about discursive change through conscious design. This implies access on the part of technologists to knowledge about language, discourse and semiosis, as well as psychological and sociological knowledge. It is predictable that discourse analysts and linguists will increasingly be expected to act as, or make available the results of their research to, discourse technologists.

Discourse technologies involve simulation: in particular, the simulation for strategic and instrumental purposes of interpersonal meanings and discursive practices. This links in with my earlier comments on democratization of discourse: the simulation of power symmetry and informality are widely used techniques on the part of institutional power-holders. One example is the sort of job interviews carried out in public services such as hospitals, local government, and universities. I have used elsewhere (Fairclough 1989a: 62) the term 'synthetic personalization' for the simulation of aspects of interpersonal meaning on the basis of strategic calculation of effects. The simulation of interpersonal meanings follows from the subordination of all other aspects of discursive practice and meaning to achieving strategic and instrumental goals – the type of interaction that Habermas calls 'strategic' in contrast to 'communicative' (see above). The technologization of discourse is associated with an extension of strategic discourse to new domains.

The technologization of discourse appears to be spreading from genres such as interview, which have a public character in the sense that they are associated with a range of public institutional functions, to the core genre of the private sphere, conversation. This reflects in part the appropriation of conversation by institutions, and its investment with specific political and ideological content. The 'alternative' medical interview above (pp. 144–9) is an example of this. It also reflects the way in which private spheres are shifting into the public domain as, in Habermas's terms, lifeworld domains come to be colonized by systems. Thus the domestic arrangements and relationships of the family are to some extent being made public, and are often referred to as a specific domain of politics.

Let me make these points more concrete by referring to a book which describes how managers in workplaces can improve their conversational skills (Margerison 1987). The book is about 'conversation control skills', though 'conversation' includes business meetings and interviews, as well as informal conversation in a more restricted sense. Some of the skills discussed, such as 'summarizing' (roughly equivalent to 'formulation' – see p. 157 above), are mainly associated with these more formal institutional types of discourse, but others also appertain to informal conversation. Indeed, 'conversation control skills' are said to be relevant not only at work, but also in managing relations within the family and amongst friends.

The book gives attention to quite a range of skills. One chapter deals with inferential skills in recognizing and reacting to verbal 'clues' and non – verbal 'signals' that point to meanings that are indirectly expressed or just hinted at. Important problems are often signposted in this way, when people feel unable to talk about them explicitly, and failing to pick up clues and signals can have serious consequences. A related issue is skills in obtaining permission to enter conversational territory – the feelings, states of mind, private thoughts, and personal motivations of others – that might be 'out of bounds'. Another chapter focuses upon techniques for turning a confrontational conversation into a collaborative and co-operative one, including techniques for 'managing' disagreement and rejection Skills in what are known in the pragmatics literature as 'positive politeness' and 'negative politeness' (see pp. 162–6 above) feature in several chapters. These include ways of showing one's appreciation and understanding of others conversationally (perhaps while trying to win consent for one's own contrary position), and ways of mitigating criticisms of others. There is a chapter dealing with how to challenge assumptions which are conversationally taken for granted, and how to be assertive without being aggressive. Another chapter discusses controlling and shifting topic, especially the shift from analysing past failures to making plans for the future.

The book claims that conversation control skills can contribute to business success and profits, safety at work, the motivation of employees, and avoidance of industrial disputes: 'Conversation control is therefore crucial to creating conditions where people work effectively together.' And in family and other social relations, 'Differences of opinion can lead to arguments and unpleasant conflicts or they can be sorted out through skilful management of conversations.' But this clear indication of the potential of conversation control as a technology is accompanied by the unconvincing claim that it is 'not about controlling the behaviour of others but getting control of our own conversation and behaviour', that it is a matter of 'influencing' people but not 'manipulating' them (pp. 193–4).

There is a close link between technologization of discourse and the skills – and competence-based view of language education and training which I discussed above as 'commodification'. The spread into private and lifeworld domains and into conversation seems to correspond to a current universalization of language skills training. Until recently, it was mainly institutional 'gatekeepers' and power-holders, and people who were in some way physically or psychologically disabled, that were exposed to communication skills training. In contemporary Britain, with the new policies for GCSE and the National Curriculum in schools and for pre-vocational education (Technical and Vocational Education Initiative, Youth Training Scheme, etc.), language and communication skills are being universally taught (see Further Education Unit 1987; Department of Education and Science 1989).

Making Sense of the Tendencies

Abstracting and isolating tendencies, as I have done above, is a way of highlighting them. But my focus throughout the book has been on orders of discourse as complex, heterogeneous, and contradictory; we must therefore try to make sense of the tendencies as they interact and cut across each other. In doing so, we need to allow for possible variations in the effects of the tendencies upon different local orders of discourse, in the degree to which they are accepted or resisted, and so forth. We also need to allow for phenomena like the 'synthetic personalization' referred to in the last section. The general point is that tendencies may have contrasting and quite different values, depending on the articulations they enter into; they are open to different political and ideological investments (see p. 67 above).

Democratization and commodification may appear to be simple opposites – the former is a weakening of control, the latter a strengthening of control – but phenomena such as synthetic personalization show that the relationship is more complex. Another reason why the tendencies cannot be regarded as simple opposites is that commodification actually implies democratization. Recall my suggestion that both the Barclaycard text of chapter 4 and the university prospectus text involve a partial shift away from traditional authoritor-authoritee relations in banking and education respectively, in favour of the 'consumer' (customer, prospective student). This shift is manifested in democratized discourse: the power of the bank and the university is not overtly expressed, and there are consequential tensions which I pointed to in both texts. Commodified texts built upon advertising models also commonly manifest other democratizing features, including informality, and a move towards conversational discourse.

This convergence between commodification and democratization is only partial and in one direction: democratization occurs without commodification, as in the 'alternative' medical interview sample of chapter 5. However, the convergence does appear to reveal common characteristics at a deeper level, in particular the way these tendencies affect the constitution of subjectivity or 'selfhood' by discourse, in the context of shifts that have been documented (by Rose MS, for instance) in the social constitution of the self in contemporary society. These shifts are towards a more autonomous, self-motivating self (a 'self-steering' self, as Rose puts it). The two tendencies appear to have in common an orientation to the 'self-steering' self: both the doctor in the 'alternative' medical interview, and the authors of the Barclaycard text and of the university prospectus, implicitly address themselves to (and therefore presuppose) versions of the self-steering self. The 'consumer', the universal addressee of advertising and its colonizing extensions into education and other spheres, is a version of the self-steering self, characterized by the capacity and the will to 'choose'. So too is the client-patient of the 'alternative' medical interview, who is also ascribed autonomy and choice. If commodification and wider processes of democratization are indeed tending to construct fundamentally the same sort of self, it would not be surprising to find them overlapping in domains such as education. Thus the potential student who is constructed as a consumer may find herself constructed on arrival as an 'autonomous learner'.

I have characterized the democratization and commodification tendencies in broad terms as properties of the contemporary societal order of discourse. As noted above, their impact upon the various more local, institutional orders of discourse is variable: some orders of discourse are coming to be heavily democratized and/or commodified, others less so. Nevertheless, what is striking is the pervasiveness of the tendencies, and the ease with which they do appear to transcend boundaries between institutions and domains. The current salience of these tendencies seems to correspond not only to the models of selfhood they implicitly project, but also to a particular state or condition of the societal order of discourse in contemporary society which makes possible the projection of new models.

This condition is one of relative 'fragmentation' of discursive norms and conventions, which affects a range of institutions and domains. What I mean by 'fragmentation' is a certain breakdown, a loss of efficacy, of more local orders of discourse, which makes them permeable by the general tendencies. To spell this out in more detail, fragmentation involves (i) greater variability of discursive practice (for example medical interviews being conducted in more varied ways); (ii) less predictability for participants in any given discursive event, and a consequent need to negotiate how a particular interview, for instance, will proceed; and (iii) greater permeability to types of discourse emanating from outside the domain in question (for example, being more open to conversational discourse), and to the general tendencies. There are indications of educational, medical, and workplace discourse becoming more fragmented in this sense.

Paradoxically, fragmentation of local orders of discourse would seem to be a condition for the increasing technologization of discourse, in the sense that the greater permeability of local orders of discourse includes being open to technologizing processes from 'outside'. The paradox is that fragmentation appears to be a relaxation of the regulation of discursive practice, whereas technologization appears to be an intensification of it. One way of interpretating the process is in terms of a shift in the nature and location of regulation. When local orders of discourse are relatively stable and autonomous, they are regulated locally and internally through overt disciplinary mechanisms or, more usually, through covert pressures. But the tendency now is for 'experts' in research and training to regulate practice in a variety of local institutions and domains. So, is the colonization of local orders of discourse by the tendencies of democratization and commodification brought about by the discourse technologists? Certainly the effect of the tendencies often comes through colonization by the major discourse technologies – advertising, interviewing, and counselling – and through training in these technologies as decontextualized skills.

However, this account is too categorical and one-sided. It suffers from the fault that Taylor (1986: 81) criticizes in Foucault's genealogical studies, of seeing change solely in terms of techniques of power which are interpreted unambiguously as tools of domination. It misses what Foucault himself refers to as the 'tactical polyvalence of discourses' – the fact that they can have different values in different 'strategies' (see above p. 59). A case in point is the reinvestment of democratization represented by synthetic personalization. Let me develop this example a little.

The argument is that democratization turns out to be ambivalent, either part of a genuine relaxation or used strategically as a technology. Even in the latter case, technologization may not be definitive. Power-holders may appropriate democratization, but the process of appropriation may itself open up a further terrain of struggle, in which defeats can be suffered by power-holders. There is a sense in which synthetic or simulated democratization for strategic purposes is a high-risk strategy, which is itself a concession to the power of democratizing forces as well as a move to combat it. Using the forms of democratized discourse – eliminating overt asymmetries in terms of address, being informal, moving onto the common ground of conversation – makes certain implicit claims about the nature of the social relationships being enacted, which are not sustainable where democratization is being simulated. The result may be a contradiction in discursive practice between the forms and the content of democratized discourse, which may become a terrain of struggle.

The tendencies, then, are caught up in processes of struggle in and over discourse practices in which they can be variously invested. As well as the possibility raised in the last paragraph of appropriating them and 'turning them around', there is also the possibility of resisting and rejecting them, or accommodating and marginalizing them. Seen as techniques in processes of discourse technologization, the tendencies give rise to a great variety of mixed or hybrid forms of discourse, in which compromises are effected between them and more traditional non-commodified or non-democratized discourse practices. The Barclaycard text and the 'alternative' medical interview were analysed earlier in these terms. One justification for an approach to discourse analysis which centres intertextuality and interdiscursivity, and associated notions such as the heterogeneity and ambivalence of discourse, is that contemporary orders of discourse are full of such hybrid texts.

However, the emphasis here is still very much upon technologization, even if resistance to it is being highlighted, and the assumption is still of relatively centred social and discursive processes. As against this, there has been an emphasis in the literature on post-modernism upon the breakdown of the social, which suggests a rather different interpretation of current processes of discursive change. Such an interpretation would highlight the fragmentation of local orders of discourse I referred to above, as a discursive dimension of a fragmentation of the social order. It would also suggest seeing the processes I have referred to as 'democratization' in terms of fragmentation, as a series of what Jameson (1984) calls 'dedifferentiations', the breaking down of distinctions and barriers, without implying that such breakdowns are merely the corollaries of unitary tendencies at other levels, be it democratization or technologization. These dedifferentiations would include the boundaries between standard and non-standard varieties of language, and imply a certain reversal of processes of standardization which have been a major feature of modern society. From this perspective, the accounts I have given so far are overinterpretations of change, premissed on assumptions about the rationality and centredness of social processes which may no longer hold in contemporary societies.

Conclusion: Relevant Models of Discourse

I have in effect offered three different interpretations of the tendencies which I have identified: interpretations in terms of unilinear colonization, hegemonic struggle, and fragmentation. Each interpretation implies a particular model of discursive practice. The account in terms of unilinear colonization implies a 'code' model of discursive practice. The classic version of a code model assumes a stable local order of discourse, and naturalized conventions which are normatively instantiated in practice: practice is simply following the norms. But unilinear colonization also implies a code model, though in this case the codes that are normatively followed are in part externally shaped through colonization by discourse technologies.

The second interpretation, in terms of hegemonic struggle, implies a hegemonic model of discursive practice, that is, a view of discursive practice as articulation: the disarticulation of existing configurations of discourse types and elements, and the rearticulation of new configurations, giving prominence to interdiscursivity and intertextuality.

The third interpretation, in terms of fragmentation, corresponds to what one might call a 'mosaic' or perhaps 'negotiative' model. Both images imply fragmentation of conventions. But the 'mosaic' image emphasizes the consequential space for creative play, for combining discourse elements in ever new ways to achieve momentary impact, for pastiche. Whereas the 'negotiation' image emphasizes that where conventions can no longer be taken as given, there is a consequential need for interactants to negotiate (almost always implicitly) which discourse elements are to be drawn upon. It is the negotiation image that has the wider applicability: not all discursive practice that is negotiative in this sense has the properties implied by 'mosaic', but discursive practice which does have these properties (the clearest examples probably come from advertising) must be negotiative, in that an implicit accord about the articulation of discourse elements must be established between producers and interpreters for a mosaic effect to 'work'.

Developing a hegemonic model of discursive practice, especially in opposition to the predominant code model, has been a major objective of this book. A hegemony model seems to make the best overall sense of the contemporary societal order of discourse. But it is not simply a preferable alternative to the other two models. Rather, each of the models gives some purchase upon the contemporary order of discourse, and each model seems to work relatively well for some domains of discursive practice, and less well for others. Rather than opting for one and rejecting the others, further research could profitably focus upon this question of which models makes most sense of which domains, and upon the tensions between the models, while keeping in play all three of the lines of interpretation for current discursive change.

8

Doing Discourse Analysis

This chapter will address the practicalities of doing discourse analysis. What follows is not to be regarded as a blueprint, as there is no set procedure for doing discourse analysis; people approach it in different ways according to the specific nature of the project, as well as their own views of discourse. The points below, therefore, should be treated as general guidelines, which identify the main elements and considerations which apply to discourse analyses, on the basis of the theoretical position I have set out above. I have occasionally acted upon the assumption that the reader is about to embark upon a major research project investigating social and discursive change, but as many readers are likely to be using discourse analysis for more modest purposes, they should not be put off by these grandiose assumptions. There are three main heads: data, analysis, and results. The focus of this book is, of course, upon analysis, but this chapter will be an opportunity to attend to other important aspects of doing discourse analysis. Readers might like to compare these guidelines with those provided in Potter and Wetherell (1987), or (for analysis only) in Fowler et al. (1979).

Data

Defining a Project

Discourse analysis ought ideally to be an interdisciplinary undertaking. This follows from the conception of discourse I have been advocating, which involves an interest in properties of texts, the production, distribution, and consumption of texts, sociocognitive processes of producing and interpreting texts, social practice in various institutions, the relationship of social practice to power relations, and hegemonic projects at the societal level. These facets of discourse impinge upon the concerns of various social sciences and humanities, including linguistics, psychology and social psychology, sociology, history, and political science.

What is specific about a particular discursive practice depends upon the social practice of which it is a facet. Research projects in discourse analysis are, therefore, most sensibly defined first in terms of questions about particular forms of social practice, and their relations to social structure; given the focus I have been adopting, in terms of particular aspects of social or cultural change. This means that it is the disciplines which deal with these questions – sociology, political science, history – that we should look to in the first instance in defining research projects. Discourse analysis should best be regarded as a method for conducting research into questions which are defined outside it. I shall give an example shortly. This is however, an inordinately 'top-down' way of seeing it: in many cases, interdisciplinary teams of researchers may be able to work with people in, for example, education or health, in investigations of issues and problems which they experience during the course of change. Indeed, it may be possible to engage in 'co-research', the individuals or groups who are the subjects of research being involved in the design, implementation, writing up, and use of the research (see Ivanic and Simpson forthcoming).

The Corpus

The perspective of specialist disciplines, and those being researched, is also important in the selection of data, the construction of a corpus of discourse samples, and in deciding what supplementary data to collect and use. The nature of the data required will vary according to the project and the research questions, but there are certain general principles to bear in mind. One can only make a sensible decision about the content and structure of a corpus in the light of adequate information on the 'archive'. (This term is used in a way which extends it beyond its historical usage, to refer to the totality of discursive practice, either recorded past practice or ongoing practice, that falls within the domain of the research project.) This is partly a practical matter of knowing what is available, and how to get access to it, but it is partly a matter of having a mental model of the order of discourse of the institution or domain one is researching, and the processes of change it is undergoing, as a preliminary to deciding upon where to collect samples for a corpus. Of course, work on the corpus may change the preliminary mental map. The discourse analyst should depend upon people in relevant disciplines, and people working within the research site, for decisions about which samples are typical or representative of a certain practice; whether the corpus adequately reflects the diversity of practice and changes of practice across different types of situation, and both normative and innovative practice; and whether the corpus includes cruces and moments of crisis (these notions are explained below). There are particular problems in collecting a corpus of material that gives access to processes of change, because one obviously needs to try to incorporate reasonable time spans in the data.

Enhancing the Corpus

There are various ways in which a corpus can be enhanced with supplementary data. One can, for instance, obtain judgements about aspects of discourse samples in the corpus from 'panels' of people who are in some significant relation to the social practice in focus. If classroom practices and classroom discourse were being studied, the panels would include teachers, pupils, parents, members of different majority and minority communities, and educational administrators (on the use of panels, see Gumperz 1982). A widely used way of enhancing a corpus is through interviews. One can interview those involved as participants in corpus samples, not only to elicit their interpretations of those samples, but also as an opportunity for the researcher to probe into issues which go beyond the sample as such, to try to discover, for example, whether a person is more conscious of the ideological investment of a particular discursive convention in some situations than in others. Or, in co-research, one may have closer and less formal access to the perspective of those being researched. The point to emphasize is that interviews, panels, and so forth, are further discourse samples, and that one way in which they enhance the corpus is simply by being added to it. The corpus should be seen not as constituted once and for all before one starts the analysis, but as open to ongoing enhancement in response to questions which arise in analysis.

An Example

An example of a possible research project will give these issues concrete instances. I shall use the example referred to in the Introduction (p. 7 above) of changes in discursive practice associated with the shift from Fordist to post-Fordist production, focusing upon a projected study of 'quality circles' (this example is based upon planning for a joint sociological and linguistic project at Lancaster University). A characteristic of post-Fordist industry is the growing importance of communication on the shop-floor. New forms of interaction between shop-floor workers, supervisers, and managers are emerging, such as 'quality circles', groups of five to ten employees who usually work together and meet regularly to discuss ways of improving quality, productivity, and other work-related issues. One unanswered question about quality circles, which may well bear upon trade union suspicions of them and their high failure rate, is whether they really break down old divisions between employees, and give shop-floor workers more power, or whether they are a management tool for using the valuable experience of shop-floor workers, and integrating them into management priorities. Research is needed into how quality circles actually function – how they select topics, how they debate issues, how they generate proposals and present them to management – and whether control of these activities is shared and negotiated, or exercized more or less overtly by management. These questions can be investigated using discourse analysis as a method. The corpus for such a study might consist of video recordings of quality circles over a one-year period from their inception. One focus might be on how conventions for conducting meetings emerge over the period, as part of a wider study of the development of power relations in quality circles. This corpus might be enhanced with recordings of the training of managers as quality circle leaders or 'facilitators', presentations of proposals by quality circles to management panels, and communication between quality circles and members of the workforce who are not involved in them. It could also be enhanced through interviews about quality circles with quality circle members, senior management, trade union representatives, and other shop-floor workers. The analyst might involve members of quality circles in arriving at definitions of research questions and analytical focus. I shall develop this example a little in discussing 'Results'.

Transcription

Spoken discourse, such as quality circle meetings, needs to be transcribed. Transcription is a difficult and time-consuming process. Depending upon the system of transcription used, it can take anything from six to twenty hours or more to transcribe one hour of recorded speech. There are a variety of transcription systems available which represent different features of speech, with different degrees of detail – intonation, stress, pausing, changes in loudness and tempo, and so forth (Atkinson and Heritage 1984: ix-xvi; Tannen 1989: 202–4). No system could conceivably show everything, and it is always a matter of judgement, given the nature of the project and the research questions, what sort of features to show, and in how much detail. A fairly minimal type of transcription, which is adequate for many purposes, shows overlaps between speakers, pauses, and silences (the transcriptions on pp. 139 and 145 are examples).

What is, perhaps, less obvious is that transcription necessarily imposes an interpretation on speech; in the words of one paper on this issue, transcription is theory (Ochs 1979). Consider a situation where three people are talking, with one of them accounting for 80 per cent of the talk. The way this is set out on paper might either represent it as a 'conversation', in which all three take turns at talking, but one happens to take longer turns and more turns than the others; or it might be represented as a monologue with various interruptions or supportive additions

from the other speakers, perhaps by setting out the more loqua-
cious speaker's talk in a column down the middle of the page
with the other contributions set out at the margins (see Edelsky
1981 for examples of this sort). Similarly, if there is silence on the
tape, the transcriber has to decide whether to attribute it to one
or other of the participants; if there is overlap, whether to represent it as one speaker interrupting another.

Coding and Selecting Samples within the Corpus

Researchers may well wish to code a whole corpus or large parts
of it in broad terms, perhaps summarizing the discourse, or code
it in terms of topics, Or they may scan the whole corpus for
particular sorts of feature – certain types of question, or formulations (see p. 157 above). However, the conception of discourse I
have presented, and the view of analysis I shall summarize below,
are especially relevant to detailed analysis of a small number of
discourse samples. This raises the problem of how to select samples for detailed analysis. The answer is broadly that samples
should be carefully selected on the basis of a preliminary survey
of the corpus, taking advice where one can get it from those being
researched, or from colleagues in relevant social science disciplines, so that they yield as much insight as possible into the
contribution of discourse to the social practice under scrutiny.
One selection strategy which has much to recommend it is to
focus on what I earlier called 'cruces' and 'moments of crisis'.
These are moments in the discourse where there is evidence that
things are going wrong: a misunderstanding which requires participants to 'repair' a communicative problem, for example through
asking for or offering repetitions, or through one participant
correcting another; exceptional disfluencies (hesitations, repetitions) in the production of a text; silences; sudden shifts of style.
In addition to the evidence of the text and of the participants'
conduct of the interaction, one might again use panel judgements
or participants' retrospective judgements about points of difficulty. Such moments of crisis make visible aspects of practices
which might normally be naturalized, and therefore difficult to
notice; but they also show change in process, the actual ways in
which people deal with the problematization of practices.

Analysis

This section consists of a summary of the sorts of analysis I have introduced and illustrated in chapters 3–7. I have not adhered exactly to the order in which topics were discussed in those chapters, but I do follow the same overall progression from (i) analysis of discourse practices (at a 'macro' level: see p. 85 above), focusing upon the intertextuality and interdiscursivity of discourse samples; to (ii) analysis of texts (plus 'micro' aspects of discourse practice); to (iii) analysis of the social practice of which the discourse is a part. These three dimensions of analysis will inevitably overlap in practice; analysts, for example, always begin with some sense of the social practice that the discourse is embedded within. But this progression is a useful one for ordering the outcome of one's engagement with a particular discourse sample before presenting it in written or spoken form. Notice that it involves a progression from interpretation to description and back to interpretation: from interpretation of the discourse practice (processes of text production and consumption), to description of the text, to interpretation of both of these in the light of the social practice in which the discourse is embedded. It is not necessary to proceed in this order, and analysts can begin from text analysis, or indeed analysis of social practice. The choice will depend upon the purposes and emphases of the analysis. 'Fronting' the analysis of discourse processes seems to be particularly appropriate, given my main concern here with process and change.

Each of the main heads in the summary below is followed by a short description of the sort of analysis it involves, and then in most cases a set of questions to act as pointers during analysis of particular discourse samples. Bear in mind that during analysis there is a constant alternation of focus from the particularity of the discourse sample, to the type(s) of discourse which it draws upon, and the configurations of discourse types to which it is oriented. Analysis should be directed at both: it should show features, patterns and structures which are typical of certain types of discourse, restructuring tendencies in orders of discourse, and ways of using these conventional resources which are specific to this sample. Note that in any particular analysis some of the categories are likely to be more relevant and useful than others, and analysts are likely to want to focus upon a small number of them.

Discourse Practice

Each of the three dimensions of discourse practice is represented below. 'Interdiscursivity' and 'Manifest Intertextuality' focus upon text production, 'Intertextual chains' upon text distribution, and 'Coherence' upon text consumption. (See chapter 4 for detailed discussion). I have added 'Conditions of discourse practice' to bring in the social and institutional aspects briefly alluded to in chapter 3 (pp. 78–80 above).

INTERDISCURSIVITY (see pp. 124–30 above) The objective is to specify what discourse types are drawn upon in the discourse sample under analysis, and how. Feel free to use the general term 'discourse type' if it is not clear whether something is a genre, activity type, style, or discourse (see pp. 125–8 above). The main way of justifying an interpretation is through text analysis, by showing that your interpretation is compatible with the features of the text, and more compatible than others. Other sorts of evidence were mentioned above under 'Enhancing the corpus'.

> Is there an obvious way of characterizing the sample overall (in terms of genre)? (if so, what does it imply in terms of how the sample is produced, distributed, and consumed?)
> Does the sample draw upon more than one genre?
> What activity type(s), style(s), discourse(s) are drawn upon? (can you specify styles according to tenor, mode, and rhetorical mode?)
> Is the discourse sample relatively conventional in its interdiscursive properties, or relatively innovative?

INTERTEXTUAL CHAINS (see pp. 130–3 above) The objective here is to specify the distribution of a (type of) discourse sample by describing the intertextual chains it enters into, that is, the series of text types it is transformed into or out of.

What sorts of transformation does this (type of) discourse sample undergo?

Are the intertextual chains and transformations relatively stable, or are they shifting, or contested?

Are there signs that the text producer anticipates more than one sort of audience?

COHERENCE (see pp. 83–4 above) The aim here is to look into the interpretative implications of the intertextual and inter-discursive properties of the discourse sample. This could involve the analyst in 'reader research', that is, research into how texts are actually interpreted.

How heterogeneous and how ambivalent is the text for particular interpreters, and consequently how much inferential work is needed? (This leads directly to intertextual dimensions of the construction of subjects in discourse: see 'Social practice' below.)

Does this sample receive resistant readings? From what sort of reader?

CONDITIONS OF DISCOURSE PRACTICE (see pp. 78–80 above) The aim is to specify the social practices of text production and consumption associated with the type of discourse the sample represents (which may be related to its genre: see the first question under 'Interdiscursivity' above).

Is the text produced (consumed) individually or collectively? (Are there distinguishable stages of production? Are animator, author, and principal the same or different people?)

What sort of non-discursive effects does this sample have?

MANIFEST INTERTEXTUALITY (see pp. 117–23 above) Manifest intertextuality is a grey area between discourse practice and text: it raises questions about what goes into producing a text, but it is also concerned with features which are 'manifest' on the surface of the text. The objective is to specify what other texts are drawn upon in the constitution of the text being analysed, and how. Genres differ in the modes of manifest intertextuality with which they are associated see (p. 128 above), and one aim here is to explore such differences.

discourse representation
Is it direct or indirect?
What is represented: aspects of context and style, or just ideational meaning?
Is the represented discourse clearly demarcated? Is it translated into the voice of the representing discourse?
How is it contextualized in the representing discourse?

presupposition
How are presuppositions cued in the text?
Are they links to the prior texts of others, or the prior texts of the text producer?
Are they sincere or manipulative?
Are they polemical (such as negative sentences)?

And one further question:

Are there instances of metadiscourse or irony?

Text

INTERACTIONAL CONTROL (see pp. 152–8 above) The objective here is to describe larger-scale organizational properties of interactions, upon which the orderly functioning and control of interactions depends. An important issue is who controls interactions at this level: to what extent is control negotiated as a joint accomplishment of participants, and to what extent is it asymmetrically exercised by one participant?

What turn-taking rules are in operation? Are the rights and obligations of participants (with respect to overlap or silence, for example) symmetrical or asymmetrical?
What exchange structure is in operation?
How are topics introduced, developed, and established, and is topic control symmetrical or asymmetrical?
How are agendas set and by whom? How are they policed and

by whom? Does one participant evaluate the utterances of others?

To what extent to participants formulate the interaction? What functions do formulations have, and which participant(s) formulate(s)?

COHESION (see pp. 174–7 above) The objective is to show how clauses and sentences are connected together in the text. This information is relevant to the description of the 'rhetorical mode' of the text (see p. 127 above): its structuring as a mode of argumentation, narrative, etc.

What functional relations are there between the clauses and sentences of the text?

Are there explicit surface cohesive markers of functional relations? Which types of marker (reference, ellipsis, conjunction, lexical) are most used?

POLITENESS (see pp. 162–6 above) The objective is to determine which politeness strategies are most used in the sample, whether there are differences between participants, and what these features suggest about social relations between participants.

Which politeness strategies (negative politeness, positive politeness, off record) are used, by whom, and for what purposes?

ETHOS (see pp. 166–7 above) The objective is to pull together the diverse features that go towards constructing 'selves', or social identities, in the sample. Ethos involves not just discourse, but the whole body. Any of the analytical categories listed here may be relevant to ethos.

GRAMMAR Three dimensions of the grammar of the clause are differentiated here: 'transitivity', 'theme', and 'modality'. These correspond respectively to the 'ideational', 'textual', and 'interpersonal' functions of language (see p. 64 above).

TRANSITIVITY (see pp. 177–85 above) The objective is to see whether particular process types and participants are favoured in the text, what choices are made in voice (active or passive), and how significant is the nominalization of processes. A major concern is agency, the expression of causality, and the attribution of responsibility.

What process types (action, event, relational, mental) are most used, and what factors may account for this?

Is grammatical metaphor a significant feature?

Are passive clauses or nominalizations frequent, and if so what functions do they appear to serve?

THEME (see pp. 183–5 above) The objective is to see if there is a discernible pattern in the text's thematic structure to the choices of themes for clauses.

What is the thematic structure of the text, and what assumptions (for example, about the structuring of knowledge or practice) underlie it?

Are marked themes frequent, and if so what motivations for them are there?

MODALITY (see pp. 158–62 above) The objective is to determine patterns in the text in the degree of affinity expressed with propositions through modality. A major concern is to assess the relative import of modality features for (a) social relations in the discourse, and (b) controlling representations of reality.

What sort of modalities are most frequent?

Are modalities predominantly subjective or objective?

What modality features (modal verbs, modal adverbs, etc.) are most used?

WORD MEANING (see pp. 185–90 above) The emphasis is upon 'key words' which are of general or more local cultural significance; upon words whose meanings are variable and changing; and upon the meaning potential of a word – a particular structuring of its meanings – as a mode of hegemony and a focus of struggle.

WORDING (see pp. 190–4 above) The objective is to contrast the ways meanings are worded with the ways they are worded in other (types of) text, and to identify the interpretative perspective that underlies this wording.

> Does the text contain new lexical items, and if so what theoretical, cultural or ideological significance do they have?
>
> What intertextual relations are drawn upon for the wording in the text?
>
> Does the text contain evidence of overwording or rewording (in opposition to other wordings) of certain domains of meaning?

METAPHOR (see pp. 194–8 above) The objective is to characterize the metaphors used in the discourse sample, in contrast to metaphors used for similar meanings elsewhere, and determine what factors (cultural, ideological, etc.) determine the choice of metaphor. The effect of metaphors upon thinking and practice should also be considered.

Social Practice (see pp. 86–96 and chapter 7 above)

The analysis of social practice is more difficult to reduce to a checklist, so the following heads should be seen only as very rough guidelines. The general objective here is to specify: the nature of the social practice of which the discourse practice is a part, which is the basis for explaining why the discourse practice is as it is; and the effects of the discourse practice upon the social practice.

SOCIAL MATRIX OF DISCOURSE The aim is to specify the social and hegemonic relations and structures which constitute the matrix of this particular instance of social and discursive practice; how this instance stands in relation to these structures and relations (is it conventional and normative, creative and innovative, oriented to restructuring them, oppositional, etc.?); and what effects it contributes to, in terms of reproducing or transforming them.

ORDERS OF DISCOURSE The objective here is to specify the relationship of the instance of social and discursive practice to the orders of discourse it draws upon, and the effects of reproducing or transforming orders of discourse to which it contributes. Attention should be paid to the large-scale tendencies affecting orders of discourse discussed in chapter 7 above.

IDEOLOGICAL AND POLITICAL EFFECTS OF DISCOURSE   It is useful to focus upon the following particular ideological and hegemonic effects (see pp. 86–96 above):

systems of knowledge and belief;
social relations;
social identities ('selves').

There are always alternative possible analyses for discourse samples, and the question arises of how analysts can justify the analyses they propose (how they can 'validate' them). There is no simple answer, and all one can do is decide, given alternative analyses, which seems to be preferable on the balance of evidence available. There are various factors to be taken into account. One is the extent to which a proposed analysis accounts for the discourse sample: does it explain even quite detailed features of it, or does it leave features unexplained, or even seem at odds with features? Another factor is whether a proposed analysis is substantiated by what participants do in an interaction. If, for example, one claims that a text is structured in a contradictory way, by drawing upon incompatible genres, do participants actually give evidence of experiencing it as problematic in their contributions? One can also take account of participants' reactions to the analysis; if it makes sense to them, and helps them explain other aspects of the type of discourse in focus, that is in its favour. A related consideration is the extent to which the analysis sheds light upon other data for the analyst, and provides a basis (even a model) for other analyses. (See Potter and Wetherell 1987: 169–72 for a more detailed discussion of issues connected with validation.)

Results

The first observation to make here is that while analysts have some control over how results are used, they never have total control once their results are in the public domain. This presents analysts with a dilemma of which I am acutely aware myself, but have not fully resolved. I argued in chapter 7 that there is a widespread process of technologization of discourse, which uses research upon discourse for redesigning discourse practices and training people to use new discourse practices. Discourse technologization is a resource for cultural and social engineering, and many discourse analysts will find the fact that it is used, and certainly some of the ways in which it is used, objectionable. Yet how do I or other analysts ensure that the research I am carrying out is not used in such contexts? The honest, if painful, answer is that I cannot: like academics in many other fields, discourse analysts are increasingly at risk of being integrated into bureaucratic and managerial agendas. As I indicated in discussing discourse technologization, this is a tendency which is at present only patchily manifested in different institutions and domains. But my feeling is that it is going to gather steam, perhaps quite rapidly, and place analysts in more pressing dilemmas in the not too distant future.

One could, of course, stop doing research, or do research into something different; but it is difficult to find areas of research that are guaranteed to be free from abuse, and these are solutions most of us find too hard to contemplate. Perhaps such pessimism should be qualified. Technologies of discourse, like other technologies, open up possibilities in various directions, some more beneficial for the majority of people than others. I have described discourse technologization as bureaucratic or managerial use of knowledge about discourse to impose change, but this knowledge could also be used in pursuit of change from below. In this connection, I have argued with colleagues elsewhere (Clark et al. 1988; Fairclough and Ivanic 1989; Fairclough forthcoming a) for a 'critical language awareness' (CLA) element in the language education of all school children, which would provide them with the knowledge to initiate change in their own discourse practices, and the discourse practices of their community.

CLA aims to draw upon learners' own language and discourse experience, to help them become more conscious of the practice they are involved in as producers and consumers of texts: of the social forces and interests that shape it; the power relations and ideologies that invest it; its effects upon social identities, social relations, knowledge, and beliefs; and the role of discourse in

processes of cultural and social change (including technologization of discourse). Through consciousness learners can become
more aware of constraints upon their own practice, and of the
possibilities, risks, and costs of individually or collectively challenging those constraints to engage in an 'emancipatory' language
practice. From this summary description it is clear how CLA
might draw upon the sort of discourse analysis I have advocated
in this book. But it also involves awareness of language variety:
historical awareness of hegemonic processes of language standardization, and the interests which lie behind them; awareness of
how the standard variety (for example, standard English) is imposed in prestigious contexts; of how such constraints disadvantage users of other varieties; of the possibilities and risks of
flouting them, and challenging the hegemony of the standard. As
this implies, CLA sees the development of language awareness
and language practice as mutually reinforcing.

Analysts may also wish to continue their relationship with
those they have been researching after the research as such is
complete. This may involve at least writing up results in a form
that is accessible to and usable by them, and perhaps entering into
dialogue with them about the results and their implications. Or it
may require longer-term involvement in action that people decide
to take in response to results. For example, if the project to
investigate quality circles in industry, referred to above, were to
show that managers largely control quality circle meetings
(perhaps in terms of the types of interactional control discussed
above, pp. 152–8), workers (or managers or both) might decide
to try to develop ways of interacting which would allow control
to be better shared and negotiated. Discourse analysts may well
be able to transform their analytical abilities into help with
design.

So there are possibilities for analysts to exercise some control
over the use of their results. But I think it would be misleading to
end upon too optimistic a note. If technologization of discourse
does gather steam, as I have predicted, discourse analysts will be
hard-pressed to prevent their well-intentioned interventions being
appropriated by those with the power, resources, and the money.

References

Althusser, L. 1971: Ideology and ideological state apparatuses. In L. Althusser (ed.), *Lenin and Philosophy and Other Essays*, London: New Left Books.

Antakki, C. 1988: *Analyzing Everyday Explanation: a casebook of methods*. London: Sage Publications.

Argyle, M. 1978: *The Psychology of Interpersonal Behaviour*, 3rd edn. Harmondsworth: Penguin Books.

Atkinson, J.M. and Drew, P. 1979: *Order in Court: the organization of verbal interaction in judicial settings*. London: Macmillan.

Atkinson, J.M. and Heritage, J. 1984: *Structures of Social Action*. Cambridge: Cambridge University Press.

Authier-Révuz, J. 1982: Hétérogénéité montrée et hétérogenéité constitutive: éléments pour une approche de l'autre dans le discours. *DRLAV*, 32.

Bagguley, P. 1990: Post-Fordism and enterprise culture: flexibility, autonomy and changes in economic organization. In Keat and Abercrombie 1990.

Bagguley, P. and Lash, S. 1988: Labour relations in disorganized capitalism: a five-nation comparison. *Environment and Planning D: Society and Space*, 6, 321–38.

Bakhtin, M. 1981: *The Dialogical Imagination*, ed. M. Holquist, trans. C. Emerson and M. Holquist. Austin: University of Texas Press.

1986: *Speech Genres and Other Late Essays*, ed. C. Emerson and M. Holquist, trans. V.W. McGee. Austin: University of Texas Press.

Barnes, D. 1976: *Teachers and Pupil Talking*. Videocasette. Milton Keynes: Open University.

Bennett, T. and Woollacott, J. 1987: *Bond and Beyond: the political career of a popular hero*. London: Macmillan.

Benson, D. and Hughes, J. 1983: *The Perspective of Ethnomethodology*. London: Longman.

Bernstein, B. 1981: Codes, modalities and the process of cultural reproduction: a model. *Language in Society*, 10, 327–67.

Billig, M., Condor, S., Edwards, D., Gane, M., Middleton, D. and Ridley, A. 1988: *Ideological Dilemmas: a social psychology of everyday thinking*. London: Sage Publications.

Bourdieu, P. 1977: *Outline of a Theory of Practice*, trans. R. Nice. Cambridge: Cambridge University Press.

1982: *Ce que Parler Veut Dire*. Paris: Fayard.

1984: *Distinction: a social critique of the judgement of taste*, trans. R. Nice. London: Routledge.

1988: *Homo Academicus*, trans. Peter Collier. Cambridge: Polity Press.

Brown, G. and Yule, G. 1983: *Discourse Analysis*. Cambridge: Cambridge University Press.

Brown, P. and Fraser, C. 1979: Speech as a marker of situation. In K. Scherer and H. Giles (eds), *Social Markers in Speech*, Cambridge: Cambridge University Press.

Brown, P. and Levinson, S. 1987: *Politeness: some universals in language usage*. Cambridge: Cambridge University Press.

Buci-Glucksmann, C. 1980: *Gramsci and the State*, trans. D. Fernbach. London: Lawrence and Wishart.

Button, G. and Casey, N. 1984: Generating topic: the use of topic initial elicitors. In Atkinson and Heritage 1984.

Button, G. and Lee, J. R. E. 1987: *Talk and Social Organization*. Clevedon: Multilingual Matters.

Cameron, D. 1985: *Feminism and Linguistic Theory*. London: Macmillan.

Chilton, P. (ed.), 1985: *Language and the Nuclear Arms Debate*. London: Pinter Publications.

Chilton, P. 1988: *Orwellian Language and the Media*. London: Pluto Press.

Clark, R., Fairclough, N., Ivanic, R. and Martin-Jones, M. 1988: Critical language awareness. *Centre for Language in Social Life Research Papers*, 1. University of Lancaster.

Coates, J. 1986: *Women, Men and Language*. London: Longman.

Coulthard, M. 1977: *An Introduction to Discourse Analysis*. London: Longman.

Courtine, J-J. 1981: Analyse du discours politique (le discours communiste adressé aux chrétiens). *Langages*, 62 (whole vol.).

Courtine, J-J. and Marandin, J-M. 1981: Quel objet pour l'analyse du discours? In *Materialités Discursives*, Lille: Presses Universitaires de Lille.

Davidson, A. I. 1986: Archaeology, genealogy, ethics. In D. C. Hoy (ed.), *Foucault: a critical reader*, Oxford: Basil Blackwell.

de Beaugrande, R. and Dressler, W. 1981: *Introduction to Text Linguistics*. London: Longman.

Debray, R. 1981: *Critique de la Raison Politique*. Paris: Gallimard.

Department of Education and Science 1988: *Report of the Committee of Inquiry into the Teaching of English Language (Kingman Report)*. London: HMSO.

1989: *English from Ages 5 to 16 (The Cox Report)*. London: HMSO.

de Saussure, F. 1959: *Course in General Linguistics*, trans. Wade Baskin. New York: McGraw Hill.

Dews, P. 1987: *Logics of Disintegration*. London: Verso.

Downes, W. 1984: *Language and Society*. London: Fontana.

Dreyfus, H. and Rabinow, P. 1982: *Michel Foucault: beyond structuralism and hermeneutics*. Brighton: Harvester Press.

Economy and Society, 18 February 1989. Special number on rhetoric.

Edelman, M. 1974: The political language of the helping professions. *Politics and Society*, 4, 295–310.

Edelsky, C. 1981: Who's got the floor? *Language in Society*, 10, 383–421.

Emerson, J. 1970: Behaviour in private places: sustaining definitions of reality in gynaecological examinations. In H. P. Dreizel (ed.), *Recent Sociology No. 2*, New York: Collier-Macmillan.

Fairclough, N. 1988a: Register, power and sociosemantic change. In D. Birch and M. O'Toole (eds), *Functions of Style*, London: Pinter Publications.

1988b: Discourse representation in media discourse. *Sociolinguistics*, 17, 125–39.

1988c: Linguistic and social change, and consequences for language education. *Centre for Language in Social Life Research Papers*, 2. University of Lancaster

1989a: *Language and Power*. London: Longman.

1989b: Language and ideology. *English Language Research Journal*, 3, 9–27.

1989c: Discourse in social change: a conflictual view. Working paper, Department of Linguistics, University of Lancaster

1990a: What might we mean by 'enterprise discourse'? In R. Keat and N. Abercrombie 1990.

1990b: Technologization of discourse. *Centre for Language in Social Life Research Papers*, 17. University of Lancaster.

(ed.), forthcoming a: *Critical Language Awareness*. London: Longman.

forthcoming b: The appropriacy of 'appropriateness'. In N. Fairclough (ed.) forthcoming a.

Fairclough, N. and Ivanic, R. 1989: Language education or language training? A critique of the Kingman model of the English language. In J. Bourne and T. Bloor (eds), *The Kingman Report*, London: Committee for Linguistics in Education.

Fishman, P. M. 1983: Interaction: the work women do. In B. Thorne, C. Kramarae and N. Thorne (eds), *Language, Gender and Society*, Rowley Mass.: Newbury House.

Foucault, M. 1971: *L'ordre du Discours*. Paris: Gallimard.

1972: *The Archaeology of Knowledge*. London: Tavistock Publications.

1979: *Discipline and Punish: the birth of the prison*. Harmondsworth: Penguin Books.

1981: *History of Sexuality*, vol. 1. Harmondsworth: Penguin Books.

1982: The subject and power. Afterword to Dreyfus and Rabinow.

1982, 1984: The order of discourse. In M. Shapiro (ed.), *Langage and Politics*, Oxford: Basil Blackwell.

Fowler, R. 1988a: Notes on critical linguistics. In R. Steele and T. Threadgold (eds), *Language Topics*, vol. 2 Amsterdam: Benjamins. 1988b: Oral models in the press. In M. MacLure et al. (eds), *Oracy Matters*, Milton Keynes: The Open University Press.

Fowler, R., Hodge, B., Kress, G. and Trew, T. 1979: *Language and Control*. Routledge: London.

Fraser, N. 1989: *Unruly Practices; power, discourse and gender in contemporary social theory*. Cambridge: Polity Press.

Frow, J. 1985: Discourse and power. *Economy and Society*, 14.

Further Education Unit 1987: *Relevance, Flexibility and Competence*. London: Further Education Unit.

Garfinkel, H. 1967: *Studies in Ethnomethodology*. Englewood Cliffs, New Jersey: Prentice Hall.

Garton, G., Montgomery, M. and Tolson A. 1988: Media discourse in the 1987 General Election: ideology, scripts and metaphors. Working paper. Programme in Literary Linguistics, Strathclyde University.

Giddens, A. 1984: *The Constitution of Society*. Cambridge: Polity Press.

Goffman, E. 1974: *Frame Analysis*. New York: Harper Colophon Books.

1981: *Forms of Talk*. Oxford: Basil Blackwell.

Graddoll, D. and Swann, J. 1989: *Gender Voices*. Oxford: Basil Blackwell.

Gramsci, A. 1971: *Selections from the prison notebooks*, ed. and trans. Q. Hoare and G. Nowell Smith. London: Lawrence and Wishart.

Gumperz, J. 1982: *Discourse Strategies*. Cambridge: Cambridge University Press.

Habermas, J. 1984: *Theory of Communicative Action*, vol. 1, trans. T. McCarthy. London: Heinemann.

Hall, S. 1988: The toad in the garden: Thatcherism among the theorists. In Nelson and Grossberg 1988.

Hall, S., Critcher, C., Jefferson, T., Clarke, J. and Roberts, B. 1978: *Policing the Crisis*. London: Macmillan.

Halliday, M. A. K. 1961: Categories of the theory of grammar. *Word*, 17, 241–92.

1966: Lexis as a linguistic level. In C. Bazell, J. C. Catford, M. A. K. Halliday and R. H. Robins (eds), *In Memory of J. R. Firth*, London: Longman.

1971: Linguistic function and literary style: an enquiry into the language of William Golding's *The Inheritors*. In M. A. K. Halliday 1973.

1973: *Explorations in the Functions of Language*. London: Edward Arnold.

1978: *Language as Social Semiotic*. London: Edward Arnold.

1985: *Introduction to Functional Grammar*. London: Edward Arnold.

Halliday, M. A. K. and Hasan, R. 1976: *Cohesion in English*. London: Longman.

1985: *Language, Context and Text: Aspects of Language in a Social-Semiotic Perspective*. Geelong, Victoria: Deakin University Press.

Harris, Z. 1963: *Discourse Analysis*. La Haye: Mouton and Company.

Hartley, J. 1982: *Understanding News*. London: Methuen.

Hasan, R. 1988: *Linguistics, Language and Verbal Art*. Oxford: Oxford University Press.

Health Education Council 1984: *Pregnancy Book*. London: Health Education Council.

Henriques, J., Hollway, W., Urwin, C., Venn, C. and Walkerdine, V. 1984: *Changing the Subject*. London: Methuen.

Heritage, J. 1985: Analyzing news interviews: aspects of the production of talk for overhearing audiences. In van Dijk 1985a, vol. 3.

Heritage, J. C. and Watson, D. R. 1979: Formulations as conversational objects. In G. Psathas (ed.), *Everyday Language: studies in ethnomethodology*, New York: Irvington.

HMSO 1985: *Fifth Report from the Home Affairs Committee*. London: HMSO.

Hodge, R. and Kress, G. 1988: *Social Semiotics*. Cambridge: Polity Press; and Ithaca: Cornell University Press.

Hoey, M. 1983: *On the Surface of Discourse*. London: George, Allen and Unwin.

Hoy, D. C. (ed.), 1986: *Foucault: a critical reader*. Oxford: Basil Blackwell.

Ivanic, R. and Simpson, J. forthcoming: Who's who in academic writing? In N. Fairclough (ed.), forthcoming a.

Jakobson, R. 1961: Concluding statement: linguistics and poetics. In T. Sebeok (ed.), *Style in Language*, Cambridge, Mass.: The MIT Press.

Jameson, F. 1984: Postmodernism, or the cultural logic of late capitalism. *New Left Review*, 146, 53–92.

Jefferson, G. and Lee, J. R. 1981: The rejection of advice: managing the problematic convergence of 'troubles-telling' and a 'service encounter'. *Journal of Pragmatics*, 5, 339–422.

Keat, R. and Abercrombie, N. (eds) 1990: *Enterprise Culture*. London: Routledge.

Kress, G. 1986: Language in the media: the construction of the domains of public and private. *Media, Culture and Society*, 8, 395–419.

Kress, G. 1987: Educating readers: language in advertising. In J. Hawthorn (ed.), *Propaganda, Persuasion and Polemic*, London: Edward Arnold.

Kress, G. 1988: *Linguistic Processes in Sociocultural Practice*. Oxford: Oxford University Press.

Kress, G. 1989: History and language: towards a social account of language change. *Journal of Pragmatics*, 13, 445–66.

Kress, G. and Hodge, R. 1979: *Language as Ideology*. London: Routledge.

Kress, G. and Threadgold, T. 1988: Towards a social theory of genre. *Southern Review*, 21, 215–43.

Kristeva, J. 1986a: Word, dialogue and novel. In T. Moi (ed.), *The Kristeva Reader*, Oxford: Basil Blackwell, 34–61.

1986b: The system and the speaking subject. In T. Moi (ed.), *The Kristeva Reader*, Oxford: Basil Blackwell. 24–33.

Labov, W. and Fanshel, D. 1977: *Therapeutic Discourse: psychotherapy as conversation*. New York: Academic Press.

Laclau, E. 1977: *Politics and Ideology in Marxist theory*. London: New Left Books.

Laclau, E. and Mouffe, C. 1985: *Hegemony and Socialist Strategy*. London: Verso.

Lakoff, G. and Johnson, M. 1980: *Metaphors We Live By*. Chicago: University of Chicago Press.

Larrain, J. 1979: *The Concept of Ideology*. London: Hutchinson.

Lecourt, D. 1972: *Pour une Critique de l'Epistemologie*. Paris: François Maspero.

Leech, G. N. 1981: *Semantics*, 2nd edn. Harmondsworth: Penguin Books.

1983: *Principles of Pragmatics*. London: Longman.

Leech, G. N., Deuchar, M. and Hoogenraad, R. 1982: *English Grammar for Today*. London: Macmillan.

Leech, G. N. and Short, M. 1981: *Style in Fiction*. London: Longman.

Leech, G. N. and Thomas, J. 1989: Language, meaning and context: pragmatics. In N. E. Collinge (ed.), *An Encyclopaedia of Language*, London: Routledge.

Leiss, W., Kline, S. and Jhally, S. 1986: *Social Communication in Advertising*. London: Methuen.

Leith, D. 1983: *A Social History of English*. London: Routledge.

Levinson, S. 1979: Activity types and language. *Linguistics*, 17, 365–99.

1983: *Pragmatics*. Cambridge: Cambridge University Press.

Looker, T. and Gregson, O. 1989: Stress and the businessman: stresswise for health success. *Business Enterprise News*, 7.

Macdonell, D. 1986: *Theories of Discourse: an introduction*. Oxford: Basil Blackwell.

Maingueneau, D. 1976: *Initiation aux Méthodes d'Analyse du Discours*. Paris: Hachette.

1987: *Nouvelles Tendances en Analyse du Discours*. Paris: Hachette.

Maldidier, D. 1984 Hommage: Michel Pecheux: une tension passionnée entre la langue et l'histoire. In *Histoire et Linguistique*. Paris: Editions de la Maison des Sciences de l'Homme.

Margerison, C. 1987: *Conversation Control Skills for Managers*. London: Mercury Books.

Martyna, W. 1978: What does *he* mean: use of the generic masculine. *Journal of Communication*, 28, 131–8.

Mey, J. 1985: *Whose Language? a study in linguistic pragmatics*. Amsterdam: John Benjamins.

Mishler, E. 1984: *The Discourse of Medicine: dialectics of medical interviews*. Norwood, New Jersey: Ablex Publishing Company.

Montgomery, M. 1990: *Meanings and the Media*. Ph.D. thesis, University of Strathclyde.

Morley, D. 1980: Texts, readers, subjects. In S. Hall, D. Hobson, A. Lowe and P. Willis (eds), *Culture, Media, Language*, London: Hutchinson.

Morris, N. (ed.), 1986: *The Baby Book*. London: Newbourne Publications Ltd.

Morris, P. 1990: Freeing the spirit of enterprise: The genesis and development of the concept of enterprise culture. In Keat and Abercombie 1990.

Nelson, C. and Grossberg, L. (eds) 1988: *Marxism and the Interpretation of Culture*. London: Macmillan.

Ochs, E. 1979: Transcription as theory. In E. Ochs and B. Schieffelin, *Developmental Pragmatics*, New York: Academic Press.

Pêcheux, M. 1982: *Language, Semantics and Ideology*. London: Macmillan

    1983: Sur les contextes épistemologiques de l'analyse de discours. *Mots*, 9, 7–17.

    1988: Discourse: structure or event? In Nelson and Grossberg 1988.

Pêcheux, M., Henry, P., Poitou, J.-P. and Haroche, C. 1979: Un exemple d'ambiguité ideologique: le rapport Mansholt. *Téchnologies, Idéologies, et Pratiques*, 1.2, 1–83.

Pomerantz, A. 1978: Compliment responses. In Schenkein 1978.

Potter, J. and Wetherell, M. 1987: *Discourse and Social Psychology: beyond attitudes and behaviour*. London: Sage Publications.

Quirk, R., Greenbaum, S., Leech, G. and Svartvik, J. 1972: *A Grammar of Contemporary English*. London: Longman.

Rabinow, P. (ed.), 1984: *The Foucault Reader*. Harmondsworth: Penguin Books.

Robin, R. 1973: *Histoire et Linguistique*. Paris: Armand Colin.

Rose, N. MS: Governing the enterprising self. Paper given at conference, Values of the Enterprise Culture, University of Lancaster, September 1989.

Rose, N. and Miller, R. MS: Rethinking the state: governing economic, social and personal life. 1989.

Sacks, H. 1967–71: *Mimeo Lecture Notes*.

    1972: On the analyzability of stories by children. In J. Gumperz and D. Hymes (eds), *Directions in Sociolinguistics*, New York: Holt, Rinehart and Winston, 325–45.

Sacks, H., Schegloff, E. and Jefferson, G. 1974: A simplest systematics for the organization of turn-taking in conversation. *Language*, 50, 696–735.

Schegloff, E. and Sacks, H. 1973: Opening up closings. *Semiotica*, 8, 289–327.

Schegloff, E., Jefferson, G. and Sacks, H. 1977: The preference for self-correction of repairs in conversation. *Language*, 53, 361–82.

Schenkein, J. (ed.), 1978: *Studies in the Organization of Conversational Interaction*. New York: Academic Press.

Schutz, A. 1962: *Collected Papers, vol. 1. The Problem of Social Reality*. The Hague: Martinus Nijhoff.

Shapiro, M. 1981: *Language and Political Understanding*. Yale: Yale University Press.

Sinclair, J. and Coulthard, M. 1975: *Towards an Analysis of Discourse: the English used by teachers and pupils*. Oxford: Oxford University Press.

Sontag, S. 1988: *Aids and its Metaphors*. Harmondsworth: Penguin Books.

Spender, D. 1980: *Man Made Language*. London: Routledge.

Sperber, D. and Wilson, D. 1986: *Relevance*. Oxford: Basil Blackwell.

Stubbs, M. 1983: *Discourse Analysis*. Oxford: Basil Blackwell.

Talbot, M. forthcoming: The construction of gender in a teenage magazine. In Fairclough forthcoming a.

Tannen, D. 1989: *Talking Voices: repetition, dialogue and imagery in conversational discourse*. Cambridge: Cambridge University Press.

Taylor, C. 1986: Foucault on freedom and truth. In D. C. Hoy (ed.), *Foucault: a critical reader*, Oxford: Basil Blackwell.

ten Have, P. 1989: The consultation as a genre. In B. Torode (ed.), *Text and Talk as Social Practice*, Dordrecht-Holland: Foris Publications, 115–35.

Thomas, J. 1988: Discourse control in confrontational interaction. *Lancaster Papers in Linguistics*, 50. University of Lancaster.

Thompson, J. B. 1984: *Studies in the Theory of Ideology*. Cambridge: Polity Press.

1990: *Ideology and Modern Culture*. Cambridge: Polity Press.

Threadgold, T. 1988a: Changing the subject. In R. Steele and T. Threadgold (eds), *Language Topics, vol. 2*, Amsterdam: Benjamins.

Threadgold, T. 1988b: Stories of race and gender: an unbounded discourse. In D. Birch and M. O'Toole, *Functions of Style*, London: Pinter Publishers.

Tolson, A. 1990: *Speaking from Experience: interview discourse and forms of subjectivity*. Ph.D. thesis, University of Birmingham.

Trew, T. 1979: Theory and ideology at work. In Fowler et al. 1979.

Urry, J. 1987: Some social and spatial aspects of services. *Society and Space*, 5, 5–26.

van Dijk, T. (ed.), 1985a: *Handbook of Discourse Analysis*, 4 vols. London: Academic Press.

1985b: *Discourse and Communication: new approaches to the analysis of mass media discourses and communication*. Berlin: Walter de Gruyter and Co.

van Dijk, T. 1988: *News as Discourse*. Hillsdale, New Jersey: Erlbaum.

Volosinov, V. I. 1973: *Marxism and the Philosophy of Language*. New York: Seminar Press.

Weedon, C. 1987: *Feminist Practice and Poststructuralist Theory.* Oxford: Basil Blackwell.

Widdowson, H. 1979: *Explorations in Applied Linguistics.* Oxford: Oxford University Press.

Williams, R. 1976: *Keywords: a vocabulary of culture and society.* London: Fontana/Croom Helm.

Zima, P. 1981: Les mécanismes discursifs de l'idéologie. *Revue de L'Institut de Sociologie (Solvay),* 4.

Index

academic writing, 162
activity type, 11, 70, 125–6, 129, 232
adjacency pair, 18, 153
advertising, 115–17, 210–11, 214, 219; mixed with financial regulations, 210
agency, social, 34, 45
agenda setting, 235
alternative medicine, 146, 166; interviews, 219
Althusser, L., 2–3, 29–30, 86–7, 90–2
ambivalence of texts, 15–16, 28, 34–5, 82, 105, 115, 131, 157–8, 188, 221, 232–8; potential, 75, 81, 188–9; reduction of, 81
ambivalence of voice, 108, 173
analysis as interpretation, 16, 19, 28, 35, 198–9
antenatal care, discourse of, 169–79
appropriacy, theories of, 68
archaeology and genealogy in Foucault, 49
archive, 227
argumentation in texts, 77, 169–77; modes of, 235

articulation of orders of discourse, 93, 223; struggles over, 70
automatic analysis of discourse, 32

Bakhtin, M., 11, 47, 100–1, 103, 126
Bernstein, B., 43, 95
Billig, M., 96
bodily hexis, 167
Bourdieu, P., 162, 167, 198
broadcasting, 201
Brown, P., 162–3

change in discourse, 5, 28, 36, 96–9, 200–24; discursive event, 96; orders of discourse, 98, 200; and social and cultural change, 5–11, 54, 102
chat in television talk shows, 68
Chilton, P., 197
classroom discourse, 13–15, 153; heterogeneity of, 16, 22; historical change, 15
clause, grammar of, 76, 177; multifunctional, 76
clause relations, elaboration, 175; ellipsis, 176; enhancement, 175;